ECONOMIC ORGANIZATIONS AS GAMES

Edited by

Ken Binmore
and Partha Dasgupta

Basil Blackwell

First published 1986

First published in paperback 1989

Basil Blackwell Ltd
108 Cowley Road, Oxford OX4 1JF, UK

Basil Blackwell Inc.
432 Park Avenue South, Suite 1503
New York, NY 10016, USA

British Library Cataloguing in Publication Data
Economic organizations as games.
    1. Economics, Mathematical 2. Game theory
    I. Binmore, K. G. II. Dasgupta, Partha
    330'.01'5193 HB144
    ISBN 0−631−14255−X
    ISBN 0−631−16888−5 Pbk

Library of Congress Cataloging in Publication Data
Economic organizations as games.
    Bibliography: p.
    Includes index.
    1. Game theory. 2. Equilibrium (Economics)
    I. Binmore, Ken. II. Dasgupta, Partha.
    HB 144.E28 1987 658.4'0355 86-11698
    ISBN 0−631−14255−X
    ISBN 0−631−16888−5 (pbk.)

Typeset in 10 on 12pt Press Roman by Unicus Graphics Ltd,
Horsham, West Sussex
Printed in Great Britain by Billing and Sons Ltd, Worcester

Contents

Preface

The Suntory–Toyota International Centre for Economics and Related Disciplines (ICERD) was established at the London School of Economics in 1978. One of its earliest initiatives was the Economic Theory Workshop which was set up as a forum for the interchange of ideas in economic theory and provided with funds from the Suntory–Toyota Foundation to finance international visits and a discussion paper series. Since that time, the Economic Theory Workshop has entertained many visitors, witnessed much heated debate and produced large numbers of discussion papers. A central theme in much of this work has been the theory of games and its applications in economics. In this and its companion volume *The Economics of Bargaining* we offer a selection of papers written by members of the workshops and our visitors on this theme. For each volume, we have written a lengthy, but we hope useful, introduction which is intended to explain the significance of the papers chosen and their place in the general development of the subject.

Finally, we should like to express our gratitude to Suntory and Toyota for their vision in supporting this truly international project and to the staff at ICERD for their assistance and guidance in running the workshop. All royalties for this and the companion volume will be donated to ICERD.

Ken Binmore
University of Michigan

Partha Dasgupta
St John's College, Cambridge

Acknowledgements

The publishers and editors acknowledge with thanks permission to reproduce in this volume material previously published elsewhere. Chapters 1 and 2 appeared in *Review of Economic Studies*, January 1986; chapters 5 and 9 in the same journal, in the January 1982 and January 1984 issues respectively. Chapter 3 appeared in *Economics Letters* (1981). Chapters 4 and 7 appeared in *Econometrica* (1983). Chapter 6 appeared in *New Developments in the Analysis of Market Structure*, edited by Joseph E. Stiglitz and G. Frank Mathewson (Macmillan/MIT Press, 1986).

INTRODUCTION

Game Theory: A Survey

K. Binmore and P. Dasgupta

A group of individuals is said to be engaged in a *game* whenever the fate of an individual in the group depends not only on his own actions, but also on the actions of the rest of the individuals in the group. Stated so broadly, it would seem that any situation of interest to social scientists is a game. More specifically, it would explain why economists have found the *theory of games* to be an appealing avenue for exploring imperfectly competitive markets. The essays collected in this volume represent a variety of such explorations. More generally, they reflect the resurgence of interest among economic theorists in analysing strategic behaviour by an appeal to the broad outlines of the theory of games.

In this Introduction, we shall briefly examine the hypotheses of game theory and its goals. Our reasons are twofold. The first is to provide a perspective within which to place the essays which follow. The second is to sound a note of caution. Game theory has come to pervade analytical economics very thoroughly in recent years but, like all specialized tools, its scope for useful application is subject to limitations. It is not true that every situation of interest to economists can be sufficiently precisely described for its study to be amenable to game-theoretic analysis. Nor, although this is less obvious, is game theory itself sufficiently well developed that it can provide an analysis for all games which can be so described. Some scrutiny of game theory, particularly in respect of its limitations and its scope, is therefore timely. An introduction to a volume of papers is admittedly a compact vehicle for such an enterprise. But we hope that at least some readers will see the necessary brevity as a virtue.

1 NASH EQUILIBRIUM

Von Neumann and Morgenstern (1944) introduced the fundamental classification of games into those of *complete information* and those of *incomplete information*.[1] The former category is basic. In so far as games of incomplete information can be handled at all, it is by reducing them to games of complete information (using the theory of Harsanyi which we discuss briefly later on).

In a game of complete information, the players are assumed to know all relevant information not explicitly forbidden by the rules. More precisely they know all about:

a The *rules* of the game. These specify the circumstances under which a player may act, the actions available at these times and the information supplied about what has happened in the game so far at these decision points. A knowledge of the rules allows each player to formulate a *strategy* for the game, i.e. a plan of action for its play which allows for all possible contingencies.

b The *players* of the game. These are specified by:

   i   their *preferences*, which are formally represented by payoff (or utility) functions defined on the set of possible *outcomes* of the game);

   ii their *beliefs*, which are formally represented by subjective probability distributions over a set of possible 'states of the world'. Usually these states of the world are attributed to 'chance moves', or, in other words, Mother Nature. Together with the strategies chosen by the players, these states of the world determine what outcome of the game results from its play.

There are three points worth making about the status of this information in a game of complete information. The first is that it is taken to be *common knowledge* (Aumann 1976). This means that, not only does each player know it, but also that each player knows that each player knows it, that each player knows that each player knows that each player knows it ... and so on *ad infinitum* (see Myerson 1984; Mertens and Zamir 1985; Brandenberger and Dekel 1985). The second point is that the players' beliefs about the world do not need to be consistent in this formulation: the players may agree to disagree. The third point is that information need not be *perfect* in a game of complete information. In a game of perfect information, like chess, the players always know everything that has happened so far in the game. In a game of *imperfect information*, like poker, a player will, in general, have only partial information about the history of the game so far. In particular, a

---

1 Recently, some authors have begun to refer to games of incomplete information as games of 'asymmetric information'. However, we find it odd to use the term 'asymmetric' when dealing with a game which may actually be symmetric in the mathematical sense.

poker player will not usually know all the cards dealt to his opponent when deciding how much to bet. Nevertheless, poker may be modelled as a game of complete information.

The informational assumptions given above are those which it is usual to make in a formal way about games of complete information. However, an analysis of how such a game would be played by rational players requires further information. In the first place, there is the possibility that players may meet before the play of the game with the aim of agreeing upon a joint course of action in the game. If such pre-play negotiations are possible, then the precise details of what can and cannot occur during the negotiation period will matter very much as regards how the game is finally played. For example, it makes a crucial difference whether or not an effective legal system exists for the enforcement of contracts or whether or not neutral referees can be called upon to assist in co-ordinating strategy choices. Nash (1951) proposed dealing with such pre-play negotiations by embedding the original game in a larger game in which the possible negotiation steps appear as formal moves. He suggested that the larger game should then be analysed on the assumption that no pre-play communication at all is allowed between the players.

This process, known currently as the *Nash program*, is discussed at much greater length in Volume 2 of this work, *The Economics of Bargaining*. The point we wish to emphasize here is that the Nash program requires that we regard the analysis of games *without pre-play communication* as fundamental. We shall sometimes stress that a game is being analysed from this point of view by calling the game a *contest*.[2]

Let us then turn to the analysis of a game without pre-play communication played by rational players. The question immediately arises: what is a rational player? Such a player is certainly rational in the sense normally understood in economics, i.e. he is a 'well-integrated' personality; his motivations are precisely defined via a preference ordering, so that he maximizes 'utility' given his subjective beliefs.

But what of his subjective beliefs? Our description of a game of complete information includes the requirement that the players' subjective beliefs over states of the world are common knowledge but leaves the players' subjective beliefs about what strategies the other players will choose to be determined by an analysis of the game. But such an analysis cannot simply be plucked from the air. As Luce and Raiffa (1957, p. 62) aptly comment, nothing

2 The word 'cooperative' means that the players may agree on any contract that they choose before the formal game is played and that the terms of this contract can be made *binding* on the players. What we have called a 'contest' is often called a 'non-cooperative game' but there is clearly a large gap between a contest and a game which is not cooperative. See Farrell (1984) for an interesting exploration of this gap.

prevents a continuation of 'If-I-think-that-he-thinks-that-I-think-that-he-thinks ...' type of reasoning to the point where all strategy choices appear to be equally reasonable. Something needs to be added in order to escape the infinite regress built into these reasoning chains. Traditional game theory cuts the Gordian knot with three further assumptions which we adjoin to the assumptions (a) and (b) that characterize a game of complete information. The new assumptions are:

c   A rational player quantifies *all* uncertainties with which he is faced using subjective probability distributions and then maximizes utility relative to these distributions. Each of these subjective probability distributions is common knowledge.

d   A rational player can duplicate the reasoning process of another rational player provided he is supplied with the same information.

e   It is common knowledge that all players are rational.

Sometimes (d) and (e) are expressed by saying that it is common knowledge that all of the individuals consult the *same*, entirely authoritative, game theory book. In particular, (d) and (e) and the common knowledge assumption regarding (a)-(c) include the possibility that two players may 'agree to disagree', provided that they generate their subjective beliefs using Bayesian updating from a common prior (Aumann 1976).

We wish to argue that, if a rational analysis of a game without pre-play communication (a contest) is able to single out an optimal strategy choice for each player, then this profile of strategy choices *must* constitute a *Nash equilibrium*[3] of the game.[4] We first define a Nash equilibrium.

Suppose that the players are labelled $i = 1, 2, \ldots, N$ and that A_i is the set of feasible strategies for player i. The elements of A_i may include mixed strategies, i.e. strategies which require player i to randomize some decisions as when bluffing in poker. A Nash equilibrium is then a strategy profile $(a_1^*, a_2^*, \ldots, a_N^*)$ with $a_i^* \in A_i$ $(i = 1, 2, \ldots, N)$ such that *each* a_i^* is a *best reply* for player i to the choices a_j^* by the players $j \neq i$. If $u_i(a_1, a_2, \ldots, a_N)$ is the expected utility that a player i derives from the use of strategy profile $(a_1, a_2, \ldots, a_N)$, then this means that

3 In honour of John Nash (1950) who proved the basic existence theorem. The opening essay of this volume by Dasgupta and Maskin explores existence problems.

4 A technical distinction ought to be made here. Aumann (1985), among others, would substitute 'correlated equilibrium' for 'Nash equilibrium' in this statement. However, the distinction is largely a verbal one. Our notion of a contest is intended to exclude co-ordinating devices which are not explicitly modelled within the game. In Aumann's terms this amounts to the requirement that the players' primeval beliefs are independent. If the players had access to co-ordinating mechanisms *external* to the game structure, then our defence of Nash equilibrium would fail and the wider notion of correlated equilibrium would be appropriate, precisely as Aumann indicates.

theory is an appropriate tool if the underlying environment is changing too rapidly for things to settle down. This last consideration imposes a severe constraint on the range of applications for game theory in economic modelling.

The second reason for emphasizing the Nash equilibrium idea lies in the fact that Nash equilibrium, and its refinements, require that account be taken of informational considerations which are not relevant in traditional economics: hence our discussion of what the players in a game are assumed to know. In traditional economics, the 'common knowledge assumption' has only a small role to play because economic transactions have been seen as being mediated, at least in part, by the price mechanism. The most pristine model is the Walrasian construct in which it is supposed, among other things, that *all* transactions are mediated by prices. One much discussed virtue of the price mechanism is that it enables agents to economize on information (see Section 5 below). It is therefore not surprising that as attention began to shift to situations in which the price mechanism does not work well, attempts should have been made to maintain the parsimony of information that individuals in the Walrasian world find adequate and hence avoid the apparent intricacies of the game-theoretic approach.

It is important, however, not to confuse these attempts to avoid a proper game-theoretic analysis with game theory itself. Such attempts are entirely laudable where successful, since they focus attention on the parameters of the problem which are of immediate relevance. But to be successful, they need to have sound microfoundations and a proper discussion of their microfoundations is seldom possible without introducing game-theoretic considerations. One might think of a game-theoretic study of the microfoundations of a model in terms of the scaffolding erected when a structure is being built. It is essential for the construction but can be discarded once the structure has been completed successfully.

As an example, consider the notion of 'conjectural equilibrium' (Hahn 1977, 1978). This is not strictly a game-theoretic notion. In theories relying on this notion, agents are seen as having models of the economy in their minds. These individual models, on the basis of which agents choose their strategies, are primitive in the constructs. As such they are necessarily *ad hoc* unless derived from empirical studies or deduced from deeper theoretical considerations. As far as we know there is to date no useful empirical evidence. But there are theoretical papers in which conjectures are refined to be 'reasonable' (Hahn 1978; Hart 1982) or 'rational' (Bresnahan 1981; Ulph 1981). However, these words are used in a sense which is weaker than a game theorist would think appropriate. In consequence, it is possible to elicit inconsistencies of one sort or another as in the spirited attack by Makowski (1983) on 'reasonable' and 'rational' conjectures.

Our own view is that conjectural equilibrium theories, as currently understood, are premature. A satisfactory theory must await developments in game theory which allow it to be founded on a firm and consistent basis. Admittedly this will not be easy as is clear from the work of Marschak and Selten (1974). However, there are enough counter-intuitive results in game theory to make it clear that attempts to anticipate what the results of a game-theoretic analysis would be are unlikely always to be accurate.

In summary, rationality, as understood in game theory, requires that each agent will *perforce* select an equilibrium strategy when choosing independently and privately. Sometimes rationality considerations can sensibly be invoked in defence of other choices in game-like situations, but only by postulating an underlying, concealed game (usually a repeated game or a super-game) which the agents are 'really playing'. This observation applies not only to 'conjectural equilibrium theories' but to a number of other theories with game-like characteristics.

Before we turn to games of incomplete information, something needs to be said about the problem of identifying the solution of a game when many equilibria exist.[8] Here it becomes necessary to be much more specific about the environment in which the game is played. If rational behaviour has been generated solely by unthinking evolutionary forces, then the problem of selecting the 'right' equilibrium will usually not even be a meaningful one. Where many equilibria are possible, in such an environment, it will typically only be possible to attribute the choice of the equilibrium actually observed to essentially random events in the history of the equilibrating process. (Consider, for example, the equilibrium represented by an ecology containing the duck-billed platypus.) At the other extreme, there is the possibility that the choice of equilibrium might be the subject of rational negotiation among the players before the game is played. (With binding contracts, neutral co-ordinating referees and the like excluded, an agreement would need to be self-enforcing and thus an equilibrium.) Under these conditions, the selection problem becomes a bargaining problem, as discussed in Volume 2 of this collection, *The Economics of Bargaining*.

The point we are seeking to make is that the selection problem, like many others in game theory, requires a preliminary classification of the game environment. Each class of environment may generate a different solution to the problem. Theories, such as Harsanyi and Selten's tracing procedure (along with the supporting apparatus for isolating a prior from which the tracing commences) which isolate a unique equilibrium need to be studied with this point in mind (see Harsanyi 1975, 1982).

So far we have been concerned with games of complete information. However, in the long run, it will be games of incomplete information which

8 This is not meant to imply that problems may not exist in games with unique Nash equilibria (see Aumann and Maschler 1972). We have claimed only that *if* a solution exists *then* it must be an equilibrium.

will be of greater significance for the development of economic theory. At first sight, the problems raised by incomplete information seem insuperable if assumptions (a) and (b) with which we began this section are relaxed.[9] These incorporate the requirements that both the rules of the game and the individual characteristics of the players are common knowledge. However, in a remarkable series of articles, Harsanyi (1967-68) showed how the theory of games of complete information can be extended to cover certain important situations in which information is incomplete. (For a mathematical exposition, see Mertens and Zamir (1985) and Brandenburger (1986).) He begins by pointing out that it is assumption (b) that is fundamental because uncertainties over the rules can be formulated, where necessary, in terms of uncertainties over payoffs. We follow Harsanyi in this and consider only how to relax assumption (b). There are several ways in which the relaxation can be achieved. We begin with a formulation which Harsanyi attributes to Selten since this emphasizes the role of Nash equilibrium.

If assumption (b) is relaxed, there will be uncertainty about the characteristics of the players. Suppose that it is common knowledge that each player i is one of a number of possible *types* $t \in T_i$. To know a player's type is to possess a complete description of that player, i.e. to know his tastes and his beliefs. But, in Harsanyi's theory, a player is assumed to know only his own type. The beliefs built into the description of a type $t \in T_i$ must therefore include probability distributions over the sets T_j ($j \neq i$) which record type i's uncertainty over whom he is playing against. Although this is not strictly necessary, we shall assume that there is no 'agreement to disagree' and so all types have *consistent* beliefs. The uncertainty over types may then be encompassed by introducing a single chance move which precedes the game of incomplete information under study. This chance move selects an n-tuple $(t_1, t_2, \ldots, t_n)$ of types to play the game according to a probability distribution which is common knowledge among all types. Each individual type then computes his own beliefs about the types against whom he is playing by conditioning on the fact that he, himself, has been chosen. Note the cunning way in which beliefs are bent back upon themselves to produce a closed system. But note also that this requires a background pool of common knowledge, i.e. the probabilities with which the opening chance move makes its selections.

The opening chance move, together with the original game of incomplete information constitute a game of *complete* information, provided the 'players' of this game are taken to be the *types* $t \in T_1 \cup T_2 \cup \ldots \cup T_n$ and not the original players $i = 1, 2, \ldots, n$. Here it is to be understood that a type who is not chosen to play by the chance move receives a zero payoff.

9 Assumptions (c), (d) and (e), concerning the nature of rationality as understood in game theory, will not be relaxed in what follows.

We can then bring our previous analysis into action and assert that rational play on the part of these types must yield a Nash equilibrium in the game of complete information we have constructed.

Suppose that, in the above discussion, type $t \in T_i$ chooses strategy $s_i(t)$, if chance calls upon him to play. We may then regard the function s_i as a strategy for player i in the original game of incomplete information. If printed in a game theory book, it would tell player i how he ought to play *contingent* on his type. The strategy profile $(s_1, s_2, \ldots, s_n)$ is called a *Bayesian equilibrium*[10] if no player i has reason to deviate from s_i after learning his type $t \in T_i$ unless some other player j deviates from s_j. A Bayesian equilibrium is therefore essentially a Nash equilibrium. Harsanyi's contribution to the study of games of incomplete information does not consist of the invention of a radically new equilibrium concept, but in observing that Nash equilibrium will do equally well for games of incomplete information provided that the latter are suitably formulated.

2   LIMITATIONS OF GAME THEORY

Section 1 makes it clear that *classification* plays an exceedingly important role in game theory. The division of games into those with complete information and those without is just one of many distinctions which need to be made with care and precision if an analysis appropriate to the problem in hand is to be possible. A game theory without an accompanying classification of games would be like biology without the Linnean scheme.

Unfortunately, the very power of the Nash equilibrium concept tends to obscure this point. In particular, the fact that the idea is relevant both to normative analyses and to positive analyses provides much room for confusion. This confusion is compounded when one begins to examine the various refinements of the Nash equilibrium idea. The choice of refinement will typically depend on the type of game under study and the nature of the environment in which it is played. A failure to classify these factors adequately is therefore likely to lead to an inappropriate choice of refinement.

In this section we propose to comment briefly on the distinction between normative (or *prescriptive*) game theory and positive (or *descriptive*) game theory. The essential points have been touched upon in Section 1 and will resurface again in Section 4. Our emphasis here is on the *limitations* inherent in the two types of theory.

As we have seen in Section 1, a game theorist needs to make numerous assumptions before he can offer prescriptions on how to play a game. Some

---

10 Chapter 8 in this volume, by Raphael Repullo, considers a model of incomplete information in which this equilibrium concept is used.

of these assumptions are far from innocuous. In particular, beliefs need to be common knowledge; individuals must be optimizers; and each person must be capable of unlimited computational ability. We consider these assumptions sequentially.

The first of these assumptions is perfectly reasonable in games like chess, bridge or backgammon. All necessary information concerning the choices of action available to the players, and the manner in which these choices interact to produce an outcome, is to be found in the official rule books of the games. Nor are there difficulties about the players' underlying motivations. To assume that it is common knowledge that each prefers to win rather than to draw and to draw rather than to lose begs no important question. But, in economic games, the common knowledge assumption is very strong indeed. Why should the beliefs held by different individuals (or types of individual) be commonly known? The fact is that our understanding of human psychology (and, indeed, of human physiology and the workings of the physical world) is hopelessly imperfect. In particular, we have little idea how individuals actually acquire beliefs. Perhaps in an 'ideal' world, it would be true that type-contingent beliefs deduced rationally from a common prior would be common knowledge. But the world is not 'ideal'.

The hypothesis that individuals optimize also requires close examination. In seeking to prescribe behaviour, a game theorist asks: what would each individual (or type) do, if each individual (or type) were to do as well for himself as he possibly could? In asking this question, the game theorist short-circuits the numerous problems of human behaviour studied by behavioural psychologists. The prescriptive game theorist does not ask: how *do* people behave? He asks: given their aims, how *should* people behave? To answer this question, we do not need to know how clever people are or how much care and attention they may devote to their decisions. The question of what is optimal is independent of these considerations.

This brings us to the third point, namely that individuals have unlimited computational abilities. It is known, for example, that chess has a solution. This is to say that either white has a winning strategy or black has a winning strategy or else both sides can force a draw. But to know that a solution *exists* is not the same as knowing what the solution *is*. Chess, in particular, is a game of such enormous complexity that it seems unlikely that the solution will ever be known. This is not because an algorithm for finding the solution cannot be constructed but simply because the execution of such an algorithm is beyond the capacity of any computing machine that can currently be envisaged.

We have stressed these limitations of the prescriptive approach because it is a commonplace to reinterpret the results of *prescriptive* theory as *descriptive* statements about the world without offering an adequate defence of such a reinterpretation. As we have argued in Section 1, the only viable defence, for the world as it is, would seem to require an appeal to evolutionary considerations. The connecting link is that, since prescriptive game theory postulates optimizing behaviour on the part of the players, it cannot invalidate itself if it were universally adopted. Given that the other individual types behave according to the theory, no individual type will have any reason to deviate from the theory's prescriptions, since the behaviour prescribed for him by the theory is already optimal. This same consideration explains why the *prescriptions* of prescriptive game theory may simultaneously serve as *descriptions* of the outcomes of long-run evolutionary processes. Once the process achieves the prescriptive outcome, the mechanism which eliminates the 'unfit' will find no candidates on which to operate and so some prospect of stability will exist.

However, it is clear that these remarks are too lame to serve as a general defence of the use of prescriptive game theory in a descriptive context. In the absence of hard experimental data, theoretical models are required in which the evolutionary process is described formally and precisely. In such models, individuals are treated as stimulus–response machines[11] and so the difficulties in prescriptive theory which relate to the beliefs and motivations of the players evaporate. Since the stimulus–response machines are usually assumed to have a very simple internal structure, the problems concerning unlimited computational complexity also disappear. If the use of prescriptive game theory is to be justified in most positive contexts, long-run behaviour in such models should approach the prescriptive outcome. Why then retain the prescriptive theory at all? The reason is that the freedom of such descriptive evolutionary models from the limitations of prescriptive theory is bought at a heavy price. Descriptive evolutionary models are bound to be highly overspecific, i.e. they will assume vastly more than our knowledge can justify. Moreover, even the simplest of evolutionary processes is likely to generate dynamic systems which are intractable to mathematical analysis.

For this reason, there have been few attempts at following the descriptive, evolutionary approach. One notable exception is the work pioneered by Maynard Smith and Price (1973) among others.[12] However, the work is more readily applicable to biology than to economics. In this approach, the players in a 'game' are defined by their strategies. In other words, an individual *is* merely a strategy. As such, he is the simplest of possible stimulus–response machines. One then studies the evolution of a population of individuals on the assumption that the numbers of a particular type of individual wax or wane according to the success or failure enjoyed by the strategy employed by that type. The fact that such models can lead to refinements of the Nash equilibrium concept is confirmed in Section 3.

11 As is familiar from 'cobweb models', e.g. Moulin (1982).

12 Maynard Smith's (1982) book *Evolution and the Theory of Games* is to be recommended. See also Nelson and Winter (1982), Selten (1983) and Axelrod (1984).

It may be objected that this approach does not allow players to learn from their experience whereas even the lowliest of life-forms are capable of adapting their behaviour to their environment. In some models, as in Friedman and Rosenthal (1985), this objection can be answered by asserting that the process by means of which the number playing a strategy is augmented or diminished includes some element of switching from less successful to more successful strategies. A more satisfactory response is to construct a model in which the strategies are 'learning rules'. Some first steps in this direction are to be found in Maynard Smith (1982). (See also Axelrod (1984), who has conducted a number of computer simulations which indicate the promise of such an approach.)

This brings us back to the problem of computational ability. How complicated is a learning strategy allowed to be? Are we to admit learning strategies whose object is to learn the learning strategies of others? Presumably increasing complexity generates costs which, if taken into account, will impose a constraint on the models of an individual which can usefully be considered. Simon (1957) has studied such limitations on complexity under the heading of *bounded rationality*. His observations are highly relevant but are not posed in a form which makes them directly applicable in game theory. For this reason, it is only recently that contributions have been made in this direction (e.g. Selten 1978; Radner 1980; Green 1982; Rubinstein 1985). However, further progress along this avenue is urgently required.

In this section we have presented prescriptive and descriptive game theory as two polar approaches to a single problem. As currently constituted, each suffers from grave deficiencies. On the other hand, they are complementary in that the vices of one are the virtues of the other. Our conjecture is that these two, polar approaches, would be drawn very much closer together if a means could be found for filtering both through a bounded rationality constraint.

We close this section by enlarging on this last point. From the prescriptive point of view, a relevant piece of information is the data processing capacity of the human brain (or, rather, that part of the total capacity which we employ when making decisions). Currently this issue is largely ignored since we know so little about it. However, ideally, one would wish to be sufficiently well informed to make it possible to construct a computer whose mental capabilities were indistinguishable from those of the individual type it is constructed to mimic. A prescriptive theory would then seek an optimal *program* for such a computer. An optimal analysis for two chimpanzees playing chess would then cease to be the same as that for two international grandmasters. A few years ago the objection that the mind of a grandmaster is far too complex for simulation would have seemed an insuperable obstacle to the use of such an example. However, recent progress in artificial intelligence has made it clear that chess can be played very well indeed by machines programmed to employ the same menu of 'heuristics' that the grandmasters use themselves in evaluating a position. From our point of view, such 'heuristics' would form part of the *specification* of a grandmaster.

A descriptive theory would envisage an evolutionary competition among game-playing programs. Bounded rationality would enter as a result of postulating that costs increase as complexity rises. Attention would then be directed at the long-run equilibria of such a system.

So far work on these issues has been largely confined to the repeated 'Prisoner's Dilemma' and related simpler games, e.g. Selten's 'Chain-store Paradox'. See, for example, Selten (1978), Rosenthal (1981), Axelrod (1984), Rubinstein (1985). But this is clearly a direction in which game theory will expand in the near future.

3   EQUILIBRIUM REFINEMENT

We have argued that, if the solution of a contest[13] exists, then it must be a Nash equilibrium. Having made this assertion, we are immediately faced with questions of *existence* and *uniqueness*. Do Nash equilibria exist? If so, is there a unique Nash equilibrium?

The classic theorem on existence is due to Nash (1950) who proved that all finite games have Nash equilibria in mixed strategies.[14] A philosopher might regard this result as closing the existence issue. In practice, however, it is seldom convenient, either conceptually or computationally, to model economic situations as finite games. Typically, agents are assumed to choose from a continuum of strategies: for example, firms may be choosing production outlays or prices. For such games, there is a well-known result of Glicksberg (1952) (see also Fan 1952). Under very general conditions, Glicksberg resolved the existence problem in the affirmative on the assumption that the players' payoffs (or utilities) are continuous functions of their strategies. The continuity assumption may appear innocuous at first blush, but by the mid-1970s, when imperfect competition entered the agenda of theoretical research in an important way, it became clear that many relevant economic games are actually discontinuous.

The first such example of which we are aware was provided by Edgeworth (1925) in his critique of Bertrand's model of price competition when applied to capacity constrained suppliers. If the market demand curve is inelastic at the competitive price, Edgeworth showed that the model has *no* equilibrium in *pure* strategies. Here a pure strategy is just a price quotation. It is

---

13 Recall that a contest is a game of complete information with no pre-play communication, explicit or implicit. Nash regarded such games as fundamental.

14 A game is finite if the number of available pure strategies is finite. A mixed strategy is a probability measure defined on a player's set of pure strategies.

therefore natural to look for an equilibrium in which each player seeks to keep the other guessing by using a *mixed* strategy by randomizing over price quotations. Unfortunately, the fact that the game is discontinuous means that Glicksberg's result does not apply.

Chapter 1 in this volume, by Dasgupta and Maskin, establishes an existence theorem for discontinuous games. The theorem is then used in chapter 2 to show that a number of well-known discontinuous economic games which have no equilibrium in pure strategies do have equilibria in mixed strategies.[15] Thus, although the conditions of the theorem are only sufficient conditions (rather than necessary and sufficient conditions), they are pretty widely applicable.[16]

The foregoing interpretation of a mixed-strategy equilibrium, that players literally randomize over their choice of pure strategies, is pervasive in the game theory literature. Since one can readily doubt the empirical plausibility of agents actually randomizing their choice, mixed strategies are often regarded as a questionable idealization. (But see Varian (1980) for an interpretation of 'sales' offered by retail stores in terms of random price quotations.) In fact there is another interpretation, which makes mixed strategies a totally compelling idea. The point is that at a mixed-strategy equilibrium any given player is indifferent between all the pure strategies to which a positive probability weight has been assigned. When playing against the equilibrium mixed strategies of all the remaining agents the player in question thus may as well choose *any one* of these pure strategies. It follows that a mixed-strategy equilibrium can be seen simply as an equilibrium at which players are *uncertain* about the choice of strategies of all the rival players and where these uncertainties are formalized as probability distributions over agents' pure strategies. In this interpretation, then, agents do not resort to random choice at all. They choose pure strategies, the equilibrium mixed strategies being merely *equilibrium beliefs* held by players about others'

15 These include models with incomplete information (since Bayesian equilibria for such games are simply Nash equilibria for a larger game of complete information). In particular, Section 5 of chapter 2 examines an incomplete information model of the insurance market which was formulated by Rothschild and Stiglitz (1976) and Wilson (1977). Competing insurance firms know each other's types but not what type (high risk or low risk) a particular buyer might be. If firms move first, the resulting game is discontinuous. Indeed, the discontinuities resemble those in the Edgeworth–Bertrand model of price competition. No equilibrium exists in pure strategies but chapter 2 establishes the existence of a mixed-strategy equilibrium.

16 Dierker and Grodel (1984) contains a model of oligopoly in which firms choose quantities on the basis of the market-clearing prices that will ensue once the quantities are produced. As (Walrasian) equilibrium prices are not unique, a selection rule must be postulated. It is shown that, no matter what the selection rules, mixed-strategy equilibria do *not* exist (the conditions of the existence theorem of chapter 1 fail to hold).

choices. Economists view mixed strategies with suspicion, born out of mis-understanding. Gabszewicz (1985) suggests that mixed strategies are a form of *deus ex machina*. Stiglitz (1985, p. 25) simply ignores them when, on discussing the problem of the non-existence of pure strategy equilibrium points in models of incomplete information, he says '... there have been several attempts to find alternative equilibrium concepts, under which ... equilibrium could be assured to exist. In my judgement, all of these have failed.' Mixed strategies do not involve any new equilibrium concept. They involve the idea that agents are not straitjacketed into having point expecta-tions about what others will be choosing. In fact, there is nothing to commend the restriction to research for pure strategy equilibria other than the mathe-matical convenience of the analyst (see chapter 2 below).

It is seldom that the question of uniqueness can be resolved so neatly as that of existence. Indeed, it is frequently the case that a game will admit a *multiplicity* of equilibria, all competing for attention. One is then faced with a *selection problem*.[17] One way of attacking this problem is through the study of refinements of the Nash equilibrium concept.

A particularly important refinement of the Nash equilibrium idea is due to Selten (1975). Selten calls this notion 'perfect' equilibrium but we shall refer to it as 'trembling-hand' equilibrium.[18] Other fruitful refinements have also been developed[19] but their study would take us too far afield.

The trembling-hand equilibria of a game are found by looking at the Nash equilibria of an auxiliary 'perturbed' game. This perturbed game has the same basic structure as the original game except that *all* actions have to be used with a certain minimum probability $\epsilon > 0$. The interpretation is that the players cannot avoid the possibility of making mistakes. Stated metaphoric-ally, each player's hand may tremble as he reaches for lever A, causing him to pull lever B by mistake. The trembling-hand equilibria in the original game are

17 In the insurance market model of footnote 15, the *uninformed* players (i.e. the firms) move first, thus providing an example of a *screening game*. In a *signalling game*, it is the *informed* players who move first by investing in something which has the potential to signal their type. Such signalling games provide good examples of multiple equilibrium problems as in Spence (1974). See Kreps (1984) for a discussion of the selection problems.

Incidentally, it may be as well to note that even the existence of a *unique* Nash equilibrium does not necessarily resolve all problems (Aumann and Maschler 1972).

18 In game theory, there is 'perfect information' and 'perfect recall' to which Selten added 'perfect equilibrium'. All relate to different things. Moreover, Selten offered *two* definitions of perfect equilibrium, intending the second definition to displace the first. The equilibrium notion specified by the first definition was then referred to as 'subgame-perfect equilibrium'. But authors sometimes continue to refer to a subgame-perfect equilibrium simply as a perfect equilibrium (as in Rubinstein's essay in volume 2).

19 For example, sequential equilibrium (Kreps and Wilson 1982), proper equilibrium (Myerson 1975), persistent equilibrium (Kalai and Samet 1982) and stable equilibrium (Kohlberg and Mertens 1982).

then the limits of Nash equilibria in the perturbed game[20] as $\epsilon \to 0$. Equivalently, a Nash equilibrium for the original game is a trembling-hand equilibrium if each of its component strategies remains optimal even when the opponents' hands tremble when selecting their equilibrium strategies.[21]

Some hesitation is appropriate before accepting the notion of a trembling-hand equilibrium as basic in prescriptive game theory. Is it possible for 'perfectly rational' players to make mistakes? This is too big a question to be tackled here, even if the mistakes are assumed to be only little ones (see Binmore 1985). However, the following example of Kreps is revealing.

Game 1

	α	β	γ
A	(50, 0)	(5, 5)	(1, −10,000)
B	(50, 50)	(5, 0)	(0, −10,000)

Player 1 chooses a row and player 2 simultaneously chooses a column. The entries on the matrix indicate the payoffs for the players depending on the strategies chosen. (Thus, if player 1 chooses A and player 2 chooses γ, then player 1 receives a payoff of 1 and player 2 receives a payoff of −10,000.)

Game 1 has two Nash equilibria in pure strategies: namely (B, α) and (A, β). It is easy to check that (A, β) is a trembling-hand equilibrium. But (B, α) is not. To see this, notice that B is a weakly-dominated strategy for player 1. (He is indifferent between A and B so long as 2 plays either α or β and he prefers A to B should 2 choose γ.) Since B is *not* an optimal response by 1 when 2 'attempts' to play α, (B, α) is not a trembling-hand equilibrium. But (A, β) yields the payoff pair $(5, 5)$, while (B, α) yields $(50, 50)$. Is the play of the latter equilibrium to be then rejected as 'irrational'?

Although the notion of a trembling-hand equilibrium is not always persuasive in a *prescriptive* context, the same objections do not apply in a

20 Of course, a proper definition requires a precise definition of a perturbed game. (Such a precise definition includes the requirement that trembles at different information sets are independent.)

21 Again, a more precise statement is necessary in general. We have interpreted a trembling-hand equilibrium as arising out of a recognition that players are always capable of making small mistakes. An alternative approach (due to Harsanyi) is to see it as a Bayesian equilibrium of a game of incomplete information where each player is nearly sure who the other players are, but is not absolutely sure. In fact, the chief purpose of resorting to the idea of trembling-hand equilibrium is to ensure that in games of imperfect information players will have consistent probability expectations about what *would* happen in the hypothetical case where some players reached information sets they in fact will not reach if all players use the strategies prescribed by the equilibrium under consideration. As such, the motivation here is the same as that underlying the Kreps–Wilson concept of sequential equilibrium.

descriptive context. Here small mistakes are a natural component of any scenario. The game-theoretic models employed in evolutionary biology provide a good illustration of this point (see Maynard Smith 1982).

Consider a two-person, symmetric game in which each player has two strategies, *a* and *b*.[22] The game is symmetric since its payoffs are to represent 'Darwinian fitness' on a competitive struggle between animals of the *same* species. Suppose that a large population of animals, all of which are programmed by strategy *a*, is invaded by a tiny group of mutants all programmed to play *b*. How will the situation evolve?

Let ϵ be the proportion of invading mutants in the total animal population. If pairs of animals from the population meet at random to play the game, then it will be as though each player were facing an opponent using a *mixed* strategy which chooses *a* with probability $1 - \epsilon$ and *b* with probability ϵ. The opponent may therefore be regarded as a player who selects *a but with a trembling hand*.

The situation therefore invites an examination of the trembling-hand equilibria of the game. A version of the trembling-hand notion which is tailor-made for such games was introduced by the biologists Maynard Smith and Price (1973). For (a, a) to be an *evolutionary stable equilibrium* in their terminology, it is required that

$$u(a, (1-\epsilon)a + \epsilon b) > u(b, (1-\epsilon)a + \epsilon b)$$

for all sufficiently small $\epsilon > 0$. The payoff function u is interpreted as the expected number of progeny, i.e. incremental Darwinian fitness. If *a* is an *evolutionary stable strategy* (ESS), then a population programmed to play *a* is immune to an invasion by a small group of mutants programmed to play *b*. On average, the mutants will have fewer progeny than the members of the original population and hence will tend to die out in the long run.

In economics, it is an old argument that, over the long haul, non-profit-maximizing firms will be weeded out in the competitive struggle and that only (truly) profit-maximizing firms will survive in the resulting stationary environment (see Winter 1971; Matthews 1984). Nelson and Winter (1982) have recently constructed complex, dynamic models of industrial production and have appealed to computer simulations to obtain an understanding of the evolution of industrial structure. In these models, firms do not optimize in the usual sense. Instead they search locally when their performance falls below some level which they regard as 'acceptable'. The long-run outcomes in the computer simulations of these models bear striking similarities to the equilibrium outcomes obtained by theoretical analysis of appropriate game-theoretic models (see, for example, Dasgupta's chapter 6 in this volume).

22 A game is symmetric if the players' strategy sets are the same and if when their strategies are permuted their payoffs are permuted as well.

We have argued earlier in this introduction that such similarities are to be expected. In particular, an evolutionary stable equilibrium, as defined above, is simply a refinement of a Nash equilibrium. Indeed, (a, a) is evolutionary stable if and only if[23]

either   (i) $u(a, a) > u(b, a)$

or   (ii) $u(a, a) = u(b, a)$ *and* $u(a, b) > u(b, b)$.

Discarding the second requirement of (ii), we are left with the condition that (a, a) be a Nash equilibrium in a symmetric game, i.e. $u(a, a) \geqslant u(b, a)$.

As the preceding paragraph indicates, an evolutionary stable equilibrium is a rather crude refinement of a Nash equilibrium.[24] Selten (1983) offers a considerably more sophisticated adaptation of his trembling-hand notion to the evolutionary context. But, at the end of the day, there is only so much that a theorist can say *in the abstract* in respect of equilibrium selection in evolutionary game theory. The reason is that the final selection will depend on fine details of the equilibrating process and on the initial conditions from which this process began. 'Abstract' reasoning may serve to narrow down the class of things which could have happened: but only empirical research can determine what actually did happen.[25]

In prescriptive theory we may hope for a sharper answer to the selection problem when multiple equilibria exist. But, as Game 1 exemplifies, we ought not to take for granted that the solution of a prescriptive selection problem is necessarily the same as the solution, if any, of a descriptive problem.

However, Selten's (1965) notion of a *subgame-perfect equilibrium* seems appropriate in *both* situations. Not only is any trembling-hand equilibrium necessarily a subgame-perfect equilibrium: subgame-perfectness embodies a persuasive rationality principle. To make the latter point, we consider the following game (see Selten 1965; Harsanyi 1976).

---

23 Both when u measures expected number of progeny and when it is a Von Neumann and Morgenstern utility function, we have that

$$u(a, (1-\epsilon)a + \epsilon b) = (1-\epsilon)u(a, a) + \epsilon u(a, b).$$

24 But see Appendix D of Maynard Smith (1982).

25 From the 'social' point of view there is nothing necessarily *optimal* about a Nash equilibrium (see the text below) and, therefore, about an evolutionary stable equilibrium. Thus suppose there is a symmetric game in which a^* is an ESS. The game may indeed possess another ESS, say, a^{**}, such that $u_i(a^{**}, a^{**}, \ldots, a^{**}) > u_i(a^*, a^*, \ldots, a^*)$ for all i. Now consider a large population, each member of which plays a^*. To this enters a small group of invading mutants, each playing a^{**}. The mutants would not survive if all were to interact randomly, for a^* is an ESS. They would survive though if they were isolated from the original population for a while: the mutants, interacting with one other, would grow at a faster rate than the original population. At some later date the barriers can be lifted and a^* would then be weeded out, since a^{**} is also an ESS. This is a form of the 'infant industry' argument for protection.

Introduction

Game 2

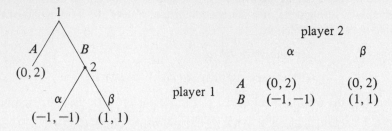

	α	β
A	$(0, 2)$	$(0, 2)$
B	$(-1, -1)$	$(1, 1)$

The game tree on the left indicates that player 1 has the first move, at which he can choose A or B. If A is chosen, the game terminates with the payoff pair $(0, 2)$. If B is chosen, player 2 gets to move. He may choose either α or β, yielding payoff pairs $(-1, -1)$ and $(1, 1)$ respectively. The table on the right indicates the normal (or strategic) form of the game. (Here the strategies labelled α and β indicate what 2 will do *if* 1 chooses B.)

The normal form has two Nash equilibria in pure strategies: namely (A, α) and (B, β). But note that the former requires player 2 to plan to choose α rather than β if he gets the opportunity to make a choice although α has a payoff of -1 and β a payoff of $+1$. Player 1 supposedly predicts this irrational plan (or, where communication is possible, believes player 2's threat to carry out the plan). Player 1 therefore chooses A. Thus player 2 does not get the opportunity to carry out his plan and so its irrationality is not exposed.

Selten (1965) pointed out that such irrational plans (or incredible threats) are inconsistent with the principle of dynamic programming and hence ought to be excluded. In the case of finite games of perfect information like Game 2, the principle of dynamic programming (or backwards induction) requires working backwards from the penultimate decision nodes, deleting irrational actions along the way. Each deletion is equivalent to the deletion of a weakly-dominated strategy from the normal form. (As one can see from the matrix of Game 2, α is a weakly-dominated strategy for player 2. Notice, therefore, that (B, β) is a trembling-hand equilibrium, whereas (A, α) is not.) The principle is the same as that employed in computing Stackelberg equilibria in two-stage models of duopoly production.[26]

For games of imperfect information, it is necessary to work backwards through *subgames* eliminating strategy n-tuples (in n-person games) which fail to require rational behaviour in each subgame. More precisely, a *subgame-perfect equilibrium* is a Nash equilibrium for the entire game which also

26 Although one should properly speak of the subgame-perfect equilibria of a Stackelberg game (in which the leader moves before the follower) rather than the Stackelberg equilibria of a two-person normal form game.

requires Nash equilibrium behaviour in *every* subgame (whether this will be reached, in equilibrium, with positive probability or not).

Selten's concept of subgame-perfect equilibrium has been surprisingly fruitful in eliminating excess equilibria across a variety of models. The dynamic oligopoly games of Shaked and Sutton (chapter 4) and the pre-emptive patenting model of Dasgupta (chapter 6, Section 5) are examples in this volume. Rubinstein's bargaining model is a notable example from the second volume.

We should not abandon the subject of refinements of the equilibrium concept without making it clear that it is a topic which is far from closed. In spite of such successes as those quoted above for subgame perfection, there remain many games for which existing refinement notions have no cutting edge. An example of major importance is found in the theory of repeated games when players discount the future at a low rate. In the 'super-game' obtained by repeating a finite, two-person game indefinitely, *any* (individually rational) outcome can be implemented by a suitable choice among the vast number of Nash equilibria. This is the so-called 'folk-theorem' of game theory (see Rubinstein 1979, 1980; Fudenberg and Maskin 1986). Attempts to eliminate some of these equilibria with the aid of various refinements have so far proved unavailing (see the general folk-theorem of Fudenberg and Maskin 1986).

4   THE AIMS OF GAME THEORY

In hypothesis testing, statisticians recognize two types of error. A type I error is to accept as true an hypothesis which is false. A type II error is to reject as false an hypothesis which is true. In mathematical modelling a similar categorization can be made. A type I error would be to accept as useful a model which is useless. A type II error would be to reject as useless a model which is useful. But what does it mean to say that a model is 'useful' or 'useless'?

There are in fact many ways in which a model can be useful. Most importantly, a model may provide a reasonably accurate picture of the way in which some section of the world works. It can then be used as a basis for policy recommendations. With this interpretation of the word 'useful', it is type I errors that are most to be feared. The purpose of Section 2, on the limitations of game theory, was to warn against type I errors when this interpretation of 'useful' is what is appropriate. The purpose of the current section is to warn against type II errors. Such errors are a commonplace amongst those social scientists who cannot conceive of any use for a model which is not a reasonably accurate representation of some real-world phenomenon. It is true that there is a narrow but important sense in which only models with a good predictive capacity are 'scientific'. For this reason we place 'prediction' at the head of the following list of aims for which a model might be constructed. If this first item is the only 'scientific' purpose for a model, then the other items are necessarily 'unscientific'. But no economist need fear being labelled 'unscientific' for adopting techniques which constitute standard (and highly successful) practice amongst theoretical physicists and other natural scientists.

From among the many possible reasons for constructing a model, we distinguish the following general aims: 0, prediction; 1, explanation; 2, criticism; 3, design. Although the methodological point we are making lies very close to the surface, it is one which is often misunderstood and so we propose to enlarge on what is involved in aims 1, 2 and 3. In seeking to achieve such aims, the models used will typically incorporate assumptions which cannot be justified in real-world terms. Such models are therefore hypothetical and it follows that the questions they address are hypothetical questions. But the answers to hypothetical questions can be very instructive: hence Roosevelt's advice to politicians that such questions not be answered. Physics undergraduates, for example, learn about fluid mechanics by initially studying two-dimensional models, although everybody agrees that space has at least three dimensions.

1   Explanation

Here we are concerned with aims in modelling which resemble those of geophysicists, evolutionary biologists, cosmologists, and meteorologists. Their fields resemble economics in that the application of classical experimental technique is not feasible. Instead use must be made of 'natural experiments' thrown up by events. Models employed in such disciplines often generate much conviction because they explain a great mass of data, albeit at a very general level, on the basis of a few plausible basic assumptions. Reductionists using such models do not claim (or should not claim) that this is the way the world *must* be: only that here is a simple model of the way the world *could* be. Usually such models are advanced with the aim of demonstrating that there is no necessity to postulate some *hidden-hand*, or *Deus ex machina* to explain complex phenomena. The fact that this is a negative aim does not make it any the less valuable.

It is natural to seek reductionist explanations of sociological, economic or political phenomena in terms of the *intentions* of the agents concerned. An agent may be an individual, a firm or some more complex organization and the intentions attributed to such an agent may be of various kinds: for example, he may be motivated by the urge to conform to some social norm or moral standard, to maximize monetary profit or simply to perpetuate his own continued existence. Game theory would seem an ideal vehicle when the aim is to offer explanations in terms of agents (or, less convincingly, of coalitions of agents) who are determined optimizers.[27] This is not necessarily a correct hypothesis but it is a simple one; and the existence of a precise, mathematical theory of games endows it with explanatory power out of all proportion to its complexity: hence the satisfaction felt when it is successfully able to provide a possible explanation for apparently complex relationships between aggregate economic variables.

It should be noted that the decision to employ a game-theoretic analysis does not necessarily require *all* agents to be modelled as optimizers. The behaviour of some agents (e.g. of a government agency) may be taken as given with no attempt being made at explaining it. Such behaviour becomes, in essence, part of the rules of the game played by those agents whose behaviour is to be explained.

Chapters 3–7 in Part II of this volume provide examples of explanations, in this sense, of certain features of industrial organization, such as the emergence of industrial concentration, the extent of product differentiation and the degree of competition among firms.

2   Criticism

The collection of data and the running of experiments in the social sciences is notoriously difficult. For this reason, economists have long used a research technique prevalent also in the natural sciences: namely, a systematic analysis of what are called 'mind-experiments'. When a mind-experiment is employed in a discipline it often does not matter at all whether the hypotheses on which it is built are realistic or even realizable. The purpose of mind-experiments is to test the *internal logic* of a theory rather than to verify or refute its conclusions. An economist, for example, may claim that, if firms may 'freely' enter an industry, then profits, of necessity, will be driven to zero. Doubtless, such an economist will have arguments with which to support his assertion. Since our knowledge of the world is incomplete, these arguments will have to apply, not only to the world as it is, but also to a variety of other worlds that might have been. In particular, most economists would agree that their arguments would remain valid in a world in which *Homo sapiens* were replaced by *Homo economicus*. Such an argument makes it possible to seek to construct a mathematical model of a theoretical economy in which the hypotheses of the economist are true but his conclusions are false. The model is then a counter-example to the general theory, i.e. it serves as a falsifying *experiment substitute*. It refutes, not the predictions of the theory, but the validity of the supporting argument.[28]

27 An exceptionally lucid and non-technical essay illustrating and emphasizing this point of view for explaining group behaviour is Schelling (1978).

28 Our understanding of the distinction between 'fixed-costs' and 'sunk-costs' has, to take only one example, been sharpened by a study of the implications of 'free-entry'. In this collection these issues are explored in chapters 3–7.

3   *Design*

Under this heading, we consider models whose purpose is to serve as a plan for the restructuring of an organization or of an activity within an organization. The organization may be a firm, an industry or, indeed, an entire economy. Similarly, the restructuring envisaged may range from the design of incentive-compatible bonus schemes for piece-workers to the construction of Utopias aimed at the total overhaul of society. As far as game theory is concerned, the organizations of interest are those in which the participants do not necessarily share the same goals and so opportunities exist, not only for mutually beneficial cooperation, but also for conflict.[29]

The point here is that it is not enough to develop criteria for social welfare. A means has to be found for implementing such criteria. The idea is to alter the rules of an existing game so as to achieve an outcome which is more desirable from the planner's point of view. (The case of a selfish or anti-social planner is not excluded, but interest centres on a planner motivated by a given and defendable criterion of social welfare.) Such an approach raises many issues, both technical and philosophical. Of these, we will consider only one: the importance of distinguishing 'group rationality' from 'individual rationality'. It is a major and fundamental error to take it for granted that, because certain cooperative behaviour will benefit every individual in a group, rational individuals will adopt this behaviour. Once all opportunities for negotiation have been modelled as formal moves in a game, rational individuals will act *strategically* and hence implement an *equilibrium* in the game. The basic problem in the design of games is therefore to construct games whose equilibria have desirable properties. As such, it can be seen as a branch of applied welfare economic theory.

As an example, consider the notion of Pareto-efficiency. For a profile of strategies, one for each player, to be Pareto-efficient, it must be the case that no other strategy profile makes at least one player better off without making any other player worse off.[30] There is no reason why an equilibrium of a game should be Pareto-efficient. In general it will not be. Dubey (1980) has studied the precise sense in which this is true. But the basic idea (of why *in general* an equilibrium is not Pareto-efficient) is very simple and so we present it below.

29 The theory of teams, as invented by Marschak and Radner (1972), is concerned with the problem of co-ordination in organizations in which members share a common goal. Two-person constant sum games offer no opportunities for enjoying mutual gains.

30 Much welfare economics is based on welfare orderings that subsume Pareto-efficiency; that is, Pareto-efficiency is regarded as necessary for optimality, though obviously it is not sufficient. One may, as has Sen (1970), question even its necessity, if non-welfare information about persons is deemed relevant in judging the desirability of outcomes.

Suppose there are N persons ($i = 1, 2, \ldots, N$) and that the feasible set of strategies for i is A_i, a closed interval of the real line. Let $u_i : \Pi_{j=1}^{N} A_j \to R^1$ be i's utility function. Write $\mathbf{a} = (a_1, \ldots, a_i, \ldots, a_N)$, where $a_i \in A_i$. Now suppose that $\mathbf{a}^*$ is an equilibrium point of the game. If u_i is differentiable and if $\mathbf{a}^*$ is an interior point of $\Pi_{j=1}^{N} A_j$, then $\mathbf{a}^*$ must be a solution of the system of N equations:

$$\partial u_i(\mathbf{a})/\partial a_i = 0, \text{ for } i = 1, \ldots, N. \tag{0.1}$$

On the other hand, suppose $\bar{\mathbf{a}}$ is Pareto-efficient. If $\bar{\mathbf{a}}$ is also an interior point of $\Pi_{j=1}^{N} A_j$, it must be the solution of the system of N equations:

$$\sum_{i=1}^{N} \lambda_i \, \partial u_i(\mathbf{a})/\partial a_j = 0, \text{ for } j = 1, \ldots, N, \tag{0.2}$$

where $(\lambda_1, \ldots, \lambda_i, \ldots, \lambda_N)$ is an N-tuple of positive numbers. Clearly (0.1) and (0.2) are not in general the same set of equations. Thus, $\mathbf{a}^*$ is not in general a solution of (0.2). So a Nash equilibrium is not Pareto-efficient, in general.

Many find it paradoxical that an equilibrium point of a game may not be group-rational. Otherwise it is difficult to see why so much intellectual energy has been invested in *philosophical* discussions of the Prisoners' Dilemma, the now-classic example of a game in which this non-congruence is sharply etched. (Recall that in this example each player has a dominant strategy, choice of which is Pareto-inefficient.) In fact, there is nothing remotely paradoxical about this. Non-cooperative games like the Prisoners' Dilemma are constructed in such a way that the players *are not able* to act jointly. It is therefore not surprising that they have to forgo the fruits of cooperation. An N-tuple of strategies is Pareto-efficient if it cannot be blocked by the coalition of all individuals. It is an equilibrium point if it cannot be blocked by any individual acting on his own. We should be surprised when the two are congruent, not when they are not.

Attempts to evade the conclusion of the Prisoners' Dilemma always reduce in the end to philosophical conjuring tricks in which the game is replaced by some other game which admits a more 'satisfactory' conclusion. Sometimes the payoffs are implicitly altered by attributing altruistic (or 'socialized') motives to the players. Sometimes the strategy spaces are altered, as in the theory of meta-games (Howard 1971). Sometimes the players are changed by implicitly treating them both as the *same* player and thus reducing the game to a one-player decision problem. It is true that, in many cases, the replacement game may be more appropriate to the situation being modelled than the Prisoners' Dilemma. Consider, for example, the phenomenon of 'kin-selection' in evolutionary models involving repetitions of the Prisoners' Dilemma (e.g. Axelrod 1984). Here, the fact that a program (or a gene package) may be playing against 'itself' becomes increasingly significant as its frequency in the population increases. In the limit, we may therefore be reduced to solving a one-player decision problem (subject to the constraint that the solution be stable in the face of invasion by the 'mutants'). But this important insight is only obscured by pretending that it can be achieved via a wrong analysis (i.e. an identification of the players) of the wrong game (i.e. the one-shot Prisoners' Dilemma).

This aside on the Prisoners' Dilemma is not made without some provocation. No game theorist will deny that *rational cooperation* in society is desirable. What will be denied is that rational cooperation can be sustainable in *all* environments. An admission of this elementary point makes it possible to concentrate on what changes in the environment are necessary to facilitate cooperation by rational individuals or to ensure that contests lead to desirable outcomes. Game *design* addresses one aspect of this class of problem. Chapters 8 and 9 in Part III discuss a few problems from this class.

5   THEORIES OF IMPERFECT COMPETITION

If non-cooperative game theory did not find much use in economic theorizing for some time it may be because of the economist's almost exclusive interest in the Walrasian economy. For there is no room for strategic behaviour in the Walrasian construct. The aim is to study an economy in which individuals treat prices as parameters. One assumes that there is a market for each and every commodity and that prices are publicly quoted. Since the hypothesis of price-taking behaviour makes sense only at equilibrium – or market clearing – prices (see Arrow 1959), we concentrate on them. These prices form part of the environment in which agents make their choices. At these prices a consumer needs only to know his endowments and his mind. Likewise, the manager of a firm needs only to know the firm's production technology. In particular, an agent needs to know nothing about who the remaining participants are, what the economy's productive capacity is, and so on. To put it more concisely, no one needs to have a model of the economy in his mind. This informational parsimony, made possible by the co-ordinating role played by the Walrasian price system, has been much commented upon. Equally emphasized has been the fact that an equilibrium allocation of goods and services in a Walrasian economy is Pareto-efficient.[31] But the Walrasian construct is designed to study resource allocation at equilibrium prices. It does not explain how the prices get established or why agents treat them as parameters. In one line of investigation an auctioneer is postulated to handle the first question, and in order to meet the second, each individual is assumed

31 The standard reference to these issues is Arrow and Hahn (1971).

to be 'small' relative to the economy.[32] In another, the socialist-pricing literature, a planner takes the auctioneer's role and agents are simply instructed to be price-takers. Neither would seem to be a suitable explanatory device for resource allocation mechanisms in private-ownership market economies.

Chapters 3–7 in Part II of this volume are all directed at *imperfectly* competitive markets, the adverb reflecting the hypothesis that not all agents are price-takers. Issues arising from incomplete information are not addressed here. It is supposed throughout that prices are public information and that goods and services are perfectly distinguishable and recognizable by all parties. Furthermore, all commodities are assumed to have a market. Market production processes are formalized as games and their equilibrium points are studied. To concentrate attention on essential matters consumers are throughout seen as price-takers. It is the production sector which is viewed as being imperfectly competitive.

The first question any such investigation must face concerns the motivation of firms. What ought they to be seen as maximizing? In a Walrasian world it seems eminently reasonable that they maximize profits. Owners would not wish it to be otherwise.[33] But in a world where firms can influence prices by their actions this is not so reasonable, at least not without justification (see Gabszewicz and Vial (1972) for an early discussion of this). Justification can be provided if the firm's shareholders spend only a small portion of their wealth on its product(s). For in this case the firm's pricing policy would not affect the shareholders' attainable utilities by virtue of these price changes; it will affect attainable utilities only through the effect on their wealth. Explicitly or implicitly, this hypothesis is maintained in each of the essays in this volume, so that firms are assumed to maximize profits.

In fact, yet more is assumed. Income effects are ignored: the models are all 'partial equilibrium'. As a recent survey by Hart (1983) demonstrates

32 In their classic article on the existence of Walrasian equilibrium Arrow and Debreu (1954) introduced an auctioneer into the economy. They assumed that the auctioneer chooses (non-negative) prices so as to maximize the value of excess demands for goods and services. Consumers and firms are by assumption price-takers, and maximize 'utilities' and profits respectively. Moreover, all the participants – including the auctioneer – move simultaneously. Thus, the Walrasian trading process is visualized explicitly as a (generalized) game. Arrow and Debreu showed that equilibrium points of such a (generalized) game are (perfectly) competitive allocations. Leaving aside the beauty of the idea, a great merit of this reformulation is that it draws one's attention to the fact that the informational parsimony in the Walrasian economy, mentioned above, is in part illusory.

33 Recall that by hypothesis all commodities have markets. It is well known that there is a problem in identifying the 'motivation' of a firm if there are missing risk markets. (See e.g. *Bell Journal of Economics and Management Science Symposium*, 5, 1974.)

implicitly, this is a sensible research strategy if we wish to *characterize* outcomes in oligopolistic industries. General equilibrium models can become
cumbersome rapidly, and in any event there are severe problems in ensuring
the existence of an equilibrium in pure strategies.

But is it reasonable to ignore income effects when studying an industry?
The answer is 'yes', provided those who purchase its product(s) spend only
a small portion of their income (or wealth) on them. For in this case the
industry's pricing policy does not affect the purchaser's *income*: only the
substitution effect prevails. This might well be true for products like tooth-
paste and restaurant services. It presumably is not true for automobiles.[34]

In modelling an imperfectly competitive industry one wants to capture the
strategic considerations that *producers* may possibly entertain. For this
reason it is sensible to allow the firms to have the first move. Consumers
can be thought of as moving next and they are seen as price-takers. In his
pioneering work on imperfect competition Cournot (1838) adopted this
modelling strategy, for each of his firms computed its profits from the market
demand function. Chapters 3–7 in Part II of this volume adopt this feature
of Cournot's work. It should be noted that even within the general confines
of this two-move structure there is a rich menu of possibilities for modelling
firm-behaviour. For example, Shaked and Sutton, in chapters 4 and 5, think
of a firm's move as being composed of several submoves: whether or not to
enter the industry, followed by a decision of what product quality to manufacture if the earlier decision has been to enter, followed by a pricing decision.
Another example is provided by Dasgupta in chapter 6 (section 5), where
some privileged firm – in the case considered, the sitting monopolist – is
allowed the first move. This is followed by a move from potential competitors. The idea is to explore the phenomenon of pre-emptive patenting, and
the move structure, as one can recognize immediately, is similar to the one
considered by von Stackelberg in his extension of Cournot's duopoly model.
But in each of the chapters firms' profits are computed from the market
demand function; that is, consumers are seen as passive agents, moving last.

In a Walrasian economy firms are by hypothesis price-takers. They therefore choose quantities of inputs and outputs, conditioned by technological
transformation possibilities. What then are the strategic variables in the
imperfectly competitive industry? In their classic contributions Cournot
(1838) saw firms choosing *quantities* and Bertrand (1883) saw them choosing
prices. The problem with Cournot's work, as he left it, is that it does not
explain the formation of prices any more than the Walrasian construct does.
In Cournot's model one may postulate an auctioneer who finds market-
clearing prices once the quantities have been produced by the firms in

34 The richer the society, the greater presumably is the number of commodities for
which the income effect is negligible.

question. Implicitly or explicitly, most of the enormous literature following Cournot's quantity-setting approach assumes this. In contrast, the question of how prices are formed is answered in one stroke by Bertrand, for the hallmark of his approach is that firms are seen as directly controlling the prices of their products.

There is a growing view that the strategic variables that firms use to compete against one another depend on the time-scale under study. Prices can be altered quickly. But production takes time and one cannot quickly alter supplies except through the holding of inventories, which is not costless. Strategic variables such as research and development require even longer lead times. This point of view has received careful attention in the work of Shaked and Sutton (chapters 4 and 5) who, as we noted earlier, see firms using prices for waging short-run competition and product quality for longrun competition. The same general view is explored by Dasgupta, Gilbert and Stiglitz in chapter 7, where research and development is seen as the strategic variable with long lead time. In a penetrating series of studies, Maskin and Tirole (1982, 1985) have developed this view the most extensively. Seen in this light, the Cournot model of quantity competition is merely a 'reduced form' of an intertemporal model in which firms first choose capacities and then compete through the use of prices.[35]

Chapters 3–7 in Part II of this volume are all directed at one broad class of interrelated questions: what are the features that determine how powerful are the forces of competition, and how are these in turn related within an industry to the nature of innovative activity undertaken and the characteristics of the commodities produced? Specifically, the essays address three sets of issues which we shall discuss briefly by way of an introduction to them.

(a) Perfect Competition as a Limit of Oligopolistic Competition in Large Markets

It has been suggested for some time that the Walrasian theory of perfect competition – culminating in the work of Arrow and Debreu – should be

35 An explicit example of this is in the interesting work of Kreps and Scheinkman (1982). They consider a two-stage game in which firms first choose their production capacities at constant marginal cost, C^*. In the second stage they compete for the market through the use of prices, as in Bertrand (1883), and it is assumed that each firm can produce at constant marginal cost, C^{**}, up to the capacity level which has been installed. In the case of a linear demand curve and a particular specification of how the commodity is allocated among consumers if the dupolistics cannot supply total demand Kreps and Scheinkman show that the model possesses a unique subgame perfect equilibrium in which each firm chooses that capacity and production level which would be chosen by the firm in a (one-stage) Cournot quantity setting model with constant marginal production cost $C^* + C^{**}$.

viewed as being a theory of imperfect competition applied to an economy in which the quantities of goods and services each firm wants to produce are 'small' *relative* to the economy. For example, consider that intermediate price-theory texts usually refer to the fees that 'super-stars' – in sports, the performing arts, or whatever – command as *competitive* rents despite the fact that such 'stars' possess unique characteristics. Why? The reasoning must be this. Suppose you are the sole producer of a commodity which is consumed by a large number of people, each of whose consumption of your product is a small portion of his total consumption of goods and services. Now you increase your output by 1 per cent. This increase is spread over your customers, and since there are many of them, the increase in consumption by each is negligible. Moreover, if the consumers' marginal rates of substitution between your good and other goods are bounded the *alteration* in the marginal rate of substitution between your good and other goods for each of your customers is negligible. This implies that you face a horizontal demand curve for your product. This does not mean your earnings are not high. They are high if your product has no near-substitutes. But such earnings constitute 'rent', not monopoly profits. You have market power but not monopoly power.[36]

The foregoing argument is simple enough, but it begs the question: one would like to know under what conditions each firm's desired production level *is* small relative to the economy. In an important contribution, Hart (1979) identified conditions – on such 'primitives' as preferences, the range of producible commodities and production possibilities – under which each firm's desired level of output becomes vanishingly small relative to the 'size of the economy' when the number of consumers in the economy is made to increase indefinitely.[37] The issue has received considerable attention in recent years. (See the Symposium on Large Economies in the *Journal of Economic Theory*, Volume 22, No. 2 (April 1980), and also Novshek (1980), Novshek and Sonnenschien (1978) and Ushio (1983).) For any such 'limit result' as we have been discussing it is useful to have some idea of the rate of convergence. This enables one to judge how good an approximation the limiting economy is. That is to say, if perfect competition is strictly valid only when the number of consumers is infinite it is worth knowing how good an approximation the hypothesis of perfect competition is when applied to a large but finite economy. Chapter 3 by Dasgupta and Ushio addresses this

36 That is, unless there are many close substitutes, price would exceed the average cost of production and we would observe for the commodity in question: marginal revenue = price = marginal cost > average cost.

37 In a pioneering essay Gabszewicz and Vial (1972) identified conditions on similar primitives, but they considered *un*differentiated products. Technological assumptions that should be noted in Hart (1979) are (a) that the space of differentiated products is compact; and (b) that firms' production sets are compact.

question in the context of a single industry producing a homogeneous product. Production by a firm involves a fixed cost and a constant marginal cost. Firms choose quantities, move simultaneously and there is free-entry. Assuming a linear market demand curve it is shown that Cournot equilibria tend to the competitive equilibrium outcome as the size of the market is enlarged, and the rate of convergence is the inverse of the square root of the size of the market. (For related results see Fraysse and Moreaux (1981), Guesnerie and Hart (1985) and Ushio (1983).) Convergence is thus slow, but it needs to be borne in mind that production sets are assumed to be un-bounded and more strongly that the average cost curve is everywhere down-ward sloping.[38] In particular, the analysis suggests a common notion of a 'natural monopoly' – one where the efficient size of a firm is comparable to the size of the market – is misleading. The industry in question here is a 'natural' monopoly with a vengeance. (The efficient size of a firm is infinity!) This, on its own, is not however an argument for discouraging competition.

(b)   Product Variety, Sunk Costs and Free-entry

For the most part (as in Salop 1979) models of imperfect competition ad-dressing the issue of product variety assume heterogeneity of consumer preferences, that if all brands are charged the same price each brand is *some* consumer's most preferred brand and that consumers are not indifferent between all brands. Armed with such an assumption it is possible to simplify and assume consumers to have the same wealth and still account for product variety in the market.

An alternative formulation is to concentrate on product *quality* by assum-ing that all consumers rank all brands the same way and then account for variety in the market by supposing that consumers differ in their ability to pay for quality, because of unequal wealth distribution. (Thus, the rich buy what all agree to be the better quality because they can afford to pay the higher price that is charged for it.) Such a formulation, studied by Gabszewicz and Thisse (1979, 1980), has been extended in different directions in a series of articles by Shaked and Sutton (chapters 4 and 5 in this volume).

Gabszewicz and Thisse (1980) assume that there is a continuum of con-sumers with differing wealth (income), and that there are m different qualities of a product offered in the market, each by a different firm. A consumer purchases a unit of his most preferred *price-adjusted* variety so long as this is better than not purchasing the product at all. Specifically, let θ_i (a positive

38 If average cost curves are U-shaped then the rate of convergence is as one should expect, faster. In fact, it is the inverse of the size of the market. This should be com-pared with Debreu (1975) where it is shown that in convex, regular economies the core converges to the set of competitive equilibria at the rate of the inverse of the size of the economy.

number exceeding unity) denote the product quality offered by the ith firm ($i = 1, \ldots, m$) and let $p(\theta_i)$ be the price charged for it. Then the utility of a consumer with wealth t, consuming θ_i, is taken to be $\theta_i(t - p(\theta_i))$. In the event the consumer does not consume the product his utility is simply t. Production costs are assumed to be nil for all firms and their strategies are their sales prices, $p(\theta_i)$, $i = 1, \ldots, m$. (Production sets are thus unbounded.) One therefore studies equilibrium outcomes, treating the product qualities on offer as exogenous. Gabszewicz and Thisse (1980) showed that the number of firms (and thus the number of product qualities) that can co-exist in the market is finite. Moreover, equilibrium profits are positive. The intuition behind the result is that if high quality products are introduced exogenously into the market, low quality firms which previously enjoyed positive profits are driven out through price competition.

In chapter 4 Shaked and Sutton extend the foregoing result about the finiteness of the number of qualities that the market can sustain by supposing that associated with each quality is a constant unit production cost.[39] They prove that if unit cost of production does not increase too rapidly with product quality the foregoing result continues to hold. (They call such an industry a Natural Oligopoly.) On the other hand, if it does increase sufficiently steeply, the number of product qualities that can find room in equilibrium is infinity, and equilibrium profits are zero; the intuition being that in this case the only way high quality firms can drive low quality ones out of the market is to lower prices to the point where they themselves make losses.

The model's shortcoming is, of course, that product quality is not 'explained': those on offer are taken to be given. This limitation is overcome completely in chapter 5 where Shaked and Sutton allow firms first to decide whether or not to enter the industry, followed by a decision about what quality to offer, conditional on entry, followed in turn by choice of price conditional on choice of product quality. Production costs are assumed nil, but it is supposed that there is an entry cost (possibly very small). Production cost being nil, we know in advance from Gabszewicz and Thisse (1980) that, provided firms produce distinct qualities, only a finite number of qualities will be on offer at an equilibrium and that firms will earn positive profits. Shaked and Sutton first prove that in subgame-perfect equilibrium no two firms will offer the same product quality, and then prove that for a particular class of parameter values there is a subgame-perfect equilibrium in which precisely two firms enter, produce distinct qualities and enjoy positive profits (Theorem 3 in chapter 5).

To see how one argues that no two firms produce the same product quality we consider a reduced form of the foregoing example by assuming

39 Firms' production sets are thus unbounded, as in Gabszewicz and Thisse (1980), cf. footnote 35.

variety away. Consider then a market for a homogeneous product whose production cost is nil. But suppose, following Shaked and Sutton, that there is an entry cost into the industry (assumed very small). Upon entry firms compete in prices. Thus the entry costs are *sunk* by the time the second stage of the move is made. It is now easy to see that if potential firms move simultaneously, the game possesses a subgame-perfect equilibrium in pure strategies in which precisely one firm enters and it charges the pure monopoly price.[40] The market is hopelessly inefficient. What are the policy implications?

A government policy which suggests itself is the imposition of a *price floor*, a designated *minimum* price that firms must comply with. It is easy to see that in the example above the government can set this minimum low enough so as to ensure that in equilibrium precisely two firms will enter, will set this minimum price via price competition, and earn zero profits net of entry costs. Indeed, social benefit under the policy just described falls short of the full optimum by (approximately) a single entry cost. Admittedly this is a mere example. But it does suggest that when sunk-costs are incurred by firms and when firms compete not only in product quality but also prices, the imposition of price *floors* on different qualities is a possible method for sustaining competition and increasing consumer welfare (see Dasgupta and Stiglitz (1984) for an analysis of this). Unfortunately the recent surge of interest in the theory of industrial organization has not reflected much passion for policy issues. Much remains to be done in this area.

One question that *has* attracted attention is the possible gains from trade in a world with differentiated products (see e.g. Krugman 1979). In their 1984 essay, Shaked and Sutton address this by extending the model of chapter 5 in this volume. They assume that upon entry a firm incurs a fixed production cost – the marginal cost of production being still zero here – and that this fixed cost (interpreted as R & D expenditure) is an increasing function of product quality. They demonstrate that under a class of parameter values similar to the one considered in chapter 5 there is a subgame-perfect equilibrium in which precisely two qualities make their appearance, and the two operating firms earn positive profits, net of entry and R & D costs. Moreover, the greater is the density of consumers the better is the quality pair that makes its appearance.[41] (This is essentially because the marginal return on R & D expenditure is higher the larger the size of the market.) In fact they prove that under certain conditions an increase in the size of the market makes *all* income groups better off. This is interpreted as a result about the gains from trade.

40 There is a symmetric mixed-strategy equilibrium among the potential firms, but nothing of substance matters for our exposition if we ignore it. We can in fact eliminate such an equilibrium entirely if we postulate that firms move sequentially. It is readily checked that the first firm to move enjoys all the advantages.

41 See Theorem 2 in Shaked and Sutton (1984).

(c)   Technological Change and Market Structure

An important channel through which firms engage in non-price competition is research and development $(R\&D)$.[42] $R\&D$ expenditure designed to locate new or improved products and to lower the manufacturing cost of existing products influences the structure of the industry. At the same time industrial structure is a determinant of the incentives that firms have for engaging in such forms of non-price competition as $R\&D$. This mutual relationship was a central theme in Schumpeter (1950), although his discussion was not in a form that is readily amenable to tests. It is somewhat paradoxical then that until recently the investigations Schumpeter's writings stimulated were for the most part empirical. Here there have been broadly two trends. One has been the case-study approach, the other an analysis of interindustry data by way of regressions undertaken between variables such as the degree of concentration, the intensity of $R\&D$ activity, the number of patents issued, growth in demand for products, and so forth. Chapter 6 in this volume, by Dasgupta, contains a summary of a number of empirical findings from the latter route. It also presents a simple theoretical construct to account for them. Although formulated in a timeless context (see Spence (1986) for a generalization) it sees $R\&D$ competition among firms as a continuous process and, more importantly, it focuses attention on that aspect of $R\&D$ output which is embodied internally within the firm.[43]

Traditionally three forces have been seen as determining the nature and extent of $R\&D$ efforts in an industry: the degree of appropriability of $R\&D$ benefits by firms (Schumpeter 1950; Arrow 1962), the extent of the market (Schmookler 1966) and innovation opportunities (Rosenberg 1976). The construction in the first part of chapter 6 accommodates all three simultaneously and thereby enables one in principle to judge the relative importance of each. But there are difficulties in doing this. Even if the latter two determining factors are treated as parameters in a model it would be misleading to so treat the first. For, the degree of appropriability depends not only on technological opportunities and the legal code: it depends as well on industrial structure, and this should not be regarded exogenous. Thus, the view emphasized in this essay (as in Dasgupta and Stiglitz 1980a) is that structure, conduct and performance are intrinsically related, but none of them 'determines' the others.

---

42 For an excellent set of recent case studies on this, see Nelson (1982). There is evidence, for example, that firms in the drug industry spend more than 10 per cent of their sales revenue on $R\&D$ and about the same on promotional outlays. See Grabowski and Vernon (1982, p. 295).

43 For a recent summary of evidence leading to the view that a substantial fraction of $R\&D$ output is of this form, see Cohen and Mowery (1984). $R\&D$ spillovers have been introduced into this model by Tandon (1984) and Levin and Reiss (1984).

The latter part of chapter 6 is devoted to simple 'patent races', a subject that has rather unfortunately dominated the recent theoretical literature. Admittedly, 'patent races' in theoretical models are not to be taken literally. What such models formalize is the fact that in certain cases what confers advantage is to be the first to *develop* a product line. Nevertheless, the short-coming of such models is that they see a single development in sight. In Dasgupta and Stiglitz (1980b) and Gilbert and Newbery (1982) an argument was developed that in certain circumstances a sitting monopolist has the greatest incentive to accomplish a further innovation in the industry. The idea here is a formalization of the one in Schumpeter (1950), to the effect that a monopolist is spurred into undertaking innovations so as to forestall entry. The latter part of chapter 6 reproduces this argument and develops conditions under which a sitting monopolist will pre-empt on *multiple* patents. These conditions are found to be extremely strong. The idea of the persistent monopolist is not to be taken seriously.

Chapter 7, by Dasgupta, Gilbert and Stiglitz, addresses a different question: What is the optimal R & D investment strategy for a resource importing country where the R & D effort is directed at developing substitute supplies? The question has received extensive concern among energy-model builders but for the most part such large-scale numerical models assume the resource price to be exogenously given, that is, uninfluenced by the domestic government's R & D policy. This obviously does not make sense. If OPEC can raise its price when it is to its advantage, it can equally lower its price should that be to its advantage. This strategic interaction, between domestic R & D policy and resource pricing policy of a foreign cartel, is formalized explicitly as an intertemporal game in chapter 7. Of particular interest is, perhaps, the result that it may well be in the interest of the importing country to use its commitment to R & D as a means of forcing the foreign cartel to lower its price today, and indeed to plan to complete the development of substitute supplies overly early in order to do so.

6   THE DESIGN OF ORGANIZATIONS

We are thinking here of society as a cooperative venture among individuals for mutual advantage. Background rules, laws, regulations and so forth, go towards *defining* a game: they help delineate individuals' feasible sets of actions. We may think of a centralized authority – the *state* – as an agency that enforces these rules etc. But in addition such an agency is required so as to co-ordinate the activities of the members of society. For at least two reasons. A central agency may be useful in disseminating information. Furthermore, we noted earlier that equilibrium points of a game typically will not satisfy even as weak a welfare criterion as Pareto-efficiency. So a central agency could be of importance in altering the rules of the game in order to help attain outcomes deemed socially desirable.

In what follows we shall suppose that society has adopted a criterion of social welfare. We need not for the moment be precise about how discriminating the criterion is. It may yield a complete ordering (as in Classical Utilitarianism). Or it may yield a partial ordering (as with Pareto-efficiency). Call a welfare optimum a *full optimum* if it 'maximizes' the social welfare criterion subject only to the technological and resource availability constraints the society faces. A welfare problem in which additional constraints have been introduced is called a second-best problem. If these additional constraints are potent we call a solution of such a problem a *second-best optimum*. Chapters 8 and 9 in Part III of this volume assume that these additional constraints arise from information asymmetries among individuals and the state. In general one would suppose that informational constraints are potent so that an optimum organization can at most sustain a second-best outcome – optimum second-best that is! But in certain circumstances the informational constraints can be rendered impotent by suitably designing the organizational structure of society, so that a full optimum can be implemented.[44]

To illustrate all this recall that the Fundamental Theorem of Welfare Economics begins by supposing that the central authority knows and can observe everything of relevance to its role. A full optimum allocation of goods and services can therefore be realized rather trivially by *command*. It is the achievement of the theorem in question that it proves that provided certain technical conditions are met regarding preferences, technology and so forth, a full optimum allocation of goods and services can be realized via a decentralized scheme in which the state is empowered to impose lump-sum transfers and to announce prices at which individuals and production units are then instructed to trade. Thus the Fundamental Theorem can be viewed as a statement about the equilibrium point of a suitably designed game (of complete information) in which the state makes the first move by simultaneously announcing prices and imposing lump-sum wealth transfer, followed by production units choosing profit maximizing activities and consumers choosing their most preferred vectors of goods and services subject to their government-imposed budget constraints. We conclude that as *instruments* for attaining a full optimum a command system and a price guided decentralized system are equally effective.[45]

It is clear that the operational significance of the Fundamental Theorem of Welfare Economics is minimal. The information that the state is assumed

44 What is often called the incentive compatibility literature is concerned with identifying such circumstances. See e.g. *Review of Economic Studies Symposium on Incentive Compatibility* (April 1979).

45 For elaboration of these issues, see Dasgupta (1980, 1982).

to possess is awesome. It is assumed to know the preferences and endowments of each and every member of society and the production possibilities available for transforming goods and services into goods and services. Questions of practical interest arise when the design of organizations takes into account the fact that the central authority possesses incomplete information. This issue is at the heart of the two chapters in Part III of this volume.

One supposes that there are certain pieces of information that are known (or which will be known) only by the individual in question; that is, they are costly (or in the extreme, impossible) to monitor publicly. These *private* pieces of information presumably include: (a) an individual's personal characteristics (e.g. his preferences and personal endowments), that is, what kind of a person he *is*; (b) the actions that he takes (e.g. how hard he works at a given task), that is, what he *does*; and (c) localized pieces of information about the state of the world (e.g. certain aspects of specialized technological possibilities). Following the insurance literature the terms *adverse selection* and *moral hazard* are often used to characterize problems in the design of organizations raised by (a) and (c), and by (b) categories of private information, respectively. One supposes as well that there are certain pieces of information that are publicly known or which can be publicly observed at relatively little cost. Thus we are invited to consider organizations in which the outcome (e.g. an allocation of goods and services) is a function of private decisions that are based on private information and public decisions that are based on publicly known information. And we are invited to choose among them on the basis of their outcomes as measured by the chosen criterion of social welfare.

By an outcome we of course mean an equilibrium point. We have already noted that an equilibrium point is defined in relation to the information structure. We are supposing here that the government possesses incomplete information. This, as we noted above, is the starting hypothesis of chapters 8 and 9 in Part III. But what do the individuals know?

Let us begin by considering problems of *pure* moral hazard. By assumption therefore the only things that are incompletely observable are *actions*. In a pure moral hazard problem everyone – including the government – knows everyone's *type*. So, provided the game is a contest (see Section 1), a rational solution must be an equilibrium point. (This is reflected in chapter 9 by Mookherjee.) But if there is adverse selection the natural assumption to make is that *individuals* as well have incomplete information about one another's type. If we now were to appeal to Harsanyi's theory (Section 1) the outcome we would be led to analyse would be a Bayesian (Nash) equilibrium. (This is reflected in chapter 8 by Repullo. But see Maskin (1977), who implicitly assumes that individuals know each other's types even though the government suffers from incomplete information. Maskin thereby studies Nash equilibria of the contests instituted by the government.)

Given the criterion of social welfare, and the technological and information constraints, the government's task is to design an optimum organization. The idea therefore is that the state assigns feasible sets of actions to individuals and to itself and makes publicly known the rules of the game it and the members of society will play. The game thus defines the organizational structure of society. On the face of it though, identifying an *optimum* organization would seem an impossible task, since there is no a priori restriction on what kinds of feasible sets the government ought to choose from when designing the organization structure. In fact, it transpires by an elementary argument that the matter is not intractable: in order to meet the adverse selection problem the government may as well ask individuals to divulge their private information. Indeed, it is possible to show that for a wide class of social welfare criteria an optimum organization has the feature that it sustains an equilibrium point in which individuals choose to tell the truth about what they know. This guiding principle, somewhat reverentially called the Revelation Principle, was proved in varying generality by Gibbard (1973), Dasgupta et al. (1979) and Myerson (1979).[46] In chapter 8, Raphael Repullo states and proves the Revelation Principle and then scrutinizes its scope and limitations by means of a set of ingenious examples. His arguments imply that the principle is less potent than is usually thought.

In actual problems of organization design both adverse selection and moral hazard are present. Not surprisingly, such combined problems are very difficult to analyse. Consequently, much of the literature treats them separately. (An exception is the optimum income tax literature inaugurated by Mirrlees (1971).) In this volume chapter 8 by Repullo is about adverse selection, and chapter 9 by Mookherjee is about moral hazard.

It would seem intuitive that in the face of incomplete information on the part of the state a full optimum cannot be guaranteed to be implemented: individuals will behave strategically so as to tilt the final outcome more in their favour than a full optimum calls for. The Revelation Principle says, roughly speaking, that there is a truth-telling equilibrium in an optimally designed organization. It does not, however, deny that the best that can be attained is only a second-best. Despite the intuition that in general incomplete information on the part of the government does entail a cost to society in terms of forgone social welfare, much of the early work on the design of organizations was aimed at identifying social welfare criteria whose *full* optima can be implemented *despite* the presence of adverse selection problems (see e.g. *Review of Economic Studies Symposium on Incentive Compatibility*, April 1979).

---

46 Among the areas of recent theoretical research where the Revelation Principle has been used is the Implicit Contract literature. See e.g. *Quarterly Journal of Economics, Symposium Issue* (1983).

Chapter 9 by Mookherjee is about moral hazard. The prototype moral hazard problem concerns a *principal* and an *agent* who wish to enter into an optimum risk-sharing arrangement. The principal owns a fixed factor of production (e.g. land or capital) and the agent supplies labour. Output is a function of labour effort and a chance factor. The principal can observe the output only, whereas the agent observes both output and his own effort (he chooses the latter). The criterion of social welfare is (*ex-ante*) efficiency. Now, it is clear that if both parties are risk-neutral moral hazard poses no problem: a full optimum can be implemented despite the fact that the principal cannot observe effort. (This is the moral hazard counterpart of the incentive compatibility results.) But if the principal (e.g. the government) is risk-neutral and the agent is risk-averse a *fully efficient* payment arrangement will have the agent receiving a fixed fee from the principal, so that the risk is absorbed entirely by the principal. However, with a fixed fee the agent has no incentive to do anything but put in the minimum of effort (the principal cannot monitor sweat), and this is not efficient. Thus, a second-best optimum payment arrangement will in general have some risk-sharing. This is the classical principal-agent result.

The question arises whether additional incentives can be provided if the principal employs more than one agent: the idea being that if the chance factors entering into the agents' production functions are correlated the contract could have the payment to each agent dependent on the *outputs* of all agents. (For note that if the chance factors are *perfectly* correlated, observing relative performances (outputs) allows one to infer relative efforts.) This captures the intuitive idea of *competition*, where *relative* performances enter into the reward structure.

Obviously the idea will work only if there is *some* correlation (otherwise observing one agent's output provides no information about other agents' efforts). Less obviously, the incentives such competition provides are greater the more correlated are the chance factors across agents' production functions. It is the merit of chapter 9 by Mookherjee that this intuition is formalized in a simple and elegant manner. (For parallel results see Holmstrom (1982).)

We have little doubt that problems in the design of organizations will continue to remain central on the agenda of theoretical economic research. It is to us surprising that the intuitive idea of competition – crystallized most sharply in *tournaments* – should have for so long remained unformalized, and that 'payment strictly according to one's contribution' should have so dominated economic thinking. It is the achievement of the recent literature on incentives to have formalized and thus improved our understanding of the variety of contractual arrangements that organizations are known to enter into. We would guess that problems associated with multiple principals and multiple agents will receive serious attention in the near future and thus improve our understanding of the idea of fiscal federalism, so central to public finance. This is of course only one set of issues. There are a great many more in the design of organizations. There remains a great deal to know.

REFERENCES

Arrow, K. J. 1959: Toward a theory of price adjustment. In M. Abramovitz et al., *The Allocation of Resources*. Stanford: Stanford University Press.

Arrow, K. J. 1962: Economic welfare and the allocation of resources for inventions. In R. R. Nelson (ed.), *The Rate and Direction of Inventive Activity*. Princeton: Princeton University Press.

Arrow, K. J. and Debreu, G. 1954: Existence of an equilibrium for a competitive economy. *Econometrica*, **22**, 265–90.

Arrow, K. J. and Hahn, F. H. 1971: *General Competitive Analysis*. San Francisco: Holden Day.

Aumann, R. 1976: Agreeing to disagree. *Annals of Statistics*, **4**, 1236–9.

Aumann, R. 1981: Survey of repeated games. In *Essays in Game Theory and Mathematical Economics in Honor of Oscar Morgenstern*. Mannheim, Wien and Zurich: Wissenschaftsverlag, Bibliographisches Institut.

Aumann, R. 1985: *Correlated Equilibrium as an Expression of Rationality*. Mimeo, Hebrew University.

Aumann, R. and Maschler, M. 1972: Some thoughts on the minimax principle. *Management Science*, **18**, 54–63.

Axelrod, R. 1984: *The Evolution of Cooperation*. New York: Basic Books.

Bernheim, D. 1984: Rationalizable strategic behaviour. *Econometrica*, **52**, 1007–28.

Bertrand, J. 1883: Théorie mathématique de la richesse sociale. *Journal des Savants*, 499–508.

Binmore, K. 1985: *Modelling Rational Players*. ICERD Discussion Paper, London School of Economics, forthcoming.

Binmore, K. and Dasgupta, P. (eds). 1986: *The Economics of Bargaining*. Oxford: Basil Blackwell.

Binmore, K., Shaked, A. and Sutton, J. 1985: Fairness or gamesmanship in bargaining? – an experimental study. *ICERD Discussion Paper 84/102*. London School of Economics.

Brandenberger, A. 1986: *Hierarchies of Beliefs in Decision Theory*. PhD dissertation, University of Cambridge.

Brandenberger, A. and Dekel, E. 1985: Hierarchies of beliefs and common knowledge, *Research Paper No. 841*. Graduate School of Business, Stanford University.

Bresnahan, T. 1981: Duopoly models with consistent conjectures. *American Economic Review*, **71**, 934–45.

Chamberlin, E. H. 1933: *The Theory of Monopolistic Competition*. Cambridge: Harvard University Press.

Cohen, W. M. and Mowery, D. C. 1984: Firm heterogeneity and R & D: an agenda for research. In B. Bozeman, M. Crow and A. Link (eds), *Strategic*

Management of Industrial R & D: Multidisciplinary Perspectives. Lexington: D. C. Heath.

Cournot, A. 1838: *Recherches sur les Principes Mathematiques de la Theorie des Richesses*. Paris: L. Hachette.

Dasgupta, P. 1980: Decentralization and rights. *Economica*, 47, 107-24.

Dasgupta, P. 1982: Utilitarianism, information and rights. In A. Sen and B. Williams (eds), *Utilitarianism and Beyond*. Cambridge: Cambridge University Press.

Dasgupta, P., Hammond, P. and Maskin, E. 1979: The implementation of social choice rules: some general results in incentive compatibility. *Review of Economic Studies Symposium on Incentive Compatibility*, 46, 183-215.

Dasgupta, P. and Stiglitz, J. 1980a: Market structure and the nature of innovative activity. *Economic Journal*, 90, 266-93.

Dasgupta, P. and Stiglitz, J. 1980b: Uncertainty, industrial structure and the speed of R & D. *Bell Journal of Economics* (Spring), 1-28.

Dasgupta, P. and Stiglitz, J. 1984: *Welfare and Competition with Sunk Costs*. Mimeo, Stanford University.

Debreu, G. 1959: *Theory of Value*. New York: Wiley.

Debreu, G. 1975: The rate of convergence of the core of an economy. *Journal of Mathematical Economics*, 2, 1-7.

Dierker, H. and Grodel, B. 1984: *Nonexistence of Cournot–Walras Equilibrium in a General Equilibrium with Two Oligopolists*. Mimeo, University of Bonn.

Dubey, P. 1980: Nash equilibrium of market games: finiteness and inefficiency. *Journal of Economic Theory*, 22, 363-76.

Edgeworth, F. M. 1925: *Papers Relating to Political Economy, I*. London: Macmillan.

Fan, Ky 1952: Fixed point and minimax theorems in locally convex topological linear spaces. *Proceedings of the National Academy of Sciences*, 38, 121-6.

Farrell, J. 1984: Communications and Nash Equilibrium. *GTE Discussion Paper*. Massachusetts: Waltham.

Fraysse, J. and Moreaux, M. 1981: Cournot equilibrium with free entry under increasing returns. *Economics Letters*, 8, 217-20.

Friedman, J. and Rosenthal, R. 1985: *A Positive Approach to Noncooperative Games*. Mimeo, Stonybrook: Department of Economics, SUNY.

Fudenberg, D. and Maskin, E. 1984: The folk theorem in repeated games with discounting and with incomplete information. *Econometrica*, 54, 533-54.

Gabszewicz, J. J. 1985: Comment. In K. Arrow and S. Honkapohja (eds), *Frontiers of Economics*. Oxford: Blackwell.

Gabszewicz, J. J. and Vial, J. P. 1972: 'Oligopoly *à la* Cournot' in General equilibrium analysis. *Journal of Economic Theory*, 4, 381-400.

Gabszewicz, J. J. and Thisse, J. F. 1979: Price competition, quality and income disparities. *Journal of Economic Theory*, 20, 340-59.

Gabszewicz, J. J. and Thisse, J. F. 1980: Entry (and exit) in a differentiated market. *Journal of Economic Theory*, 22, 327-38.

Gibbard, A. 1973: Manipulation of voting schemes: a general result. *Econometrica*, 41, 587-602.

Gilbert, R. and Newbery, D. 1982: Preemptive patenting and the persistence of monopoly. *American Economic Review*, **72**, 514–26.

Glicksberg, I. L. 1952: A further generalization of the Kakutani fixed point theorem with application to Nash equilibrium points. *Proceedings of the National Academy of Sciences of the U.S.A.*, **38**, 170–4.

Grabowski, H. G. and Vernon, J. M. 1982: The pharmaceutical industry. In Nelson (ed.).

Green, E. 1982: *Internal Costs and Equilibrium: The Case of Repeated Prisoner's Dilemma*. Mimeo, California Institute of Technology.

Guesnerie, R. and Hart, O. 1985: Welfare losses due to imperfect competition: asymptotic results for Cournot–Nash equilibria with free-entry. *International Economic Review*, **26**, 525–46.

Guth, W., Schmittberger, K. and Schwarze, B. 1982: An experimental analysis of ultimatum bargaining. *Journal of Economic Behaviour and Organization*, **3**, 367–88.

Hahn, F. H. 1977: Exercises in conjectural equilibria. *Scandinavian Journal of Economics*, **79** (2), 210–24.

Hahn, F. H. 1978: On non-Walrasian equilibria. *Review of Economic Studies*, **45**, 1–17.

Harsanyi, J. C. 1967–1968: Games with incomplete information played by Bayesian players, Parts I, II, III. *Management Science*, **14** (3, 5, 7).

Harsanyi, J. C. 1975: The tracing procedure: a Bayesian approach to defining a solution for n-person non-cooperative games. *International Journal of Game Theory*, **4**, 61–95.

Harsanyi, J. C. 1976: *Essays on Ethics, Social Behaviour and Scientific Explanations*. Boston: D. Reidel.

Harsanyi, J. C. 1977: *Rational Behaviour and Bargaining Equilibrium in Games and Social Situations*. Cambridge: Cambridge University Press.

Harsanyi, J. 1982: Solutions for some bargaining games under the Harsanyi–Selten solution theory, Parts I–II. *Mathematical Social Sciences*, **3**, 179–91 and 259–89.

Hart, O. 1979: Monopolistic competition in a large economy with differentiated commodities. *Review of Economic Studies*, **46**, 1–30.

Hart, O. 1982: Reasonable conjectures. *ICERD Discussion Paper No. 82/61*. London School of Economics.

Hart, O. 1983: Imperfect competition in general equilibrium: an overview of recent work. *ICERD Discussion Paper No. 83/64*. London School of Economics.

Holmstrom, B. 1982: Moral hazard in teams. *Bell Journal of Economics*, Autumn, 326–40.

Howard, N. 1971: *Paradoxes of Rationality: Theory of Metagames and Political Behaviour*. Cambridge, Mass.: MIT Press.

Kalai, E. and Samet, D. 1982: Persistent equilibria. *Discussion Paper No. 515*. Northwestern University: Department of Economics.

Kohlberg, E. and Mertens, J. F. 1982: On the strategic stability of equilibria. *CORE Discussion Paper No. 8248*. Université Catholique de Louvin.

Kreps, D. 1984: *Signalling Games and Stable Equilibria*. Mimeo, Graduate School of Business, Stanford University.

Kreps, D. and Scheinkman, J. 1982: *Cournot Pre-Commitment and Bertrand Competition Yield Cournot Outcomes*. Mimeo, Department of Economics, University of Chicago.

Kreps, D. and Wilson, R. 1982: Sequential equilibria. *Econometrica*, **50**, 863–94.

Krugman, P. 1979: Increasing returns, monopolistic competition, and international trade. *Journal of International Economics*, **9**, 469–79.

Levin, R. and Reiss, P. C. 1984: Tests of a Schumpeterian model of R & D and market structure. In Z. Griliches (ed.) *R & D, Patents and Productivity*. Chicago: University of Chicago Press.

Luce, R. D. and Raiffa, H. 1957: *Games and Decisions*. New York: Wiley.

Makowski, L. 1983: 'Rational conjectures' aren't rational, 'Reasonable conjectures' aren't reasonable. *Discussion Paper No. 66, SSRC Research Project on Risk, Information and Quantity Signals in Economics*. Cambridge: Department of Applied Economics.

Marschak, J. and Radner, R. 1972: *Economic Theory of Teams*. New Haven: Yale University Press.

Marschak, T. and Selten, R. 1978: Restabilizing responses, inertia supergames and oligopolistic equilibria. *Quarterly Journal of Economics*, **92**, 71–93.

Maskin, E. 1977. *Nash Equilibrium and Welfare Optimality*. Mimeo. MIT.

Maskin, E. and Tirole, J. 1982: *A Theory of Dynamic Oligopoly, Part 1: Overview and Quantity Competition with Large Fixed Costs*. MIT Working Paper.

Maskin, E. and Tirole, J. 1985: *A Theory of Dynamic Oligopoly, Part 2: Price Competition*. MIT Working Paper.

Matthews, R. C. O. 1984: Darwinism and economic change. *Oxford Economic Papers*, **36**, 91–117.

Maynard Smith, J. 1982: *Evolution and the Theory of Games*. Cambridge: Cambridge University Press.

Maynard Smith, J. and Price, G. R. 1973: The logic of animal conflict. *Nature*, **246**, 15–18.

Maynard Smith, J. and Price, G. R. 1974: The theory of games and the the evolution of animal conflict. *Journal of Theoretical Biology*, **47**, 209–21.

Mertens, J.-F. and Zamir, S. 1985: Formulations and analysis for games with incomplete information. *International Journal of Game Theory*, **14**.

Mirrlees, J. A. 1971: An exploration in the theory of optimal income taxation. *Review of Economic Studies*, **38**, 175–208.

Moulin, H. 1982: *Game Theory for the Social Sciences*. New York: New York University Press.

Myerson, R. 1975: Refinement of the Nash equilibrium concept. *International Journal of Game Theory*, **7**, 73–80.

Myerson, R. 1979: Incentive compatibility and the bargaining problem. *Econometrica*, **47**, 61–74.

Myerson, R. 1984: An introduction to game theory. *Discussion Paper No. 623*. Northwestern University.

Nash, J. F. 1950: Equilibrium points in n-person games. *Proceedings of the National Academy of Sciences of the U.S.A.*, **36**, 48–9.

Nash, J. 1951: Non-cooperative games. *Annals of Mathematics*, **54**, 286–95.

Nelson, R. (ed.) 1982: *Government and Technical Progress: A Cross-Industry Analysis*. New York: Pergamon Press.

Nelson, R. and Winter, S. 1982: *An Evolutionary Theory of Economic Change*. Cambridge: Harvard University Press.

Novshek, W. 1980: Cournot equilibrium with free entry. *Review of Economic Studies*, **47**, 473–86.

Novshek, W. and Sonnenschein, H. 1978: Cournot and Walras equilibrium. *Journal of Economic Theory*, **19**, 223–66.

Pearce, D. G. 1984: Rationalizable strategic behaviour and the problem of perfection. *Econometrica*, **52**, 1029–50.

Radner, R. 1980: Collusive behaviour in noncooperative epsilon-equilibria of oligopolies with long but finite lives. *Journal of Economic Theory*, **22** (2), 136–54.

Rosenberg, N. 1976: *Perspectives in Technology*. Cambridge: Cambridge University Press.

Rosenthal, R. 1981: Games of perfect information, predatory pricing and the chain-store paradox. *Journal of Economic Theory*, **25**, 92–100.

Rothschild, M. and Stiglitz, J. E. 1976: Equilibrium in competitive insurance markets: an essay on the economics of imperfect information. *Quarterly Journal of Economics*, **90**, 629–49.

Rubinstein, A. 1979: Equilibrium in supergames with the overtaking criterion. *Journal of Economic Theory*, **21**, 1–9.

Rubinstein, A. 1980: Strong perfect equilibria in supergames. *International Journal of Game Theory*, **9**.

Rubinstein, A. 1985: Finite automata play the repeated Prisoner's Dilemma. *ICERD Discussion Paper*. London School of Economics.

Salop, S. 1979: Monopolistic competition with outside goods. *Bell Journal of Economics*, **10** (Spring), 141–56.

Schelling, T. 1978: *Micromotives and Macrobehaviour*. New York: W. W. Norton.

Schmookler, J. 1966: *Invention and Economic Growth*. Cambridge: Cambridge University Press.

Schumpeter, J. 1950: *Capitalism, Socialism and Democracy*. 3rd Edition. New York: Harper and Row.

Selten, R. 1965: Spieltheoretische Behandlund eines Oligopolmodels mit Nachfragetragheit, *Zeitschrift fur die Gesamte Staatswissenschaft*, **121**, 401–24 and 667–89.

Selten, R. 1975. Re-examination of the perfectness concept for equilibrium points in extensive games. *International Journal of Game Theory*, **4**, 25–55.

Selten, R. 1978: The chain-store paradox. *Theory and Decision*, **9**, 127–59.

Selten, R. 1983: *Evolutionary Stability in Extensive 2-Person Games*. Mimeo, University of Bielefeld.

Sen, A. 1970: *Collective Choice and Social Welfare*. San Francisco: Holden Day.

Shaked, A. and Sutton, J. 1984: Natural oligopolies and international trade. In H. Kierkowski (ed.), *Monopolistic Competition and International Trade*, 34–50.

Simon, H. 1957: *Models of Man*. New York: John Wiley.

Spence, A. M. 1974: *Market Signalling: Informational Transfer in Hiring and Related Screening Processes*. Cambridge, Mass.: Harvard University Press.

Spence, A. M. 1986: Cost reduction, competition and industry performance. In J. E. Stiglitz and F. Mathewson (eds), *New Developments in the Analysis of Market Structure*. London: Macmillan.

Stiglitz, J. E. 1985. Information and economic analysis: a perspective. *Economic Journal*, supplement, **95**, 21–41.

Tandon, P. 1984: Innovation, market structure and welfare. *American Economic Review*, **74**, 394–403.

Ulph, D. 1981: Rational conjectures in the theory of oligopoly. *International Journal of Industrial Organization*, forthcoming.

Ushio, Y. 1983: Cournot equilibrium with free entry: the case of decreasing average cost functions. *Review of Economic Studies*, **50**, 347–54.

Varian, H. 1980: A model of sales. *American Economic Review*, **70**, 651–9.

Von Neumann, J. and Morgenstern, O. 1944: *Theory of Games and Economic Behaviour*. Princeton: Princeton University Press.

Wilson, C. 1977: A model of insurance markets with incomplete information. *Journal of Economic Theory*, **16**, 167–207.

Winter, S. 1971: Satisficing, selection, and the innovating remnant. *Quarterly Journal of Economics*, **85**, 237–61.

I

EQUILIBRIUM THEORY

1

The Existence of Equilibrium in Discontinuous Economic Games, I: Theory

P. Dasgupta and E. Maskin

1 INTRODUCTION

In this paper and its sequel (Dasgupta and Maskin 1986; chapter 2 in this volume) we study the existence of Nash equilibrium in games where agents' payoff (or utility) functions are discontinuous. Our enquiry is motivated by a number of recent studies that have uncovered serious existence problems in seemingly innocuous economic games. These examples include models of spatial competition (Eaton and Lipsey 1975; Shaked 1975), Hotelling's model of price competition (d'Aspremont et al. 1979), and models of market-dependent information (e.g. the insurance-market example of Rothschild and Stiglitz (1976) and Wilson (1977)). In fact, the non-existence of Nash equilibrium in simple economic models was noted long ago by Edgeworth (1925) in his critique of Bertrand's (1883) analysis of price setting duopolists (see Chamberlin 1956, pp. 34–6).

These examples can be readily cast as games in normal form with continuous strategy sets (see the sequel to this paper). Since they fail in general to possess an equilibrium they must obviously violate one or more of the hypotheses of the classical existence theorem for games of this type (e.g. Debreu 1952; Glicksberg 1952; Fan 1952). These hypotheses typically include *continuity* and a limited form of *quasi-concavity* of the payoff functions (in addition to the usual convexity and compactness assumptions on strategy sets). To understand better a model that does not possess an equilibrium it is helpful to identify the failure – violation of quasi-concavity or

For helpful discussions and comments we are grateful to Kenneth Arrow, Oliver Hart, Andreu Mas-Colell, Leo Simon and two referees. Avner Shaked made several suggestions on an earlier draft which helped in the development of our main theorem.

of continuity – to which the non-existence can be attributed. Drawing such a distinction allows us to construct a taxonomy of 'equilibrium failure' and to highlight the structural similarities or differences among models. It also enables us to see how the models may be plausibly modified to restore the existence of equilibrium. This is important because the failure of an economic model to possess an equilibrium has sometimes led economists to cast doubt on the validity – and even the internal consistency – of the construct.

In the sequel to this paper we shall see that the utility functions in the economic games referred to earlier are neither continuous nor quasi-concave.[1] However, we demonstrate that the payoff functions in mildly modified versions of these constructs exhibit two weaker forms of continuity which, together with the requirement of quasi-concavity, suffice for the existence of an equilibrium (Theorem 2, below). From this we may conclude that, at least in the modified versions of these models, discontinuities in the payoff functions are not the real source of the problem. Rather, it is the failure of the payoff functions to be quasi-concave which is 'responsible' for the non-existence of equilibrium.

These observations bear on the existence of Nash equilibrium in *pure strategies*. In this study, however, we are concerned, in the main, with the existence of Nash equilibrium in *mixed (random) strategies*. For games in which payoff functions are not quasi-concave, mixed strategies may offer an escape route from the problem of non-existence. Yet, the classical existence theorems on mixed-strategy equilibrium (e.g. Glicksberg 1952) typically hypothesize continuous utility functions, and are, therefore, not applicable to the economic games we have mentioned. In this study we show that the classical theorems can be suitably generalized. In the sequel to this paper we observe that a significant feature shared by the simplest versions of most of these economic models is that their discontinuities occur only at points where two or more agents use the *same* strategy. We also note that even in the more general versions of these models the set of discontinuities is of a dimension lower than that of the strategy space. Thus, in particular, the set of discontinuities is of (Lebesgue) measure zero. In this paper we establish equilibrium existence theorems (Theorems 4 and 5) for games possessing discontinuity sets of this kind. Theorem 4 examines a sequence of successively finer finite approximations of a game with a continuous strategy set. The theorem asserts that if the limiting strategies of a sequence of equilibrium strategy vectors for these finite games are themselves atomless on the closure of the set of

---

1 The non-existence problem may therefore appear to be more complex than in the examples exhibited by McManus (1964) and Roberts and Sonnenschein (1977), where payoff functions fail to be quasi-concave but are continuous. See, however, Dierker and Grodal (1984), who show that there are examples in the Roberts–Sonnenschein framework where discontinuities are so severe that even a mixed strategy equilibrium fails to exist.

discontinuities, then they constitute an equilibrium (mixed) strategy vector for the game in question.

Another important feature shared by these economic models is that, although agents' utility functions are discontinuous, their sum is an upper semi-continuous function of strategies. (This is not quite true of all the examples to be studied in the sequel, but nearly enough to suffice for our purpose.) Moreover, at the points of discontinuity, the utility functions satisfy some limited form of *lower* semi-continuity. Theorem 5, our main result, states, roughly speaking, that with a discontinuity set of the type mentioned above, an (upper semi) continuous-sum game in which individual utility functions satisfy a weak form of lower semi-continuity possesses a mixed-strategy equilibrium. Theorem 5a extends our main result to cases in which a player has a strategy where his payoff function is discontinuous regardless of other agents' strategies. Theorem 5b shows that we may be able to dispense with the requirement that the sum of payoffs be upper semi-continuous, if a downward jump in one player's payoff is always accompanied by an upward jump in another player's payoff. (See also the interesting paper by Simon (1984), who calls such pairs of jumps 'complementary discontinuities'.) In addition to the assumptions of Theorem 5, Theorem 6 hypothesizes that the game is symmetric. The theorem asserts the existence of a symmetric equilibrium – one in which all agents choose the same probability measure. More important, it also provides conditions under which an equilibrium measure is atomless on the discontinuity set.

In the sequel to this paper, where we explore economic applications of these results, we shall appeal to Theorems 5 and 6 to establish the existence and some of the qualitative features of mixed-strategy equilibrium in the economic models mentioned above.

The idea of exploring mixed-strategy equilibria in discontinuous games has occurred to many. The only general existence theorem that we are aware of is due to Glicksberg (1950) who showed that a two-person zero-sum game on the unit square always has a minimax value if the payoff function is either upper or lower semi-continuous (see Definitions 2 and 4 below). In all the other studies known to us the approach has been to demonstrate the existence of equilibrium by construction. Thus Karlin (1959) has analysed what are called 'games of timing', which are discontinuous two-person zero-sum games.[2] In the economics literature Beckmann (1965) has demonstrated, by construction, the existence of a mixed-strategy equilibrium in the symmetric version of the Bertrand–Edgeworth model with a linear market demand

2 The games of timing that have been most frequently discussed are 'duels' (see Karlin 1959; Owen 1968; Jones 1980). The payoff functions in these games are neither upper nor lower semi-continuous, and so Glicksberg's (1950) theorem does not apply to them. (See example 2 in Section 5 below.)

curve. (See also Shubik 1955; Shapley 1957). More recently Shilony (1977) and Varian (1980), also constructively, have demonstrated the existence of mixed-strategy equilibrium in certain symmetric models of price-setting firms. The limitations of these constructive approaches are fairly obvious. Not only are the existence results necessarily specific rather than general, but one fails to learn why the discontinuities in the model (which are, after all, what is crucial) do not prevent the existence of equilibrium.[3] Furthermore, the demonstrations, so far as we are aware, apply in the main to symmetric games; and it is not clear that they extend to asymmetric versions. It bears emphasis that Theorems 4 and 5, our main existence theorems, do not assume that the game is symmetric.

The plan of this paper is as follows. In Section 2 we introduce much of the notation and present two theorems (Theorems 1 and 2) on the existence of pure-strategy equilibrium. Theorem 1, due to Debreu (1952), is well known. Theorem 2, which postulates only a weak form of continuity for the utility functions, is a straightforward extension. We have included it because the payoff functions of many economic models, including slightly modified versions of the ones mentioned above, fail to satisfy continuity but are continuous in our weaker sense (see the sequel). Theorem 2 thus places the 'blame' for the non-existence of pure-strategy equilibrium squarely on the lack of quasi-concavity of these payoff functions. The fact that non-existence can be ascribed to a failure of quasi-concavity, and not to continuity, makes the existence of mixed-strategy equilibrium more plausible. In Section 3 mixed-strategies are introduced formally, and we state Glicksberg's (1952) theorem for continuous payoff functions as Theorem 3. We then provide an example (due to Sion and Wolfe 1957) of a game with discontinuous payoff functions that does not possess even an ϵ-equilibrium. In Section 4 we present existence results (Theorems 4, 5, 5a and 5b) for games with discontinuous payoff functions. Before proving them in detail in Sub-sections 4.3 and 4.4, we provide an outline of the argument in Sub-section 4.2. These theorems have been strongly motivated by the economic models of the sequel. Nevertheless, we believe that they cannot be generalized much further. Indeed, as the examples of Section 6 demonstrate, the theorems are 'tight', in the sense that dropping any of their hypotheses renders them invalid. Finally, Section 5 treats symmetric games.

To simplify the exposition and notation, we suppose in Sections 4–6 that the strategy set of each agent is one-dimensional. In fact, this is so in all the economic examples mentioned earlier, except for the two-dimensional location model of Shaked (1975) and the insurance-market example of Rothschild, Stiglitz and Wilson. In the Appendix we present the multi-dimensional generalizations of Theorems 4, 5, and 6.

---

3 Rosenthal (1980) also demonstrates, by construction, the existence of a symmetric mixed-strategy equilibrium in a model of oligopolistic international trade.

2 EQUILIBRIUM IN PURE STRATEGIES

Agents are assumed to be N in number, indexed by i or $j = 1, \ldots, N$. $A_i \subseteq R^m$ denotes the set of feasible actions (strategies) from which agent i may choose.[4] A typical element of A_i is a_i. Write a for an N-tuple of actions. Thus $a \in \Pi_{j=1}^N A_j$. Define $a_{-i} \equiv (a_1, a_2, \ldots, a_{i-1}, a_{i+1}, \ldots, a_N)$ as the vector of actions of all agents other than i. We shall often write $a = (a_i, a_{-i})$, $A = \Pi_{j=1}^N A_j$ and $A_{-i} = \Pi_{j \neq i} A_j$.

Let $U_i : \Pi_{j=1}^N A_j \to R^1$ be the *payoff (utility) function* of agent i. A *game* is summarized as $[(A_i, U_i); i = 1, \ldots, N]$, where A_i is agent i's feasible set of (pure) strategies, and U_i is his payoff (utility) function. Define $\psi_i(a_{-i}) = \{a_i \in A_i \mid U_i(a_i, a_{-i}) = \max_{a_i' \in A_i} U_i(a_i', a_{-i})\}$. $\psi_i(a_{-i})$ is called agent i's reaction correspondence.

Definition 1. $a^* \in A$ is a Nash equilibrium in pure strategies of the game $[(A_i, U_i); i = 1, \ldots, N]$ if $U_i(a_i^*, a_{-i}^*) = \max_{a_i \in A_i} U_i(a_i, a_{-i}^*)$ for all $i = 1, \ldots, N$; (or, equivalently if $a^* \in \Pi_{i=1}^N \psi_i(a_{-i}^*)$).

The following is a basic result.

Theorem 1 (Debreu, Glicksberg, Fan). *Let $A_i \subseteq R^m$, $(i = 1, \ldots, N)$ be nonempty, convex and compact. If, $\forall i$, $U_i : A \to R^1$ is continuous in a and quasiconcave in a_i, the game $[(A_i, U_i); i = 1, \ldots, N]$ possesses a pure-strategy Nash equilibrium.*

In the sequel we shall note that each of the economic models mentioned in the Introduction violates both the continuity and quasi-concavity requirements. This prompts us to extend Theorem 1 so that it applies to games with a limited form of continuity.

In what follows we shall always suppose that $A_i (i = 1, \ldots, N)$ is nonempty and compact.

Definition 2. $U_i : A \to R^1$ is *upper semi-continuous* (u.s.c.) if for any sequence

$$\{a^n\} \subseteq A \text{ such that } a^n \to a, \lim \sup_{n \to \infty} U_i(a^n) \leqslant U_i(a).$$

Definition 3. $U_i : A \to R^1$ is *graph continuous* if for all $\bar{a} \in A$ there exists a function $F_i : A_{-i} \to A_i$ with $F_i(\bar{a}_{-i}) = \bar{a}_i$ such that $U_i(F_i(a_{-i}), a_{-i})$ is continuous at $a_{-i} = \bar{a}_{-i}$.

We call the property described in Definition 3 graph continuity, because, if one graphs a player's payoff as a function of his own strategy (holding the strategies of the other players fixed), and if this graph changes continuously as one varies the strategies of the other players, then the player's payoff function is graph continuous in the sense of Definition 3. (Actually, graph continuity, as we have defined it, is a bit weaker than this.)

---

4 R^m is m-dimensional Euclidean space ($m \geqslant 1$).

We can now state and prove

Theorem 2. *Let $A_i \subseteq R^m$ $(i = 1, \ldots, N)$, be non-empty, convex and compact. If $\forall i$, $U_i : A \to R^1$ is quasi-concave in a_i, upper semi-continuous in a and graph continuous, then the game $[(A_i, U_i); i = 1, \ldots, N]$ possesses a pure-strategy Nash equilibrium.*

Proof. We prove the Theorem for the case $N = 2$: (extension to $N > 2$ is immediate). Let ψ_1 and ψ_2 be the reaction correspondences of the two agents. They exist and are compact-valued because U_1 and U_2 are upper semi-continuous. Moreover, they are convex-valued because U_1 and U_2 are quasi-concave in a_1 and a_2 respectively. We need now only verify that the ψ_i's are upper hemi-continuous correspondences.[5]

Consider the sequences $\{a_2^n\} \subseteq A_2$ and $\{a_1^n\} \subseteq A_1$ such that $a_2^n \to \bar{a}_2$, $a_1^n \to \bar{a}_1$ and $\forall n, a_1^n \in \psi_1(a_2^n)$. If $\bar{a}_1 \notin \psi_1(\bar{a}_2)$ there exists $a_1^* \in A_1$ such that $U_1(a_1^*, \bar{a}_2) > U_1(\bar{a}_1, \bar{a}_2)$. Let $\epsilon = [U_1(a_1^*, \bar{a}_2) - U_1(\bar{a}_1, \bar{a}_2)]/2$. Then there exists F with $F(\bar{a}_2) = a_1^*$ and $\delta > 0$ such that $\|a_2 - \bar{a}_2\| < \delta$ implies $|U_1(F_1(a_2), a_2) - U_1(a_1^*, \bar{a}_2)| < \epsilon$. It follows that, for n sufficiently large, $|U_1(F_1(a_2^n), a_2^n) - U_1(a_1^*, \bar{a}_2)| < \epsilon$. But $U_1(F_1(a_2^n), a_2^n) \leq U_1(a_1^n, a_2^n)$. Therefore, $U_1(a_1^n, a_2^n) \geq U_1(F_1(a_2^n), a_2^n) \geq U_1(\bar{a}_1, \bar{a}_2) + \epsilon$ for n sufficiently large. But $U_1(\bar{a}_1, \bar{a}_2) \geq \lim \sup_{n \to \infty} U_1(a_1^n, a_2^n)$, a contradiction. Therefore, $\bar{a}_1 \in \psi_1(\bar{a}_2)$, and so ψ_1 is upper hemi-continuous. Similarly for ψ_2. We may therefore apply the Kakutani fixed point theorem to the correspondence $\psi_1 \times \psi_2$ to conclude that a Nash equilibrium exists. $\parallel$

In fact we can obtain a result very similar to Theorem 2 by recalling the following:

Definition 4. A function $g : A \to R^1$ is *lower semi-continuous* (l.s.c.) if for all sequences $\{a^n\} \subseteq A$ such that $a^n \to \bar{a}$, $\lim \inf_{n \to \infty} g(a^n) \geq g(\bar{a})$.

We now have the following.

Corollary. *$\forall i$, let $A_i \subseteq R^m$, $(i = 1, \ldots, N)$ be non-empty, convex and compact, and let $U_i : A \to R^1$ be quasi-concave in a_i and u.s.c. Define $V_i(a_{-i}) = \max_{a_i} U_i(a_i, a_{-i})$; ($V_i$ is well defined because U_i is u.s.c.). If $\forall i$, V_i is l.s.c., then the game $[(A_i, U_i); i = 1, \ldots, N]$ possesses a pure-strategy Nash equilibrium.[6]*

Proof. Virtually identical to the proof in Theorem 2. $\parallel$

In the sequel we will note that the payoff functions in the models of product and price competition referred to earlier here violate both upper semi-

---

5 $\psi_i : A_{-i} \to A_i$ is *upper hemi-continuous* if $\{a_{-i}^n\} \subseteq A_{-i}$ and $a_{-i}^n \to \bar{a}_{-i}$; $a_i^n \in \psi_i(a_{-i}^n)$ and $a_i^n \to \bar{a}_i$ imply $\bar{a}_i \in \psi_i(\bar{a}_{-i})$. An upper hemi-continuous and compact-valued correspondence is sometimes called a *closed* correspondence.

6 It is simple to show that graph continuity and u.s.c. of U_i imply that V_i is l.s.c.

continuity and quasi-concavity, although they satisfy graph continuity. We will also observe that it is possible to modify the payoff functions slightly, and plausibly, so that the resulting payoff functions satisfy the u.s.c. requirement. Nevertheless, even in such modified versions, an equilibrium in pure strategies fails to exist in general. Theorem 2 suggests, therefore, that the explanation for the non-existence in these modified examples is solely the lack of quasi-concavity; the failure of the payoff functions to be continuous is irrelevant. We turn therefore to mixed strategies to convexify the payoff functions. In Section 4 we develop two theorems, one of which (Theorem 5) is used in the sequel to demonstrate the existence of mixed-strategy equilibrium in each of the models cited in the Introduction.

3 NASH EQUILIBRIUM IN MIXED STRATEGIES

Let $A_i \subseteq R^m$, $(i = 1, \ldots, N)$, be non-empty, convex and compact. Let $U_i = A \to R^1$ be bounded and measurable for all i. Let $D(A_i)$ for the space of all (Borel) probability measures on A_i.[7]

Definition 5. A mixed-strategy (Nash) equilibrium of the game $[(A_i, U_i); i = 1, \ldots, N]$ is an N-tuple of probability measures $(\mu_1^*, \ldots, \mu_i^*, \ldots, \mu_N^*)$, with $\mu_i^* \in D(A_i)$, such that for all $i = 1, \ldots, N$

$$\int U_i(a_i, a_{-i}) \, d(\mu_i^*(a_i) \times \boldsymbol{\mu}_{-i}^*(a_{-i}))$$

$$= \max_{\mu_i \in D(A_i)} \int U_i(a_i, a_{-i}) \, d(\mu_i(a_i) \times \boldsymbol{\mu}_{-i}^*(a_{-i})),$$

where $\boldsymbol{\mu}_{-i}^*(a_{-i}) \equiv \Pi_{j \neq i} \mu_j^*(a_j)$.

In what follows we shall often denote by $\boldsymbol{\mu}$ the product measure $\mu_1 \times \ldots \times \mu_N$. That is, if $E \subseteq A$ is a (Borel) measurable set, then we write $\boldsymbol{\mu}(E) = (\mu_1 \times \ldots \times \mu_N)(E)$. Likewise, we shall often write

$$\int_A U_i(a) \, d\boldsymbol{\mu} = \int_A U_i(a_1, \ldots, a_N) \, d(\mu_1(a_1) \times \ldots \times \mu_N(a_N)),$$

and also

$$\int_{A_{-i}} U_i(\bar{a}_i, a_{-i}) \, d\boldsymbol{\mu}_{-i} = \int_{A_{-i}} U_i(\bar{a}_i, a_{-i}) \, d(\mu_1(a_1) \times \ldots \times \mu_{i-1}(a_{i-1})$$

$$\times \mu_{i+1}(a_{i+1}) \times \ldots \times \mu_N(a_N)).$$

---

7 In what follows we shall always endow $D(A_i)$ with the topology of weak convergence; i.e. a sequence of measures $\{\mu_i^n\} \subseteq D(A_i)$ converges to $\mu_i^* \in D(A_i)$ if $\int_{A_i} f(a_i) \, d\mu_i^n \to \int_{A_i} f(a_i) \, d\mu_i^*$ for all real-valued continuous functions f defined on A_i.

Where there is no risk of confusion we shall not explicitly indicate the domain over which the integration is being carried out. Thus, for $\int U_i(a)d\boldsymbol{\mu}$ it will be understood that the domain is $A \equiv \Pi_{i=1}^N A_i$.

Now, we know from Nash (1950) that if A_i is a *finite* set a mixed-strategy equilibrium exists. For our purposes the more relevant existence theorem is

Theorem 3 (Glicksberg 1952). *Let $A_i \subseteq R^m$, $(i = 1, \ldots, N)$ be non-empty and compact. Let $U_i : A \to R^1$ be continuous. Then there exists a mixed-strategy equilibrium for the game $[(A_i, U_i); i = 1, \ldots, N]$.*

The remainder of this paper is devoted to extending Theorem 3 by relaxing the requirement that payoff functions be continuous. The theorems that follow are motivated by the economic models to be analysed in the sequel. In these models we shall note that payoff functions are bounded, and are in fact continuous except on a set of measure zero (with respect to the Lebesgue measure) in the strategy space. One might conjecture that such games are assured of at least an ϵ-equilibrium in mixed strategies, for all positive ϵ.[8] That this speculation is ill-founded is borne out by

Example 1 (Sion and Wolfe 1957). Consider a two-person zero-sum game played on the unit square. Thus $A_1 = A_2 = [0, 1]$. The payoff $U_1(a_1, a_2)$ to agent 1 is given by the function

$$U_1(a_1, a_2) = \begin{cases} -1 & \text{if } a_1 < a_2 < a_1 + \frac{1}{2} \\ 0 & \text{if } a_1 = a_2 \text{ or } a_2 = a_1 + \frac{1}{2} \\ +1 & \text{otherwise.} \end{cases} \tag{1.1}$$

See figure 1.1.

Define

$$V_1 \equiv \sup_{\mu_1 \in D([0,1])} \inf_{\mu_2 \in D([0,1])} \int U_1(a_1, a_2) \, d\mu_1 \, d\mu_2$$

and

$$V_2 \equiv \inf_{\mu_2 \in D([0,1])} \sup_{\mu_1 \in D([0,1])} \int U_1(a_1, a_2) \, d\mu_1 \, d\mu_2$$

as the 'values' of the game for the two players. It can in fact be shown that $V_1 = \frac{1}{3}$ and $V_2 = \frac{3}{7}$, establishing therefore that no equilibrium exists and, indeed, that for ϵ sufficiently small not even an ϵ-equilibrium exists. It can also be confirmed that the value pair $(\frac{1}{3}, \frac{3}{7})$ is attained if the mixed strategy chosen by the first agent puts probability weight only on the points $\{0, \frac{1}{2}, 1\}$, and that of the second agent puts weight only on $\{\frac{1}{4}, \frac{1}{2}, 1\}$.

8 $(\mu_1^*, \ldots, \mu_i^*, \ldots, \mu_N^*)$ is an ϵ-equilibrium if for all i, μ_i^* results in an expected payoff to agent i not more than ϵ less than the supremum when j $(j \neq i)$ plays μ_j^*.

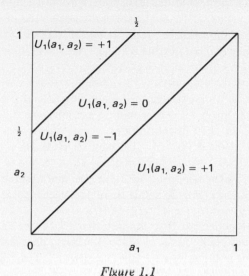

$\frac{1}{2}$

$U_1(a_1, a_2) = +1$

$U_1(a_1, a_2) = 0$

$\frac{1}{2}$ $U_1(a_1, a_2) = -1$

$U_1(a_1, a_2) = +1$

a_2

0   a_1 1

Figure 1.1

4   THE EXISTENCE OF MIXED-STRATEGY EQUILIBRIUM

4.1   Characterization of Discontinuity Set

Theorem 3 establishes that the non-existence of equilibrium in Example 1 is due to discontinuities in the payoff functions. Note that the discontinuities occur only when either the players' strategies are the same, or they differ by $\frac{1}{2}$: that is, they occur on a set of dimension one less than that of the joint strategy space. But this is precisely the kind of discontinuity set possessed by the economic models referred to earlier, which, we shall show in the sequel to this paper, *do* have equilibria. We must, therefore, investigate what distinguishes these economic games from Example 1. Theorems 4 and 5 below make the differences clear.

Let $[(A_i, U_i); i = 1, \ldots, N]$ be a game, where $A_i \subseteq R^1$ is a closed interval.[9] In what follows, we shall suppose that for each i, the discontinuities of U_i are confined to a subset of a continuous manifold of dimension less than N. To be precise, for each pair of agents $i, j \in \{1, \ldots, N\}$, let $D(i)$ be a positive integer, and for each integer d, with $1 \leqslant d \leqslant D(i)$, let $f_{ij}^d : R^1 \to R^1$ be a *one-to-one, continuous* function with the property that $f_{ij}^d = (f_{ji}^d)^{-1}$. Finally, for each $i \in \{1, \ldots, N\}$ define

$$A^*(i) = \{(a_1, \ldots, a_N) \in A \mid \exists j \neq i, \exists d, 1 \leqslant d \leqslant D(i) \text{ such that } a_j = f_{ij}^d(a_i)\}$$

$$(1.2)$$

---

9 In the Appendix we consider games in which (pure) strategy sets are multi-dimensional.

We shall suppose that the discontinuities of $U_i(a)$ are confined to a subset $A^{**}(i)$ of $A^*(i)$. In other words, $A^{**}(i)$ is the set of discontinuities of $U_i(a)$, *and* $\forall i$, $A^{**}(i) \subseteq A^*(i)$. Note in particular from (2) that $A^*(i) \subseteq R^N$ is of (Lebesgue) measure zero. Finally, $\forall a_i \in A_i$ define $A^*_{-i}(a_i) = \{a_{-i} \in A_{-i} | (a_i, a_{-i}) \in A^*(i)\}$, and $A^{**}_{-i}(a_i) = \{a_{-i} \in A_{-i} | (a_i, a_{-i}) \in A^{**}(i)\}$.

Observe that the discontinuity set is defined so that a player's payoff is discontinuous only when his strategy is 'related' to that of another (through the function f_{ij}^d). In many of the economic examples mentioned, f_{ij}^d is the identity function, so that discontinuities occur only when two players' strategies coincide. Notice that for the game in Example 1, we may take $D(1) = D(2) = 2$, $f_{12}^1(a_1) = a_1$, $f_{12}^2(a_1) = a_1 + \frac{1}{2}$, and define $A^*(i)$ by (1.2). In this case $A^*(1.1)$ is the same as $A^*(1.2)$, i.e. the union of the two $45°$ lines in the diagram accompanying Example 1. In fact, each point of $A^*(i)$ is a point of discontinuity of U_i, i.e. $A^{**}(i) = A^*(i)$.

Note that the requirement that the function f_{ij}^d be one-to-one does not rule out a non-monotonic curve of discontinuities; since each monotonic subcurve can be made to correspond to a different f_{ij}^d. The real force of the assumption is to exclude f_{ij}^d's that are 'vertical' or 'horizontal' on some interval. (See Example 4 of Section 6 for the explanation of why this restriction is in some sense necessary. See also Theorem 5a below.)

4.2 An Outline of the Argument

Consider a game $[(A_i, U_i); i = 1, \ldots, N]$, where $A_i \subseteq R^1$ is a closed interval, and suppose that $U_i(a)$ is bounded, and is continuous except on a subset, $A^{**}(i)$, of $A^*(i)$, as defined by (1.2). We wish to state conditions under which the game possesses a mixed-strategy equilibrium. In this sub-section we provide an idea of the arguments we use to prove our main existence theorem (Theorem 5).

Consider a sequence of finite approximations (lattices) of A_i. We denote the nth finite approximation by $A_i^n (n > 0)$, and we suppose that the lattice is finer the larger the value of n, and that $A_i^n \to A_i$ as $n \to \infty$. We denote the finite game defined on the nth lattice by $[(A_i^n, U_i); i = 1, \ldots, N]$, where it is understood that for the finite game the payoff function of agent i is the restriction of U_i to the set $\Pi_{i=1}^N A_i^n$. By Nash's theorem we know that this game possesses a mixed-strategy equilibrium. Let $(\mu_1^n, \ldots, \mu_i^n, \ldots, \mu_N^n) = \boldsymbol{\mu}^n$ be an equilibrium. Since the space of (Borel) probability measures is sequentially compact under the topology of weak convergence, we may as well suppose that the sequence $\{\boldsymbol{\mu}^n\}$ itself converges. Let $(\mu_1^*, \ldots, \mu_i^*, \ldots, \mu_N^*) = \boldsymbol{\mu}^*$ be the limit of this sequence; i.e. $\lim_{n \to \infty} \boldsymbol{\mu}^n = \boldsymbol{\mu}^*$.[10] We would like to ensure that $\boldsymbol{\mu}^*$ is in fact a mixed-strategy equilibrium of the limiting game $[(A_i, U_i); i = 1, \ldots, N]$.

10 To be precise, $\boldsymbol{\mu}^*$ is the limit of some subsequence $\{\boldsymbol{\mu}^{nk}\}$.

Let $\bar{A}^{**}(i)$ denote the closure of $A^{**}(i)$. Since $A^*(i)$ is closed we conclude that $\bar{A}^{**}(i) \subseteq A^*(i)$. Let $A_i^{**}(i)$ (resp. $\bar{A}_i^{**}(i)$, $A_i^*(i)$) be the projection of $A^{**}(i)$ (resp. $\bar{A}^{**}(i)$, $A^*(i)$) onto A_i. (Thus, for example, $\forall \bar{a}_i \in A_i^{**}(i)$, $\exists a_{-i} \in A_{-i}$ such that $(\bar{a}_i, a_{-i})$ is a point of discontinuity of U_i.). Theorem 4 says that if $\forall i$, μ_i^* is atomless on $\bar{A}_i^{**}(i)$, then μ^* is an equilibrium of $[(A_i, U_i); i = 1, \ldots, N]$. This is intuitively appealing. If for large enough n, the equilibrium mixed-strategy, μ_i^n, places very little probability weight on points that lie in $\bar{A}_i^{**}(i)$, then the fact that U_i is discontinuous at points in $A^{**}(i)$ does not matter for the limiting game.

But Theorem 4 is not very helpful in determining whether a game has an equilibrium: in order to verify whether μ_i^* is atomless on $\bar{A}_i^{**}(i)$ we need to compute μ_i^n. It is desirable to put conditions directly on the payoff functions, U_i, that guarantee that the limiting vector of measures, μ^*, is an equilibrium. This is what Theorem 5 does.

In addition to the requirement that the discontinuity sets, $A^{**}(i)$, be contained in $A^*(i)$, where $A^*(i)$ is defined by (1.2), Theorem 5 requires that the *sum* of the utility functions be *upper* semi-continuous (see Definition 2 above), and that each player's utility function satisfies a weak form of *lower* semi-continuity as a function of his own strategy (see Definition 6 below). We now present a road-map of the arguments leading to Theorem 5.

Once again, consider a sequence, $\{\mu^n\}$, of equilibria in successively finer finite approximations to the game $[(A_i, U_i); i = 1, \ldots, N]$. Let $\mu^* = \lim_{n \to \infty} \mu^n$. Because U_i is bounded and A_i is compact, the sequence $\{\int U_i(a) d\mu^n\}$ has a convergent sub-sequence. Without loss of generality, therefore, we may assume that it converges itself. Via Lemmas 1–3 we will show that for any given player i there *cannot* be more than a *countable* number of pure strategies, $\bar{a}_i$, such that

$$\int_{A_{-i}} U_i(\bar{a}_i, a_{-i}) \, d\mu_{-i}^* > \lim_{n \to \infty} \int U_i(a) \, d\mu^n. \tag{1.3}$$

(This demonstration relies only on the fact that U_i is continuous *off* the set $A^{**}(i)$, where $A^{**}(i)$ is a subset of $A^*(i)$, defined by (1.2). It does not require that the game be an upper-semi-continuous-sum game, nor that U_i satisfy the weak form of lower-semi-continuity.) Now, of course, Lemmas 1–3 are only an intermediate stage of the argument, because we will wish finally to prove that there exists *no* $\bar{a}_i$ such that (1.3) holds. In order to prove this we will need the further conditions on the payoff functions that we have alluded to. To see this, note that because $\Sigma_{i=1}^N U_i(a)$ is upper-semi-continuous, we have

$$\lim_{n \to \infty} \int \Sigma U_i(a) \, d\mu^n \leqslant \int \Sigma U_i(a) \, d\mu^*, \tag{1.4}$$

and therefore, $\exists i$ such that

$$\lim_{n \to \infty} \int U_i(a) \, d\mu^n \leqslant \int U_i(a) \, d\mu^*. \tag{1.5}$$

From (5) one may conclude that $\mathbf{E}\bar{a}_i \in A_i$ such that

$$\lim_{n \to \infty} \int U_i(a) \, d\mu^n \leqslant \int U_i(\bar{a}_i, a_{-i}) \, d\mu^*_{-i}. \tag{1.6}$$

In Lemma 4 it is argued that (1.5) must hold with *equality* for this i. For if not, then $\exists \bar{a}_i \in A_i$ such that (1.6) is a strict inequality. Therefore, the fact that U_i is weakly lower semi-continuous in a_i (see Definition 6 below), would imply that there is an interval in A_i containing $\bar{a}_i$ such that (1.3) holds for all $\bar{a}_i$ in this interval. But this contradicts the conclusion that (1.3) can hold for only countably many $\bar{a}_i$. Thus (1.5) must be an equality for all i.[11] Theorem 5 establishes that μ^* is an equilibrium of the limiting game. For if it is not, then $\exists i$ and $\exists \bar{a}_i \in A_i$ such that

$$\int U_i(\bar{a}_i, a_{-i}) \, d\mu^*_{-i} > \int U_i(a) \, d\mu^*.$$

But this, in conjunction with the fact that (1.5) holds with equality implies that (1.6) holds with strict inequality, generating the same contradiction as before.

4.3 Equilibrium when Points of Discontinuity are not Atoms

In this sub-section we prove Theorem 4 via two lemmas that are also useful in the proof of Theorem 5. Lemma 1 is straightforward, but its proof is tedious.

Lemma 1. Let $A_i \subseteq R^1$, $(i = 1, \ldots, N)$, be a closed interval, and let μ_i be a (Borel) probability measure defined on A_i. Let $A^*(i) \subseteq A$ be defined by (1.2), and let $A^{**}(i)$ be a subset of $A^*(i)$. If $\forall i$, μ_i is atomless on $A_i^{**}(i)$ (i.e. $\forall a_i \in A_i^{**}(i)$, $\mu_i(\{a_i\}) = 0$), then $\forall i$, $\mu(A^{**}(i)) = 0$. Furthermore, if for $\bar{a}_i \in A_i$, $\mu_j(\{f_{ij}^d(\bar{a}_i)\}) = 0$, $\forall j \neq i$ and $\forall d$, $1 \leqslant d \leqslant D(i)$, then $\mu_{-i}(A^*_{-i}(\bar{a}_i)) = 0$, where $A^*_{-i}(\bar{a}_i) \equiv \{a_{-i} \in A_{-i} \mid (\bar{a}_i, a_{-i}) \in A^*(i)\}$.

Proof. Note that $\forall i$, we have

$$\mu(A^{**}(i)) \equiv (\mu_1 \times \ldots \times \mu_N)(A^{**}(i))$$

$$\leqslant \Sigma_{s \neq i} \Sigma_{1 \leqslant d \leqslant D(i)} (\mu_1 \times \ldots \times \mu_N)(\{(a_1, \ldots, a_N) \in A \mid a_s$$

$$= f_{is}^d(a_i)\} \cap A^{**}(i)). \tag{1.7}$$

---

11 Note that if U_i were continuous on A_i, (1.5) would hold with equality by the definition of the topology of weak convergence of probability measures.

We now construct a lattice on $A^*(i)$ as follows: Let $a_i^* \equiv \min A_i$ and $a_i^{**} \equiv \max A_i$. For each i, j and d as above, each positive integer n, and $r \in \{0, \ldots, (n-1)\}$, let

$$B_i^n(r) \equiv A_i^{**}(i) \cap \left\{ a_i \in A_i \, \middle| \, a_i^* + \frac{r}{n}(a_i^{**} - a_i^*) \leqslant a_i \leqslant a_i^* + \frac{(r+1)}{n}(a_i^{**} - a_i^*) \right\},$$

and

$$B_j^n(r, i, d) \equiv A_j^{**}(j) \cap \left\{ a_j \in A_j \, \middle| \, f_{ij}^d \left(a_i^* + \frac{r}{n}(a_i^{**} - a_i^*) \right) \right.$$

$$\left. \leqslant a_j \leqslant f_{ij}^d \left(a_i^* + \left(\frac{r+1}{n}\right)(a_i^{**} - a_i^*) \right) \right\}.$$

Because $\forall i$, μ_i is atomless on $A_i^{**}(i)$ and because of the continuity of the functions f_{ij}^d, $\forall \epsilon > 0$, $\exists \bar{n}$ such that $\forall n > \bar{n}$, $\forall j$, $\forall d$ with $1 \leqslant d \leqslant D(i)$, and $\forall r \in \{0, \ldots, n-1\}$,

$$\mu_i(B_r^n(r)) < \epsilon \quad \text{and} \quad \mu_j(B_j^n(r, i, d)) < \epsilon. \tag{1.8}$$

From (1.7) it follows that

$$\boldsymbol{\mu}(A^{**}(i)) \leqslant \Sigma_{j \neq i} \left\{ \Sigma_{1 \leqslant d \leqslant D(i)} \, \Sigma_{r=0}^{n-1} \mu_i(B_i^n(r)) \, \mu_j(B_j^n(r, i, d)) \right.$$

$$\left. \times \, \Pi_{s \neq i, j} \mu_s(A_s^{**}(s)) \right\}. \tag{1.9}$$

Using (1.8) and the facts that

$$\Sigma_{r=0}^{n-1} \mu_j(B_j^n(r, i, d)) \leqslant \mu_j(A_j^{**}(j)) \quad \text{and} \quad \mu_j(A_j^{**}(j)) \leqslant 1 \quad \text{for } \forall j,$$

we can transform (1.9) to $\boldsymbol{\mu}(A^{**}(i)) \leqslant D(i)N\epsilon$. Since ϵ is arbitrary, we conclude that $\boldsymbol{\mu}(A^{**}(i)) = 0$.

Next suppose that for $\bar{a}_i \in A_i$, $\mu_j(f_{ij}^d(\bar{a}_i)) = 0$ for all $j \neq i$ and $1 \leqslant d \leqslant D(i)$. We then have

$$\boldsymbol{\mu}_{-i}(A_{-i}^*(\bar{a}_i)) \leqslant \Sigma_{j \neq i} \Sigma_{1 \leqslant d \leqslant D(i)} \boldsymbol{\mu}_{-i}(\{a_{-i} \in A_{-i} \,|\, a_j = f_{ij}^d(\bar{a}_i)\})$$

$$\leqslant \Sigma_{j \neq i} \Sigma_{i \leqslant d \leqslant D(i)} \mu_j(\{f_{ij}^d(\bar{a}_i)\}) \, \Pi_{s \neq i, j} \mu_s(A_s) = 0,$$

as desired. $\parallel$

Lemma 2. *Let $A_i \subseteq R^1$, $(i = 1, \ldots, N)$ be a closed interval and let $U_i : A \to R^1$, $(i = 1, \ldots, N)$, be continuous, except on a subset $A^{**}(i)$, of $A^*(i)$, where $A^*(i)$ is defined by (1.2). Suppose $\forall i$, U_i is bounded. Let A_i^n be a finite subset of A_i with the property that*

$$\sup_{a_i \in A_i} \inf_{a_i^n \in A_i^n} |a_i - a_i^n| \leqslant 1/n.$$

Let $(\mu_1^n, \ldots, \mu_N^n)$ be an equilibrium vector of mixed strategies for the finite

game $[(A_i^n, U_i); i = 1, \ldots, N]$, *and let* $(\mu_1^*, \ldots, \mu_N^*) = \lim_{n \to \infty} (\mu_1^n, \ldots, \mu_N^n).$[12]
If for some i, $\exists \bar{a}_i \in A_i$ *such that*

$$\int_{A_{-i}} U_i(\bar{a}_i, a_{-i}) \, d\mu_{-i}^* > \lim_{n \to \infty} \int_A U_i(a) \, d\mu^n + \epsilon \quad \text{for some } \epsilon > 0, \quad (1.10)$$

then $\mu_{-i}^*(\bar{A}_{-i}^{**}(\bar{a}_i)) > 0$, *where* $\bar{A}_{-i}^{**}(\bar{a}_i)$ *is the closure of the set*

$$A_{-i}^{**}(\bar{a}_i) \equiv \{a_{-i} \in A_{-i} \mid (\bar{a}_i, a_{-i}) \in A^{**}(i)\}.[13]$$

Remark. From Lemma 2 we may conclude that $\forall \bar{a}_i \notin A_i^{**}(i)$,

$$\int U_i(\bar{a}_i, a_{-i}) \, d\mu_{-i} \leq \lim_{n \to \infty} \int U_i(a) \, d\mu^n.$$

Proof. Suppose that the hypotheses of the Lemma are satisfied, but that $\mu_{-i}^*(\bar{A}_{-i}^{**}(\bar{a}_i)) = 0$. Because $\bar{A}_{-i}^{**}(\bar{a}_i)$ is closed, for each $\epsilon > 0$, $\exists$ an open set $A_{-i}^{**} \supseteq \bar{A}_{-i}^{**}(\bar{a}_i)$ such that

$$\mu_{-i}^*(\bar{A}_{-i}^{**}) < \epsilon/4M, \quad (1.11)$$

where $M > \sup |U_i|$, and $\bar{A}_{-i}^{**}$ is the closure of A_{-i}^{**}.
Using (1.10) and (1.11) we may obtain

$$\int_{\tilde{A}_{-i}} U_i(\bar{a}_i, a_{-i}) \, d\mu_{-i}^* > \lim_{n \to \infty} \int_A U_i(a) \, d\mu^n + 3\epsilon/4 \quad (1.12)$$

where $\tilde{A}_{-i} \equiv A_{-i} - A_{-i}^{**}$.

Choose an open neighbourhood $B(\bar{a}_i)$ of $\bar{a}_i$, such that if $a_i \in B(\bar{a}_i)$ then $A_{-i}^{**}(a_i) \subseteq A_{-i}^{**}$. Then U_i is continuous when restricted to $B(\bar{a}_i) \times \tilde{A}_{-i}$. From (1.11) and (1.12) we conclude that $\exists t > 0$ and $\bar{a}_i^t \in A_i^t \cap B(\bar{a}_i)$ such that

$$\int_{\tilde{A}_{-i}} U_i(\bar{a}_i^t, a_{-i}) \, d\mu_{-i}^* > \lim_{n \to \infty} \int_A U_i(a) \, d\mu^n + 3\epsilon/4. \quad (1.13)$$

Because U_i is continuous on $\{\bar{a}_i^t\} \times \tilde{A}_{-i}$ we can invoke the Tietz extension lemma to continuously extend U_i as a function of a_{-i} to $\{\bar{a}_i^t\} \times A_{-i}$. If $\tilde{U}_i$ is the extension, then we may assume that $\sup |\tilde{U}_i| < M$.
From (1.11) and (1.13) we have

$$\int_{A_{-i}} \tilde{U}_i(\bar{a}_i^t, a_{-i}) \, d\mu_{-i}^* > \lim_{n \to \infty} \int_A U_i(a) \, d\mu^n + \epsilon/2. \quad (1.14)$$

---

12 We know that $\{\mu^n\}$ possesses a sub-sequence which converges. Thus we are supposing that μ^* is the limit of some sub-sequence of $\{\mu^n\}$.

13 From the boundedness of U_i we may conclude that a sub-sequence of $\{\int U_i(a) \, d\mu^n\}$ converges. Thus, without loss of generality we suppose that $\lim_{n \to \infty} \int U_i(a) \, d\mu^n$ exists.

But from the hypotheses, inequalities (1.12) and (1.14) and the continuity of $\bar{U}_i$, we may conclude that $\exists \bar{n} > 0$ such that for $n > \bar{n}$,

$$\int_{A_{-i}} \bar{U}_i(\bar{a}_i^t, a_{-i}) \, d\mu_{-i}^n > \int_A U_i(a) \, d\mu^n + \epsilon/2 \tag{1.15}$$

and from (1.11) that

$$\mu_{-i}^n(\bar{A}_{-i}^{**}) < \epsilon/4M. \tag{1.16}$$

Therefore, from (1.15) and (1.16) we obtain, for $n > \bar{n}$,

$$\int_{A_{-i}} U_i(\bar{a}_i^t, a_{-i}) \, d\mu_{-i}^n > \int_A U_i(a) \, d\mu^n + \epsilon/4. \tag{1.17}$$

But for $n > t$, (1.17) contradicts the hypothesis that $\mu^n = (\mu_1^n, \ldots, \mu_N^n)$ constitutes an equilibrium for the game $[(A_i^n, U_i); i = 1, \ldots, N]$. Thus $\mu_{-i}^*(\bar{A}_{-i}^{**}(\bar{a}_i)) > 0$. ‖

We may now use Lemmas 1 and 2 to state and prove:

Theorem 4. *Let $A_i \subseteq R^1$, $(i = 1, \ldots, N)$, be a closed interval, and let $U_i : A \to R^1$, $(i = 1, \ldots, N)$, be continuous, except on a subset $A^{**}(i)$ of $A^*(i)$, where $A^*(i)$ is defined by (1.2).*

Suppose $\forall i$, U_i is bounded. Let A_i^n be a finite subset of A_i with the property that

$$\sup_{a_i \in A_i} \inf_{a_i^n \in A_i^n} |a_i - a_i^n| < 1/n.$$

Let $(\mu_1^n, \ldots, \mu_N^n)$ be an equilibrium vector of mixed strategies for the finite game $[(A_i^n, U_i); i = 1, \ldots, N]$, and let $(\mu_1^*, \ldots, \mu_N^*) = \lim_{n \to \infty}(\mu_1^n, \ldots, \mu_N^n)$; (see footnote 12, p. 63). Suppose, $\forall ij$, d and $\forall \bar{a}_i \in \bar{A}_i^{**}(i)$, $\mu_j^*(\{f_{ij}^d(\bar{a}_i)\}) = 0$. Then $(\mu_1^*, \ldots, \mu_N^*) \equiv \mu^*$ constitutes an equilibrium for the infinite game $[(A_i, U_i); i = 1, \ldots, N]$.

Proof. Suppose that the hypotheses of the theorem are satisfied, but that $(\mu_1^*, \ldots, \mu_N^*)$ is not an equilibrium. Then some agent, say agent i, can do better by playing some strategy other than μ_i^*. That is, $\exists \bar{a}_i \in A_i$, and $\epsilon > 0$ such that

$$\int_{A_{-i}} U_i(\bar{a}_i, a_{-i}) \, d\mu_{-i}^* > \int_A U_i(a) \, d\mu^* + \epsilon. \tag{1.18}$$

Obviously, $\{\bar{a}_i\} \times A_{-i}^{**}(\bar{a}_i) \subseteq A^{**}(i)$.

Therefore, by hypothesis and Lemma 1, we have

$$\mu_{-i}^*(A_{-i}^{**}(\bar{a}_i)) = 0, \tag{1.19}$$

and

$$\mu^*(A^{**}(i)) = 0. \tag{1.20}$$

Since U_i is continuous on $A - A^{**}(i)$, we may conclude from (1.20) that

$$\lim_{n \to \infty} \int_A U_i(a) \, d\mu^n = \int_A U_i(a) \, d\mu^*.$$

Thus, from (1.18) we have

$$\int_{A_{-i}} U_i(\bar{a}_i, a_{-i}) \, d\mu^*_{-i} > \lim_{n \to \infty} \int_A U_i(a_i, a_{-i}) \, d\mu^n + \epsilon. \tag{1.21}$$

But (1.19) and (1.21) together contradict the conclusion of Lemma 2. Therefore $\mu^* = (\mu^*_1, \ldots, \mu^*_N)$ is an equilibrium for the game $[(A_i, U_i); i = 1, \ldots, N]$.   ‖

Remark. If $\forall i$, $A^{**}(i)$ is empty, (i.e. U_i is continuous on A), Theorem 4 asserts that the game $[(A_i, U_i); i = 1, \ldots, N]$ possesses a mixed-strategy equilibrium. This is Theorem 3 above.

Remark. We have noted that in Example 1, where $N = 2$ and $A_1 = A_2 = [0, 1]$, we may take $D(1) = D(2) = 2$, $f^1_{12}(a_1) = a_1$ and $f^2_{12}(a_1) = a_1 + \frac{1}{2}$. We also noted that for this game $A^*(i) = A^{**}(i)$, $(i = 1, 2)$, and therefore, that $\bar{A}^{**}_1(1) = \bar{A}^{**}_2(2) = [0, 1]$. Theorem 4 implies that the limits of a sequence of equilibria of successively finer finite approximations of Example 1 must possess atoms.

4.4   The Main Existence Theorem

In this section we state and prove our main result (Theorem 5). First, we prove two lemmas which will be useful. In Section 4.2 we presented a verbal account of them and their motivation.

Lemma 3. *Let $A_i \subseteq R^1$, $(i = 1, \ldots, N)$ be a closed interval, and let $U_i : A \to R^1$, $(i = 1, \ldots, N)$, be continuous except on a subset $A^{**}(i)$ of $A^*(i)$, where $A^*(i)$ is defined by (1.2). Suppose $\forall i$, U_i is bounded. Let A^n_i be a finite subset of A_i with the property that*

$$\sup_{a_i \in A_i} \inf_{a^n_i \in A^n_i} |a_i - a^n_i| < 1/n.$$

Let $(\mu^n_1, \ldots, \mu^n_N)$ be an equilibrium vector of mixed strategies for the finite game $[(A^n_i, U_i); i = 1, \ldots, N]$, and let $(\mu^*_1, \ldots, \mu^*_N) = \lim_{n \to \infty}(\mu^n_1, \ldots, \mu^n_N)$; (see footnote 12, p. 62). Then, $\forall i$

$$\int_{A_{-i}} U_i(\bar{a}_i, a_{-i}) \, d\mu^*_{-i} \leqslant \lim_{n \to \infty} \int_A U_i(a) \, d\mu^n$$

for all but countably many $\bar{a}_i \in A_i$.

Proof. Suppose that the hypotheses of the lemma hold but that $\exists i$ such that

$$\int_{A_{-i}} U_i(\bar{a}_i, a_{-i})\, d\boldsymbol{\mu}^*_{-i} > \lim_{n \to \infty} \int_A U_i(a)\, d\boldsymbol{\mu}^n \tag{1.22}$$

for uncountably many $\bar{a}_i \in A_i$.

By Lemma 2 we conclude that for each $\bar{a}_i \in A_i$ which satisfies (1.22), $\mu^*_{-i}(\bar{A}^{**}_{-i}(\bar{a}_i)) > 0$. But then, by Lemma 1 we know that for each such $\bar{a}_i$, $\exists j$ $(j \neq i)$ and $\exists d$ with $1 \leqslant d \leqslant D(i)$ such that

$$\mu^*_j(\{f^d_{ij}(\bar{a}_i)\}) > 0. \tag{1.23}$$

Since we are supposing here that the number of $\bar{a}_i$'s satisfying (1.22) is un-countable, there must exist j and d such that (1.23) holds for uncountably many $\bar{a}_i$'s. But f^d_{ij} is one-to-one, so that we may conclude that μ^*_j has uncountably many atoms. But this is an impossibility. Thus (1.22) can hold for only countably many $\bar{a}_i$'s. $\|$

The hypotheses of Lemma 3 are satisfied by Example 1. The economic games that we study in the sequel are (upper semi)-continuous-sum games. Moreover, Example 1, being a zero-sum game is, of course, an upper semi-continuous-sum game. We now come to a property of payoff functions, however, that is satisfied by the games in the sequel, but *not* by Example 1.

Definition 6. $U_i(a_i, a_{-i})$ is *weakly lower semi-continuous* in a_i if $\forall \bar{a}_i \in A^{**}_i(i)$, $\exists \lambda \in [0, 1]$ such that $\forall a_{-i} \in A^{**}_{-i}(\bar{a}_i)$, $\lambda \lim \inf_{a_i \to \bar{a}_i} U_i(a_i, a_{-i}) + (1 - \lambda) \lim \inf_{a_i \overset{+}{\to} \bar{a}_i} U_i(a_i, a_{-i}) \geqslant U_i(\bar{a}_i, a_{-i})$.[14]

(If $\bar{a}_i$ is the right end point of A_i and, therefore, $\lim \inf_{a_i \overset{+}{\to} \bar{a}_i} U_i(a_i, a_{-i})$ is not defined, the definition reduces to the condition $\lim \inf_{a_i \to \bar{a}_i} U_i(a_i, a_{-i}) \geqslant U_i(\bar{a}_i, a_{-i})$; i.e. that $U_i(a_i, a_{-i})$ is left lower semi-continuous in a_i at $\bar{a}_i$. Similarly, if $\bar{a}_i$ is the left end point of A_i, then the definition reduces to the condition $\lim \inf_{a_i \overset{+}{\to} \bar{a}_i} U_i(a_i, a_{-i}) \geqslant U_i(\bar{a}_i, a_{-i})$; i.e. that $U_i(a_i, a_{-i})$ is right lower semi-continuous in a_i at $\bar{a}_i$.)

Remark. Notice that in Example 1 $U_1(a_1, a_2)$ is not weakly lower semi-continuous in a_1 at the point $(1, 1)$.

Lemma 4. Let $A_i \subseteq R^1$, $(i = 1, \ldots, N)$, be a closed interval, and let $U_i : A \to R^1$, $(i = 1, \ldots, N)$, be continuous, except on a subset $A^{**}(i)$ of $A^*(i)$, where $A^*(i)$ is defined by (1.2). Suppose $\Sigma^N_{i=1} U_i(a)$ is upper semi-continuous, $\forall i\, U_i(a_i, a_{-i})$ is bounded, and is weakly lower semi-continuous in a_i. Let A^n_i be a finite subset of A_i with the property that

$$\sup_{a_i \in A_i} \inf_{a^n_i \in A^n_i} |a_i - a^n_i| < 1/n.$$

---

14 '$a_i \to \bar{a}_i$' (resp. '$a_i \overset{+}{\to} \bar{a}_i$') denotes that a_i approaches $\bar{a}_i$ from the left (resp. right). Notice that if $U_i(a_i, a_{-i})$ is lower semi-continuous in a_i, it is weakly lower semi-continuous in a_i.

Let $(\mu_1^n, \ldots, \mu_N^n)$ be an equilibrium vector of mixed strategies for the finite game $[(A_i^n, U_i); i = 1, \ldots, N]$, and let $(\mu_1^*, \ldots, \mu_N^*) = \lim_{n \to \infty}(\mu_1^n, \ldots, \mu_N^n)$; (see footnote 12, p. 62). Then, $\forall i$

$$\lim_{n \to \infty} \int_A U_i(a) \, d\mu^n = \int_A U_i(a) \, d\mu^*. \tag{1.24}$$

Proof. Suppose that the hypotheses of the Lemma hold. Then $\forall i$ there exists a subsequence of $\{\int U_i(a) \, d\mu^n\}$ which converges. Thus without loss of generality we may assume that $\forall i$, $\lim_{n \to \infty} \int_A U_i(a) \, d\mu^n$ exists. Now suppose $\exists i$ such that (1.24) is not satisfied. Then $\exists \epsilon > 0$ such that either

$$\lim_{n \to \infty} \int U_i(a) \, d\mu^n \geqslant \int U_i(a) \, d\mu^* + \epsilon, \tag{1.25}$$

or

$$\lim_{n \to \infty} \int U_i(a) \, d\mu^n \leqslant \int U_i(a) \, d\mu^* - \epsilon. \tag{1.26}$$

Suppose (1.25) holds for this i. Then since $\Sigma_{i=1}^N U_i(a)$ is upper semi-continuous we may conclude that

$$\int \Sigma_{i=1}^N U_i(a) \, d\mu^* \geqslant \lim_{n \to \infty} \int \Sigma_{i=1}^N U_i(a) \, d\mu^n.$$

It follows therefore that $\exists j \neq i$ such that (1.26) holds for agent j. We conclude therefore that if (1.24) does not hold for all agents then there exists at least one agent for whom (1.26) holds. For this agent, j, $\exists \bar{a}_j \in A_j$ such that

$$\int_{A_{-j}} U_j(\bar{a}_j, a_{-j}) \, d\mu_{-j}^* \geqslant \lim_{n \to \infty} \int U_j(a) \, d\mu^n + \epsilon. \tag{1.27}$$

Now suppose U_j is weakly lower semi-continuous in a_j. Then it follows that $\int_{A_{-j}} U_j(a_j, a_{-j}) \, d\mu_{-j}^*$ is either right or left lower semi-continuous as a function of a_j at $\bar{a}_j$. Without loss of generality assume that it is right lower semi-continuous. Then it follows from (1.27) that

$$\liminf_{a_j \overset{+}{\to} \bar{a}_j} \int_{A_{-j}} U_j(a_j, a_{-j}) \, d\mu_{-j}^* \geqslant \int_{A_{-j}} U_j(\bar{a}_j, a_{-j}) \, d\mu_j^*$$

$$\geqslant \lim_{n \to \infty} \int U_j(a) \, d\mu^n + \epsilon. \tag{1.28}$$

It follows that $\exists \delta > 0$ such that $\forall \tilde{a}_j \in [\bar{a}_j, \bar{a}_j + \delta]$,

$$\int_{A_{-j}} U_j(\tilde{a}_j, a_{-j}) \, d\mu_{-j}^* > \lim_{n \to \infty} \int U_j(a) \, d\mu^n.$$

But this contradicts Lemma 3. Therefore (1.24) must hold for all agents. ‖

Theorem 5. *Let $A_i \subseteq R^1$ ($i = 1, \ldots, N$) be a closed interval and let $U_i : A \to R^1$ ($i = 1, \ldots, N$) be continuous except on a subset $A^{**}(i)$ of $A^*(i)$, where $A^*(i)$ is defined by (1.2). Suppose $\Sigma_{i=1}^N U_i(a)$ is upper semi-continuous and $U_i(a_i, a_{-i})$ is bounded and weakly lower semi-continuous in a_i. Then the game $[(A_i, U_i); i = 1, \ldots, N]$ possesses a mixed-strategy equilibrium.*

Proof. Suppose the hypotheses of the theorem are satisfied. $\forall i$, and $n > 0$, let A_i^n be a finite subset of A_i with the property that

$$\sup_{a_i \in A_i} \inf_{a_i^n \in A_i^n} |a_i - a_i^n| < 1/n.$$

For each $n > 0$, let $(\mu_1^n, \ldots, \mu_N^n)$ be a mixed-strategy equilibrium of the game $[(A_i^n, U_i); i = 1, \ldots, N]$. Let $(\mu_1^*, \ldots, \mu_N^*) = \lim_{n \to \infty} (\mu_1^n, \ldots, \mu_N^n)$; (see footnote 12, p. 62). If $\pmb{\mu}^*$ is not an equilibrium of the game $[(A_i, U_i); i = 1, \ldots, N]$, then $\exists i$ and $\exists \bar{a}_i \in A_i$ such that

$$\int_{A_{-i}} U_i(\bar{a}_i, a_{-i}) \, d\pmb{\mu}_{-i}^* > \int_A U_i(a) \, d\pmb{\mu}^*. \tag{1.29}$$

From Lemma 4, (1.29) implies

$$\int_{A_{-i}} U_i(\bar{a}_i, a_{-i}) \, d\pmb{\mu}_{-i}^* > \lim_{n \to \infty} \int_A U_i(a) \, d\pmb{\mu}^n. \tag{1.30}$$

Now we can use an argument identical to the one used in Lemma 4 to show that if (1.30) holds then there is an uncountable set of $\bar{a}_i$'s, with $\bar{a}_i \in A_i$ such that

$$\int U_i(\bar{a}_i, a_{-i}) \, d\pmb{\mu}_{-i}^* > \lim_{n \to \infty} \int U_i(a) \, d\pmb{\mu}^n,$$

and this contradicts Lemma 3. Therefore $\pmb{\mu}^*$ is an equilibrium of the game $[(A_i, U_i); i = 1, \ldots, N]$. ‖

Our sets $A^*(i)$ rule out discontinuities in agent i's payoff that occur independently of other agents' payoffs. This is limiting. For suppose that a quantity-setting firm must bear a set-up cost to produce any positive output level. Then its profit will be discontinuous at zero output regardless of what the other firms do.

We wish to modify Theorem 5 to allow for this sort of discontinuity. This is achieved in

Theorem 5a. *Suppose that the game $[(A_i, U_i); i = 1, \ldots, N]$ satisfies the hypotheses of Theorem 5, except that for some i there exists a strategy $\hat{a}_i \in A_i$ such that for all $\bar{a}_{-i} \in A_{-i}$,*

(i) $\lim_{a_i \to \hat{a}_i, a_{-i} \to \bar{a}_{-i}} U_i(a_i, a_{-i})$ *exists and equals* $U(\hat{a}_i, \bar{a}_{-i})$

(ii) $\lim_{a_i \overset{+}{\to} \hat{a}_i} U_i(a_i, \bar{a}_{-i})$ *exists, is less than or equal to* $U(\hat{a}_i, \bar{a}_{-i})$ *and is continuous in* $\bar{a}_{-i}$.

Then the game has a mixed-strategy equilibrium.

Proof. The proof consists of enlarging player's i's strategy space, extending the U_i's so that the game satisfies the hypotheses of Theorem 5 on the enlarged space, and then showing that an equilibrium of the modified game corresponds to an equilibrium of the original game.

Let $A_i = [a_i^*, a_i^{**}]$ and take $\hat{A}_i = [a_i^*, a_i^{**} + 1]$. Define $\hat{U}_j : \hat{A}_i \times A_{-i} \to R^1$, $j = 1, \ldots, N$, so that

$$\hat{U}_i(a_i, a_{-i}) = \begin{cases} U_i(a_i, a_{-i}), & \text{if } a_i \leqslant \hat{a}_i \\ (a_i - \hat{a}_i) \lim_{\bar{a}_i \overset{+}{\to} \hat{a}_i} U_i(\bar{a}_i, a_{-i}) + (1 - a_i + \hat{a}_i) U_i(\hat{a}_i, a_{-i}) \\ \qquad \text{if } \hat{a}_i < a_i \leqslant \hat{a}_i + 1, \\ U_i(a_i - 1, a_{-i}), & \text{if } a_i > \hat{a}_i + 1 \end{cases} \tag{1.31}$$

and for $j \neq i$

$$\hat{U}_j(a_i, a_{-i}) = \begin{cases} U_j(a_i, a_{-i}), & \text{if } a_i \leqslant \hat{a}_i \\ U_j(\hat{a}_i, a_{-i}), & \text{if } \hat{a}_i < a_i \leqslant \hat{a}_i + 1 \\ U_j(a_i - 1, a_{-i}), & \text{if } a_i > \hat{a}_i + 1. \end{cases} \tag{1.32}$$

Because $\lim_{\bar{a}_i \overset{+}{\to} \hat{a}_i} U_i(\bar{a}_i, a_{-i})$ exists, this modified game is well defined. Furthermore, because $(a_i - \hat{a}_i) \lim_{\bar{a}_i \overset{+}{\to} \hat{a}_i} U_i(\bar{a}_i, a_{-i}) + (1 - a_i + \hat{a}_i) U_i(\hat{a}_i, a_{-i})$ is continuous at any point where $\hat{a}_i \leqslant a_i \leqslant \hat{a}_i + 1$ and converges to $U_i(\hat{a}_i, \bar{a}_{-i})$ as (a_i, a_{-i}) tends to $(\hat{a}_i, \bar{a}_{-i})$, $\hat{U}_i$ is continuous at all points (a_i, a_{-i}), where $\hat{a}_i \leqslant a_i \leqslant \hat{a}_i + 1$. Notice too that (1.32) introduces no new discontinuities in the payoff functions of players other than i. Hence the modified game satisfies the hypotheses of Theorem 5. We conclude that there exists an equilibrium $(\hat{\mu}_1, \ldots, \hat{\mu}_N)$. For any set $E \subseteq A_i$, let

$$\mu_i^*(E) = \begin{cases} \hat{\mu}_i(E \cap [a_i^*, \hat{a}_i)) + \hat{\mu}_i([\hat{a}_i, \hat{a}_i + 1]) \\ \qquad + \hat{\mu}_i(\{a_i \mid a_i - 1 \in E \text{ and } a_i - 1 > \hat{a}_i\}) & \text{if } \hat{a}_i \in E \\ \hat{\mu}_i(E \cap [a_i^*, \hat{a}_i)) + \hat{\mu}_i(\{a_i \mid a_i - 1 \in E \text{ and } a_i - 1 > \hat{a}_i\}) & \text{if } \hat{a}_i \notin E. \end{cases}$$

Take $\mu_j^* = \hat{\mu}_j$ for all $j \neq i$. Notice that μ_i^* shifts all the probability mass of $\hat{\mu}_i$ in $[\hat{a}_i, \hat{a}_i + 1]$ to $\hat{a}_i$. Thus because $U_i(\hat{a}_i, a_{-i}) \geqslant \lim_{\bar{a}_i \overset{+}{\to} \hat{a}_i} U_i(a_i, a_{-i})$ we see from (1.31) that μ_i^* must be an optimal strategy for i in the original game given that $\hat{\mu}_i$ is optimal in the modified game. Because this shift in mass does not affect the payoffs of agents other than i, $\hat{\mu}_j$ is optimal in the original game for each $j \neq i$. Hence $(\mu_1^*, \ldots, \mu_N^*)$ is an equilibrium for the original game. ‖

Remark. Theorem 5a implies that an equilibrium exists in the Cournot model with set-up costs studied by Novshek (1980) and others, even when set-up costs are large.

Theorem 5a generalized Theorem 5 in one direction – roughly speaking, that the f_{ij}^d's are not restricted to be one-to-one mappings. In Theorem 5b below we generalize Theorem 5 in another direction. Notice that, in the proof of Theorem 5, the hypothesis that the sum of agents' payoff functions is upper semi-continuous is invoked only to show that if $\{\mu^n\}$ is a sequence of vectors of measures converging to μ^*, there exists an agent i for whom (1.25) holds. We can guarantee the existence of such a player, however, without requiring upper semi-continuity. What is needed is that at any point where one player's payoff falls, another's rises. To formalize this idea we restrict attention to the case of two agents and of a discontinuity set consisting of the main diagonal.

Theorem 5b. *Suppose that $N = 2$ and that $A_1 = A_2 = [a^*, a^{**}]$. For $i = 1, 2$ suppose that $U_i : A \to R^1$ is bounded and continuous except on the subset $\{(a_1, a_2) \mid a_1 = a_2\}$. For each $a \subset [a^*, a^{**}]$ assume that there exists $i \in \{1, 2\}$ such that*

$$\text{(i)} \quad \lim_{a_1 \to a, a_2 \xrightarrow{+} a} U_i(a_1, a_2) \geqslant U_i(a, a) \geqslant \lim_{a_1 \xrightarrow{+} a, a_2 \to a} U_i(a_1, a_2)$$

and

$$\text{(ii)} \quad \lim_{a_1 \to a, a_2 \xrightarrow{+} a} U_j(a_1, a_2) \leqslant U_j(a, a) \leqslant \lim_{a_1 \xrightarrow{+} a, a_2 \to a} U_j(a_1, a_2), \quad j \neq i,$$

where the left (right) inequality in (i) is strict if and only if the right (left) inequality in (ii) is strict. Then the game $[(A_i, U_i); i = 1, 2]$ has a mixed-strategy equilibrium.

Proof. For each $a \subset [a^*, a^{**}]$ choose $\bar{u}_i(a)$ and $\bar{u}_j(a)$ and define

$$\hat{U}_i(a, a) = \begin{cases} U_i(a, a), & \text{if the left inequality in (i) holds with equality} \\ \bar{u}_i(a), & \text{if the left inequality in (i) holds strictly} \end{cases} \tag{1.33}$$

and

$$\hat{U}_j(a, a) = \begin{cases} U_j(a, a), & \text{if the right inequality in (ii) holds with equality} \\ \bar{u}_j(a), & \text{if the right inequality in (ii) holds strictly} \end{cases} \tag{1.34}$$

where

$$\lim_{a_1 \to a, a_2 \xrightarrow{+} a} U_i(a_1, a_2) > \bar{u}_i(a) > U_i(a, a), \tag{1.35}$$

$$\lim_{a_1 \xrightarrow{+} a, a_2 \to a} U_j(a_1, a_2) > \bar{u}_j(a) > U_j(a, a), \tag{1.36}$$

and

$$\bar{u}_i(a) + \bar{u}_j(a) \geqslant \begin{cases} \lim_{a_1 \to a, a_2 \xrightarrow{+} a}(U_i(a_1, a_2) + U_j(a_1, a_2)) \\ \lim_{a_1 \xrightarrow{+} a, a_2 \to a}(U_i(a_1, a_2) + U_j(a_1, a_2)) \end{cases}. \tag{1.37}$$

For $a_1 \neq a_2$ take

$$\hat{U}_i(a_1, a_2) = U_i(a_1, a_2) \qquad (1.38)$$

and

$$\hat{U}_j(a_1, a_2) = U_j(a_1, a_2). \qquad (1.39)$$

Because U_i and U_j are continuous where $a_1 \neq a_2$, (1.38) and (1.39) imply that $\hat{U}_1 + \hat{U}_2$ is also continuous there. From (1.33), (1.34) and (1.37), $\hat{U}_1 + \hat{U}_2$ is upper semi-continuous at points where $a_1 = a_2$. From (1.33) and (1.35), $\hat{U}_i$ is either left or right lower semi-continuous at (a, a) and from (1.34) and (1.36), so is $\hat{U}_j$. Hence, the game $[(A_i, \hat{U}_i); i = 1, 2]$ has a mixed-strategy equilibrium $(\hat{\mu}_1, \hat{\mu}_2)$. We will now show that $(\hat{\mu}_1, \hat{\mu}_2)$ is an equilibrium for the original game.

Choose $\hat{a}_1 \in \text{supp } \hat{\mu}_1$. Then,

$$\int \hat{U}_1(\hat{a}_1, a_2) \, d\hat{\mu}_2 \geqslant \int \hat{U}_1(a_1, a_2) \, d\hat{\mu}_2 \quad \text{for all } a_1 \in A_1. \qquad (1.40)$$

If $\hat{\mu}_2(\hat{a}_1) > 0$ and if U_1 is discontinuous at $(\hat{a}_1, \hat{a}_1)$, then from (1.33) and (1.34), there exists a'_1 close to $\hat{a}_1$ such that $\int \hat{U}_1(a'_1, a_2) \, d\hat{\mu}_2 > \int \hat{U}_1(a_1, a_2) \, d\mu_2$, a contradiction of (1.40). Hence

$$\int \hat{U}_1(\hat{a}_1, a_2) \, d\hat{\mu}_2 = \int U_1(\hat{a}_1, a_2) \, d\hat{\mu}_2. \qquad (1.41)$$

But from (1.33)–(1.36), $\hat{U}_1(a_1, a_2) \geqslant U_1(a_1, a_2)$ for all (a_1, a_2). Therefore,

$$\int \hat{U}_1(a_1, a_2) \, d\hat{\mu}_2 \geqslant \int U_1(a_1, a_2) \, d\hat{\mu}_2. \qquad (1.42)$$

But (1.41) and (1.42) imply that

$$\int U_1(\hat{a}_1, a_2) \, d\hat{\mu}_2 \geqslant \int U_1(a_1, a_2) \, d\hat{\mu}_2,$$

i.e. $\hat{\mu}_1$ is best response to $\hat{\mu}_2$ in the original game. Similarly $\hat{\mu}_2$ is a best response to $\hat{\mu}_1$. ‖

5   SYMMETRIC GAMES

Definition 7. Let $\bar{\bar{A}} \subseteq R^m \, (m \geqslant 1)$ be non-empty and compact, and let

$$A = \underbrace{\frac{\bar{\bar{A}} \times \ldots \times \bar{\bar{A}}}{}}_{N \text{ times}}.$$

For $U_i: A \to R^1$, $i = 1, \ldots, N$, $[(\bar{\bar{A}}, U_i); i = 1, \ldots, N]$ is a symmetric game if for all permutations, π, on the set $\{1, \ldots, N\}$, all $a \in A$ and all i,

$$U_i(a_1, \ldots, a_i, \ldots, a_N) = U_{\pi(i)}(a_{\pi(1)}, \ldots, a_{\pi(i)}, \ldots, a_{\pi(N)}).$$

The central result of this section, Theorem 6, states that under suitable assumptions mixed-strategy equilibria of discontinuous symmetric games are atomless on the set of discontinuities.

Definition 8. An equilibrium in mixed strategies, $(\mu_1^*, \ldots, \mu_i^*, \ldots, \mu_N^*)$ is symmetric if μ_i^* is independent of i.

Lemma 5 (Fan). *Let* $X \subseteq R^n$, $(n \geqslant 1)$, *be non-empty, convex and compact. Let* $F: X \times X \to R^1$ *be continuous, and concave in its first argument, and suppose that* $F(x, x) = 0$ *for* $x \in X$. *Then* $\exists x^* \in X$ *such that* $\max_{y \in X} F(y, x^*) = 0$.

Proof. $\forall y \in X$, let $\phi(y) \equiv \{x \in X \,|\, F(x, y) = \max_{x' \in X} F(x', y)\}$. It is immediate that ϕ is non-empty, convex- and compact-valued and upper hemi-continuous. Therefore, by Kakutani fixed-point theorem, $\exists y^* \in X$ such that $y^* \in \phi(y^*)$; that is,

$$\max_{x \in X} F(x, y^*) = F(y^*, y^*) = 0. \quad \|$$

We can now establish a simple result on symmetric, finite games.

Lemma 6. *Let* $[(\bar{\bar{A}}, U_i); i = 1, \ldots, N]$ *be a symmetric game, where* $\bar{\bar{A}} \subseteq R^m$ $(m \geqslant 1)$, *is non-empty and finite. Then the game possesses a symmetric mixed-strategy equilibrium.*[15]

Proof. Let $D(\bar{\bar{A}})$ be the set of all (Borel) probability measures on $\bar{\bar{A}}$. For $\mu, \nu \in D(\bar{\bar{A}})$ define

$$F(\mu, \nu) \equiv \int U_1(a_1, \ldots, a_N) \, d(\mu(a_1) \times \nu(a_2) \times \ldots \times \nu(a_N))$$

$$- \int U_1(a_1, \ldots, a_N) \, d(\nu(a_1) \times \nu(a_2) \times \ldots \times \nu(a_N)).$$

Clearly, F is continuous in μ and ν and linear (and therefore concave) in μ. Moreover, $F(\mu, \mu) = 0$. Therefore F satisfies the hypotheses of Lemma 5. Thus $\exists \mu^* \in D(\bar{\bar{A}})$ such that $\max_{\mu \in D(\bar{A})} F(\mu, \mu^*) = F(\mu^*, \mu^*) = 0$. It follows that μ^* is the best response for agent 1 if each of the remaining agents uses μ^*. By symmetry, μ^* is the best response of any agent i if each of the remaining agents μ^*. Thus $(\mu^*, \ldots, \mu^*)$ is an equilibrium. $\|$

---

15 This result is well known among game theorists. We are including a proof here because we have been unable to find a reference. We are indebted to Hervé Moulin for suggesting the use of the Fan lemma here.

We can now state

Lemma 7. *Let* $[(\bar{A}, U_i); i = 1, \ldots, N]$ *be a symmetric game, where* $\bar{A} \subseteq R^1$ *is non-empty and compact, and where* U_i *satisfies the conditions of Theorem 5. Then the game possesses a symmetric mixed-strategy equilibrium.*

Proof. Use the proof of Theorem 5 and Lemma 6. ‖

Theorem 6 below presents a set of conditions which ensures the existence of equilibrium mixed strategies that are atomless on discontinuity sets. The computation of equilibrium strategies is particularly simplified when this is so. The examples analysed by Karlin (1959), Beckmann (1965), Rosenthal (1980) and Varian (1980) satisfy the postulates of Theorem 6. The theorem, therefore, also provides an explanation of why the computational techniques these authors rely on actually work for their models.

We are now concerned with symmetric games $[(\bar{A}, U_i); i = 1, \ldots, N]$, with $\bar{A} \subseteq R^1$, possessing the property that $\forall \bar{a}_i \in A_i^{**}(i)$, the corresponding point on the 'diagonal',

$$\underbrace{(\bar{a}_i, \bar{a}_i, \ldots, \bar{a}_i)}_{N\text{-times}},$$

is a point of discontinuity of U_i. As we shall see in the sequel, several well-known economic games share this property. What we require is that the inequality in the definition of weak lower semi-continuity (Definition 6) be strict on the diagonal. We shall call this stronger condition property (α).

Property (α). $\forall \bar{a}_i \in A_i^{**}(i)$, $\exists \lambda \in [0, 1]$ *such that for all* $a_{-i} \in A_{-i}^{**}(\bar{a}_i)$

$$\lambda \liminf_{a_i \to \bar{a}_i} U_i(a_i, a_{-i}) + (1 - \lambda) \liminf_{a_i \to \bar{a}_i} U_i(a_i, a_{-i}) \geqslant U_i(\bar{a}_i, a_{-i}),$$

where the inequality is strict if

$$a_{-i} = \underbrace{(\bar{a}_i, \ldots, \bar{a}_i)}_{N-1 \text{ times}}.$$

We may now prove

Theorem 6. *Let* $\bar{A} \subseteq R^1$ *be non-empty and compact, and let* $[(\bar{A}, U_i); i = 1, \ldots, N]$ *be a symmetric game, where* $\forall i$,

$$U_i : \underbrace{\bar{A} \times \ldots \times \bar{A}}_{N\text{-times}} \to R^1 \text{ is continuous,}$$

except on a subset $A^{**}(i)$ *of* $A^*(i)$, *where* $A^*(i)$ *is defined by* (1.2). *Suppose* $\Sigma_{i=1}^{N} U_i(a)$ *is upper semi-continuous, and* $\forall i \, U_i(a_i, a_{-i})$ *is bounded and satisfies Property* (α). *Then there exists a symmetric mixed-strategy equilibrium* $(\mu^*, \ldots, \mu^*)$ *with the property that* $\forall i$ *and* $\forall \bar{a}_i \in A_i^{**}(i)$, $\mu^*(\{\bar{a}_i\}) = 0$.

Proof. Let μ^* be the limit of some sub-sequence of a sequence of probability measures, $\{\mu^n\}$, where

$$\underbrace{(\mu^n, \ldots, \mu^n)}_{N\text{-times}}$$

is a symmetric mixed-strategy equilibrium of the finite game $[(\bar{\bar{A}}^n, U_i); i = 1, \ldots, N]$, where $\bar{\bar{A}}^n(n > 0)$ is a finite subset of $\bar{A}$ with the property $\sup_{a \in \bar{A}} \inf_{a^n \in \bar{\bar{A}}n} |a - a^n| < 1/n$. By the proof of Lemma 6, we know that $(\mu^*, \ldots, \mu^*)$ is a symmetric mixed-strategy equilibrium of the game $[(\bar{A}, U_i); i = 1, \ldots, N]$. Suppose $\exists \bar{a}_i \in A_i^{**}(i)$ such that $\mu^*(\{\bar{a}_i\}) > 0$. Because $U_i(a)$ satisfies (α) and $\mu^*(\{\bar{a}_i\}) > 0$, there exists $\lambda \in [0, 1]$ such that

$$\lambda \liminf_{a_i \to \bar{a}_i} \int U_i(a_i, a_{-i}) \, d\mu_{-i}^*(a_{-i})$$

$$+ (1 - \lambda) \liminf_{a_i \overset{+}{\to} \bar{a}_i} \int U_i(a_i, a_{-i}) \, d\mathbf{\mu}_{-i}^*(a_{-i}) > \int U_i(\bar{a}_i, a_{-i}) \, d\mathbf{\mu}_{-i}^*(a_{-i}).$$

Without loss of generality we may therefore suppose that

$$\liminf_{a_i \to \bar{a}_i} \int U_i(a_i, a_{-i}) \, d\mathbf{\mu}_{-i}^*(a_{-i}) > \int U_i(\bar{a}_i, a_{-i}) \, d\mathbf{\mu}_{-i}^*(a_{-i}).$$

But this contradicts the conclusion that μ^* is an equilibrium strategy for player i.   ‖

Example 2. It will be useful to exemplify Theorem 6 by reviewing games of 'timing', or 'duels', which have been much studied by game theorists (see Karlin 1959; Owen 1968; Jones 1980).[16] These are symmetric two-person zero-sum games on the unit square. The version called the 'silent duel' has player 1's payoff function of the form:

$$U_1(a_1, a_2) = \begin{cases} a_1 - a_2 + a_1 a_2 & \text{if } a_1 < a_2 \\ 0 & \text{if } a_1 = a_2 \\ a_1 - a_2 - a_1 a_2 & \text{if } a_1 > a_2. \end{cases}$$

Note first that $A_i^{**}(i) = (0, 1]$ for $i = 1, 2$. Note also that for each $a_2 > 0$, $U_1(a_1, a_2)$ is *left* lower semi-continuous as a function of a_1 at $a_1 = a_2$. Likewise, for each $a_1 > 0$, $U_2(a_1, a_2)$ is *left* lower semi-continuous as a function of a_2 at $a_1 = a_2$. Thus $U_i(i = 1, 2)$ is weakly lower semi-continuous as a function of a_i. Note in particular that U_i satisfies property (α). We conclude that the game satisfies the hypotheses of Theorem 6. Now Theorem 6 says that the game therefore has a symmetric equilibrium where the mixed strategy is

---

16 We are grateful to J.-F. Mertens for drawing our attention to these games.

atomless on $(0, 1]$. This is indeed the case; for it is known (see Karlin 1959; Owen 1968), that the probability density function $p(a_i) = 0$ if $0 \leqslant a_i < \frac{1}{3}$ and $p(a_i) = \frac{1}{4}a_i^3$ if $\frac{1}{3} \leqslant a_i \leqslant 1$ (for $i = 1, 2$) is an equilibrium of this game.

The version which is called the 'noisy duel' has player 1's payoff function of the form:

$$U_1(a_1, a_2) = \begin{cases} 2a_1 - 1 & \text{if } a_1 < a_2 \\ 0 & \text{if } a_1 = a_2 \\ 1 - 2a_2 & \text{if } a_1 > a_2. \end{cases}$$

Note first that $A_i^{**}(i) = [0, 1] - \{\frac{1}{2}\}$ for $i = 1, 2$. Note also that for each $a_2 > (<)\frac{1}{2}$, $U_1(a_1, a_2)$ is *left* (*right*) lower semi-continuous as a function of a_1 at $a_1 = a_2$. Likewise, for each $a_1 > (<)\frac{1}{2}$, $U_2(a_1, a_2)$ is *left* (*right*) lower semi-continuous as a function of a_2 at $a_1 = a_2$. Thus U_i ($i = 1, 2$) is weakly lower semi-continuous in a_i. Clearly U_i satisfies property (α). We conclude that the game satisfies the hypotheses of Theorem 6. It is easy to check (see Karlin 1959; Owen 1968) that the pair of pure strategies $a_1 = a_2 = \frac{1}{2}$ is an equilibrium of this game.

6   THE TIGHTNESS OF THE HYPOTHESES OF THEOREM 5

In this section we present examples to demonstrate that the hypotheses of Theorem 5 are 'tight', in the sense that dropping any of them renders the theorem invalid.

Observe first that Example 1 in Section 3 fulfils all the hypotheses of Theorem 5 except for the requirement that U_i is weakly lower semi-continuous in a_i. The example therefore demonstrates that some lower semi-continuity condition is essential to guarantee the existence of an equilibrium. We next present examples in which the two other major assumptions are in turn dropped.

Example 3 (dropping the assumption that $\Sigma_{i=1}^N U_i$ is upper semi-continuous). Let $i = 1, 2$, let $A_1 = A_2 = [0, 1]$, and let

$$U_i(a_1, a_2) = \begin{cases} 0 & \text{if } a_1 = a_2 = 1 \\ a_i & \text{otherwise.} \end{cases}$$

The game thus defined satisfies all the hypotheses of Theorem 5 except upper semi-continuity of the sum ΣU_i. The game does not possess a mixed-strategy equilibrium because, for any choice of a mixed strategy on the part of one agent that places positive probability on unity, the other will wish to choose a pure strategy as close to unity as possible, but will avoid unity itself. However, if the mixed strategy places zero probability on unity, the other will wish to play unity. Notice finally that the example violates the assumptions of Theorem 5b.

Example 4 (dropping the assumption that the functions f_{ij}^d in the definition of the set $A^*(i)$ are one-to-one). Let $i = 1, 2$, let $A_1 = A_2 = [0, 1]$, and let

$$U_1(a_1, a_2) = \begin{cases} a_1, & \text{for } 0 \leqslant a_1 \leqslant \frac{1}{2} \text{ and } 0 \leqslant a_2 \leqslant \frac{1}{2} \\ a_1 + 3a_2 - 2, & \text{for } 0 \leqslant a_1 \leqslant \frac{1}{2} \text{ and } 1 \geqslant a_2 > \frac{1}{2} \\ -2a_1 + 2, & \text{for } 1 \geqslant a_1 > \frac{1}{2} \text{ and } 0 \leqslant a_2 \leqslant \frac{1}{2} \\ -2a_1 + 3a_2, & \text{for } 1 \geqslant a_1 > \frac{1}{2} \text{ and } 1 \geqslant a_2 > \frac{1}{2} \end{cases}$$

and

$$U_2(a_1, a_2) = \begin{cases} a_2, & \text{for } 0 \leqslant a_1 \leqslant \frac{1}{2} \text{ and } 0 \leqslant a_2 \leqslant \frac{1}{2} \\ -2a_2 + 2, & \text{for } 0 \leqslant a_1 \leqslant \frac{1}{2} \text{ and } 1 \geqslant a_2 > \frac{1}{2} \\ a_2 + 3a_1 - 2, & \text{for } 1 \geqslant a_1 > \frac{1}{2} \text{ and } 0 \leqslant a_2 \leqslant \frac{1}{2} \\ -2a_2 + 3a_1, & \text{for } 1 \geqslant a_1 > \frac{1}{2} \text{ and } 1 \geqslant a_2 > \frac{1}{2} \end{cases}$$

The game thus defined satisfies all the hypotheses of Theorem 5 except for the requirement that the functions f_{ij}^d in the definition of $A^*(i)$ in (1.2) be one-to-one. Notice that in this example

$$A^*(i) = \{(a_1, a_2) \mid a_1 = \tfrac{1}{2}, 0 \leqslant a_2 \leqslant 1\} \cup \{(a_1, a_2) \mid 0 \leqslant a_1 \leqslant 1, a_2 = \tfrac{1}{2}\},$$

for $i = 1, 2$. It is clear that the game does not possess an equilibrium. For any choice of a mixed strategy on the part of one player the other will wish to choose a pure strategy as close to $\frac{1}{2}$ from the right as possible but avoiding $\frac{1}{2}$. Note finally that the example violates the assumptions of Theorem 5a.

APPENDIX

In this Appendix we establish the counterparts of the results of this paper for the case where agents' strategy sets are multi-dimensional. Thus, assume $A_i \subseteq R^m$ $(m \geqslant 1)$ for $i = 1, \ldots, N$. A typical element of A_i is a_i, and we write a_{ik} for the kth component of a_i, $(k = 1, \ldots, m)$. Similarly, A_{ik} is the kth projection of A_i. Otherwise, the notation is the same as in the text.

We begin by characterizing the discontinuity set, as in Section 4.1 of the text. Let $[(A_i, U_i); i = 1, \ldots, N]$ be a game, where $A_i \subseteq R^m$ is non-empty, convex, and compact for all i. Let $Q \subseteq \{1, \ldots, m\}$. For each pair of agents $i, j \in \{1, \ldots, N\}$, let $D(i)$ be a positive integer. For each integer d, with $1 \leqslant d \leqslant D(i)$ let $f_{ij}^d : R^1 \to R^1$ be a one-to-one, continuous function with the property that $f_{ij}^d = (f_{ji}^d)^{-1}$. Finally, $\forall i$, define

$$A^*(i) = \{(a_1, \ldots, a_N) \in A \mid \exists j \neq i, \exists k \in Q, \exists d, 1 \leqslant d \leqslant D(i)$$

$$\text{such that } a_{jk} = f_{ij}^d(a_{ik})\}. \quad (\text{A1.1})$$

As in the text, we suppose that $\forall i$ the discontinuities of $U_i(a)$ are confined to a subset $A^{**}(i)$ of $A^*(i)$.

In what follows the multi-dimensional version of a given result in the text is denoted by the corresponding starred number.

Lemma 1*. *Let $A_i \subseteq R^m$ $(m \geqslant 1)$ be non-empty, convex, and compact for all i, and let $\mu_i \in D(A_i)$. Let $A^*(i) \subseteq A$ be defined by* (A1.1) *and let $A^{**}(i) \subseteq A^*(i)$. If $\forall i$, $\forall k \in Q$ and $\bar{a}_{ik} \in A_{ik}$, $\mu_i(\{a_i \in A_i^{**}(i) \mid a_{ik} = \bar{a}_{ik}\}) = 0$, then $\forall i$, $\mu(A^{**}(i)) = 0$. Furthermore, if $\forall \bar{a}_i \in A_i$, $\forall j \neq i$, $\forall d$ $(1 \leqslant d \leqslant D(i)$ and $\forall k \in Q$, $\mu_j(\{a_j \in A_j \mid a_{jk} = f_{ij}^d(\bar{a}_{ik})\}) = 0$, then $\mu_{-i}(A_{-i}^*(\bar{a}_i)) = 0$, where $A_{-i}^*(\bar{a}_i) = \{a_{-i} \in A_{-i} \mid (\bar{a}_i, a_{-i}) \in A^*(i)\}$.*

Proof. The proof of the first part is virtually identical to its counterpart in the text. In place of the initial inequality (1.7) we now have

$$\mu(A^{**}(i)) \leqslant \Sigma_{s \neq i} \Sigma_d \Sigma_{k \in Q} [(\mu_1 \times \ldots \times \mu_N)(\{(a_1, \ldots, a_N) \in A \mid a_{sk}$$

$$= f_{is}^d(a_{ik})\} \cap A^{**}(i))]$$

and the remaining argument is the same as in the text.

To prove the second part we note that

$$\mu_{-i}(A_{-i}^*(\bar{a}_i)) \leqslant \Sigma_{j \neq i} \Sigma_d \Sigma_{k \in Q} \mu_{-i}(\{a_{-i} \in A_{-i} \mid a_{jk} = f_{ij}^d(\bar{a}_{ik})\})$$

$$\leqslant \Sigma_{j \neq i} \Sigma_d \Sigma_{k \in Q} u_j(\{a_j \in A_j \mid a_{jk} = f_{ij}^d(\bar{a}_{ik})\}) \Pi_{s \neq i,j} \mu_s(A_s)$$

$$= 0. \quad \|$$

The proof of Lemma 2 in the text does not assume that A_i is one-dimensional. It therefore applies without change to the multi-dimensional case. We may now state

Theorem 4*. *For $i = 1, \ldots, N$, let $A_i \subseteq R^m (m \geqslant 1)$ be non-empty, convex, and compact, and let $U_i : A \to R^1$ be continuous, except on a subset of $A^*(i)$, where $A^*(i)$ is defined by* (A1.1). *Suppose $\forall i$, U_i is bounded. Let A_i^n be a finite subset of A_i with the property that*

$$\sup_{a_i \in A_i} \inf_{a_i^n \in A_i^n} \| a_i - a_i^n \| < 1/n.$$

Let $\mu^n = (\mu_1^n, \ldots, \mu_N^n)$ be an equilibrium vector of mixed strategies for the finite game $[(A_i^n, U_i); i = 1, \ldots, N]$, and let $\mu^n \to \mu^*$ as $n \to \infty$; (see footnote 12, p. 62). Suppose $\forall i, j (i \neq j)$, $\forall d$, $\forall k \in Q$ and $\forall \bar{a}_i \in A_i^{**}(i)$, $\mu_j^*(\{a_j \in A_j \mid a_{jk} = f_{ij}^d(\bar{a}_{ik})\}) = 0$. Then $\mu^* = (\mu_1^*, \ldots, \mu_N^*)$ is an equilibrium for the infinite game $[(A_i, U_i); i = 1, \ldots, N]$.

Proof. Identical to the proof of Theorem 4 in the text. $\quad \|$

We turn next to the generalization of Lemma 3.

Lemma 3*. *Let $A_i \subseteq R^m (m \geqslant 1)$, $(i = 1, \ldots, N)$, be non-empty, convex, and compact, and let $U_i: A \to R^1$ be continuous, except on a subset $A^{**}(i)$ of $A^*(i)$, where $A^*(i)$ is defined by* (A1.1). *Suppose $\forall i$, U_i is bounded. Let A_i^n be a finite subset of A_i with the property that*

$$\sup_{a_i \in A_i} \inf_{a_i^n \in A_i^n} \| a_i - a_i^n \| < 1/n.$$

Let $(\mu_1^n, \ldots, \mu_N^n)$ be an equilibrium vector of mixed strategies for the finite game $[(A_i^n, U_i); i = 1, \ldots, N]$, and let $(\mu_1^*, \ldots, \mu_N^*) = \lim_{n \to \infty} (\mu_1^n, \ldots, \mu_N^n)$; (see footnote 12, p. 62). Then $\forall i$, a set of pure strategies $\bar{a}_i \in A_i$ that differ from one another in every component $\bar{a}_{ik}$[17] $(k = 1, \ldots, m)$ and that satisfy

$$\int_{A_{-i}} U_i(\bar{a}_i, a_{-i}) \, d\mu_{-i}^* > \lim_{n \to \infty} \int_A U_i(a) \, d\mu^n \qquad \text{(A1.2)}$$

contains at most countably many members.

Proof. Suppose $\exists i$ for which there are uncountably many pure strategies that differ from one another in every component and that satisfy (A1.2). By Lemma 2 we conclude that $\mu_{-i}^*(\bar{A}_{-i}^{**}(\bar{a}_i)) > 0$ for each such $\bar{a}_i$, where $\bar{A}_{-i}^{**}(\bar{a}_i)$ is the closure of the set $A_{-i}^{**}(\bar{a}_i) = \{a_{-i} \in A_{-i} \,|\, (\bar{a}_i, a_{-i}) \in A^{**}(i)\}$. But $\bar{A}_{-i}^{**}(\bar{a}_i) \subseteq A_{-i}^*(\bar{a}_i)$. Therefore, from Lemma 1* we can conclude that for each such $\bar{a}_i$, $\exists j \neq i$, $\exists d$ $(1 \leqslant d \leqslant D(i))$ and $\exists k \in Q$ such that

$$\mu_j^*(\{a_j \in A_j \,|\, a_{jk} = f_{ij}^d(\bar{a}_{ik})\}) > 0. \qquad \text{(A1.3)}$$

Thus, there exist j and d and k such that for uncountably many $a_i (i = j)$, (A1.3) holds. But the functions f_{ij}^d are by hypothesis one-to-one. Therefore, the sets $\{a_j \in A_j \,|\, a_{jk} = f_{ij}^d(\bar{a}_{ik})\}$ are disjoint. We thus conclude that there are uncountably many disjoint subsets of A_j of positive measure, a contradiction. ∥

In what follows we shall consider games which satisfy the hypotheses of Lemma 3* and for which $\Sigma_{i=1}^N U_i(a)$ is upper semi-continuous. We now generalize the (weakly) lower semi-continuous property (see Definition 6). Let B^m be the surface of the unit sphere in R^m with the origin as its centre. Let $e \in B^m$, and let θ be a positive number. Then we say that $U_i(a_i, a_{-i})$ is weakly lower semi-continuous in a_i if for all $\bar{a}_i \in A_i^{**}(i)$ there exists an absolutely continuous measure ν on B^m such that for all $a_{-i} \in A_{-i}^{**}(\bar{a}_i)$,

$$\int_{B^m} [\liminf_{\theta \to 0} U_i(\bar{a}_i + \theta e, a_{-i}) \, d\nu(e)] \geqslant U_i(\bar{a}_i, a_{-i}).$$

---

17 By differing in every component, we mean that if $\bar{a}_i$ and $\bar{a}_i'$ are two such pure strategies, then $\bar{a}_{ik} \neq \bar{a}_{ik}'$ for all k.

Lemma 4*. $\forall i$, let $A_i \subseteq R^m$ $(m \geqslant 1)$ be non-empty, convex and compact, and let $U_i : A \to R^1$ $(i = 1, \ldots, N)$ be continuous, except on a subset $A^{**}(i)$ of $A^*(i)$, where $A^*(i)$ is defined by (A1.1). Suppose $\Sigma_{i=1} U_i(a)$ is upper semi-continuous, $U_i(a_i, a_{-i})$ is bounded and is weakly lower semi-continuous in a_i. Let A_i^n be a finite subset of A_i with the property that

$$\sup_{a_i \in A_i} \inf_{a_i^n \in A_i^n} \| a_i - a_i^n \| < 1/n.$$

Let $(\mu_1^n, \ldots, \mu_N^n)$ be an equilibrium vector of mixed strategies for the finite game $[(A_i^n, U_i); i = 1, \ldots, N]$, and let $(\mu_1^*, \ldots, \mu_N^*) = \lim_{n \to \infty} (\mu_1^n, \ldots, \mu_N^n)$. Then $\forall i$

$$\lim_{n \to \infty} \int_A U_i(a) \, d\mu^n = \int_A U_i(a) \, d\mu^*. \tag{A1.4}$$

Proof. Suppose $\exists i$ for which (A1.4) does not hold. Then by an argument identical to the one in Lemma 4 we conclude that $\exists j$, $\exists \bar{a}_j \in A_j$ and $\exists \epsilon > 0$ such that

$$\int_{A_{-j}} U_j(\bar{a}_j, a_{-j}) \, d\mu_{-j}^* > \lim_{n \to \infty} \int U_j(a) \, d\mu^n + \epsilon. \tag{A1.5}$$

But U_j is weakly lower semi-continuous in a_j. Therefore from (A1.5) we can conclude that

$$\int_{B^m} \left[\liminf_{\theta \to 0} \int_{A_{-j}} U_j(\bar{a}_j + \theta e, a_{-j}) \, d\mu_{-j}^* \right] d\nu(e)$$

$$> \lim_{n \to \infty} \int U_j(a) \, d\mu^n + \epsilon. \tag{A1.6}$$

But ν is an absolutely continuous distribution on B^m. Therefore, (A1.6) implies that there exist uncountably many pure strategies, $\tilde{a}_j$, that differ from one another in every component k and that satisfy

$$\int_{A_{-j}} U_j(\tilde{a}_j, a_{-j}) \, d\mu_{-j}^* > \lim_{n \to \infty} \int U_j(a) \, d\mu^n.$$

This contradicts Lemma 3*. ∥

Theorem 5*. For all i, let $A_i \subseteq R^m$ $(m \geqslant 1)$ be non-empty, convex and compact, and let $U_i : A \to R^1$ be continuous except on a subset $A^{**}(i)$ of $A^*(i)$, where $A^*(i)$ is defined by (A1.1). Suppose $\Sigma U_i(a)$ is upper semi-continuous, for all i $U_i(a_i, a_{-i})$ is bounded and is weakly lower semi-continuous in a_i. Then the game $[(A_i, U_i); i = 1, \ldots, N]$ possesses a mixed-strategy equilibrium.

Proof. Simple adaptation of the proof of Theorem 5, but using Lemmas 3* and 4* instead of 3 and 4. ‖

In the text, symmetric games have been defined for the case where agents' strategy sets are multi-dimensional. Indeed, the existence of symmetric mixed-strategy equilibria for symmetric games which satisfy the hypotheses of Theorem 5* follows directly from Lemma 5 and Theorem 5*. We proceed, therefore, to a generalization of Theorem 6. We first state the multi-dimensional version of condition (α). We call this (α^*).

Property (α^*). $\forall \bar{a}_i \in A_i^{**}(i)$, $\exists$ a non-atomic measure ν on B^m such that for all $a_{-i} \in A_{-i}^{**}(\bar{a}_i)$

$$\int_{B^m} [\lim_{\theta \to 0} \inf U_i(\bar{a}_i + \theta e, a_{-i}) \, d\nu(e)] \geqslant U_i(\bar{a}_i, a_{-i}),$$

where the inequality is strict if

$$a_{-i} = \frac{(\bar{a}_i, \ldots, \bar{a}_i)}{(N-1) \text{ times}}.$$

We may now state

Theorem 6*. *Let* $\bar{A} \subseteq R^m$ ($m \geqslant 1$) *be non-empty, convex and compact, and let* $[(\bar{A}, U_i); i = 1, \ldots, N]$ *be a symmetric game, where* $\forall i$,

$$U_i : \underbrace{\bar{A} \times \ldots \times \bar{A}}_{N \text{ times}} \to R^1$$

is continuous, except on a subset $A^{**}(i)$ *of* $A^*(i)$; *where* $A^*(i)$ *is defined by* (A1.1). *Suppose* $\Sigma_{i-1}^N U_i(a)$ *is upper semi-continuous, and for all* i, U_i *is bounded and satisfies Property* (α^*).

Then there exists a symmetric mixed-strategy equilibrium ($\mu^*, \ldots, \mu^*$) *with the property that* $\forall i$ *and* $\forall \bar{a}_i \in A_i^{**}(i)$, $\mu^*(\{\bar{a}_i\}) = 0$.

Proof. Virtually identical to the proof of Theorem 6. ‖

REFERENCES

d'Aspremont, C., Gabszewicz, J. and Thisse, J. 1979: On Hotelling's 'stability in competition'. *Econometrica*, **47** (5), 1145–50.

Beckmann, M. J. 1965: 'Edgeworth–Bertrand duopoly revisited'. In Henn, R. (ed.) *Operations Research-Verfahren*, III (Meisenheim: Sonderdruck, Verlag, Anton Hein), 55–68.

Bertrand, J. 1883: Review of Cournot's 'Rechercher sur la theoric mathematique de la richesse'. *Journal des Savants*, 499–508.

Chamberlin, E. 1956: *The Theory of Monopolistic Competition*. Cambridge: Harvard University Press.

Dasgupta, P. and Maskin, E. 1977: The existence of economic equilibria: continuity and mixed strategies. *IMSS Technical Report No. 252*. Stanford University.

Dasgupta, P. and Maskin, E. 1986: The existence of equilibrium in discontinuous economic games, 2: Applications. *Review of Economic Studies*, January 1986 (chapter 2 in this volume).

Debreu, G. 1952: A social equilibrium existence theorem. *Proceedings of the National Academy of Sciences*, **38**, 886–93.

Dierker, H. and Grodal, B. 1984: Nonexistence of Cournot Walras equilibrium in a general equilibrium model with two oligopolists. Mimeo.

Eaton, B. C. and Lipsey, R. 1975: The principle of minimum differentiation reconsidered: some new developments in the theory of spatial competition. *Review of Economic Studies*, **42**, 27–50.

Edgeworth, F. M. 1925: *Papers Relating to Political Economy, I*. London: Macmillan.

Fan, K. 1952: Fixed point and minimax theorems in locally convex topological linear spaces. *Proceedings of the National Academy of Sciences*, **38**, 121–6.

Glicksberg, I. L. 1950: Minimax theorem for upper and lower semi-continuous payoffs. *Research Memorandum RM-478*. Rand Corporation.

Glicksberg, I. L. 1952: A further generalization of the Kakutani fixed point theorem with application to Nash equilibrium points. *Proceedings of the American Mathematical Society*, **38**, 170–4.

Jones, A. J. 1980: *Game Theory: Mathematical Models of Conflict*. Chichester: Ellis Horwood Limited.

Karlin, S. 1959: *Mathematical Methods and Theory in Games, Programming and Economics, Vol. II*. London: Pergamon Press.

McManus, M. 1964: Equilibrium, numbers and size in Cournot oligopoly. *Yorkshire Bulletin of Economic Society Research*, 68–75.

Nash, J. F. 1950: Equilibrium points in N-person games. *Proceedings of the National Academy of Sciences, U.S.A.*, **36**, 48–9.

Novshek, W. 1980: Cournot equilibrium with free entry. *Review of Economic Studies*, **47**, 473–86.

Owen, G. 1968: *Game Theory*. Philadelphia: W. B. Saunders Company.

Roberts, J. and Sonnenschein, H. 1977: On the foundations of the theory of monopolistic competition. *Econometrica*, **45**, 101–14.

Rosenthal, R. 1980: A model in which an increase in the number of sellers leads to a higher price. *Econometrica*, **48**, 1575–80.

Rothschild, M. and Stiglitz, J. E. 1976: Equilibrium in competitive insurance markets: an essay on the economics of imperfect information. *Quarterly Journal of Economics*, **90**, 629–49.

Shaked, A. 1975: Non-existence of equilibrium for the 2-dimensional 3-firms location problem. *Review of Economic Studies*, **42**, 51–6.

Shapley, L. S. 1957: A duopoly model with price competition. *Econometrica*, **25**, 354–5.

Shiloney, Y. 1977: Mixed pricing in oligopoly. *Journal of Economic Theory*, **14** (2), 373–88.

Shubik, M. 1955: A comparison of treatments of a duopoly problem; Part II, *Econometrica*, **23**, 417–31.

Simon, L. 1984: Games with discontinuous payoffs, Part 1: theory. Berkeley: Department of Economics, University of California.

Sion, M. and Wolfe, P. 1957: On a game without a value. *Contributions to the Theory of Games, III*. Princeton: Annals of Mathematical Studies No 39, 299–306.

Varian, H. 1980: A model of sales. *American Economic Review*, **70**, 651–9.

Wilson, C. A. 1977: A model of insurance markets with incomplete information. *Journal of Economic Theory*, **16**, 167–207.

2

The Existence of Equilibrium in Discontinuous Economic Games, II: Applications

P. Dasgupta and E. Maskin

1 INTRODUCTION

In Part I of this study (chapter 1 in the present volume) we established two existence theorems for mixed-strategy equilibrium in games with discontinuous payoff functions (see Theorems 4(4*) and 5(5*) in chapter 1). In this second part we use the second of these two theorems to prove the existence of mixed-strategy equilibrium in some well-known discontinuous economic games that fail to have pure steategy equilibria. The models we analyse are the Bertrand–Edgeworth example of price setting duopolists with capacity constraints (see Section 2.2); price competition among firms producing differentiated products (Hotelling 1929; d'Aspremont et al. 1979; see Section 2.3); spatial competition (Eaton and Lipsey 1975; Shaked 1975; see Section 3); and models of market dependent information (Rothschild and Stiglitz 1976; Wilson 1977; Section 4). The paper concludes (Section 5) with a classification of these models.

2 PRICE COMPETITION

2.1 Introduction

Consider a market for N (possibly differentiated) products, where commodity i is supplied by firm i. Firms choose prices as strategic variables, and a given consumer purchases from that firm which charges the lowest price, corrected for his perception of product quality. In this section we present two well-

We thank Kenneth Arrow, Martin Hellwig, David Salant, and Avner Shaked for their helpful comments.

known special cases of such a market, the Bertrand–Edgeworth and Hotelling duopoly models which are known for failing, in general, to have pure strategy equilibria. We show, however, that these models satisfy the hypotheses of Theorem 5, and so have equilibria where firms choose prices randomly.

2.2   The Bertrand-Edgeworth Duopoly Model[1]

We consider a market for a single commodity with a continuum of consumers represented by the unit interval $[0, 1]$. Consumers are identical, and the representative consumer's demand for the commodity is a continuous, monotonically decreasing function, $Q(a)$, where a ($\geqslant 0$) is the price. We assume that the demand curve cuts both axes and denote by $\bar{\bar{a}}$ (> 0) the choke-off price for the representative consumer (i.e. $Q(a) = 0$ for $a \geqslant \bar{\bar{a}}$, and $Q(a) > 0$ for $0 \leqslant a < \bar{\bar{a}}$).

There are two firms in the industry $i = 1, 2$. (It is easy to generalize all the results that follow to any number of firms.) Firm i has an endowment of S_i units of the commodity; (alternatively we can think of S_i as the capacity of a zero-cost technology). Firms choose prices and play non-cooperatively. It is assumed that the firm quoting the lower price serves the entire market up to its capacity, and that the residual demand is met by the other firm. The residual demand depends, of course, on which consumers purchase from which firm. We assume that all consumers are identical and that rationing at the lower price is on a first-come-first-serve basis. On the other hand, if the duopolists set the same price they share the market demand in proportion to their capacities, so long as their capacities are not met.

Formally, let $\bar{a}$ be the *competitive* price of the commodity; that is, $\bar{a}$ solves the market clearing equation $Q(a) = S_1 + S_2$ if $S_1 + S_2 < Q(0)$, and equals zero otherwise. Let a_i be the price chosen by firm i. We may as well suppose that $a_i \in A_i = [\bar{a}, \bar{\bar{a}}]$. We define the profit functions, $U_1(a_1, a_2)$ and $U_2(a_1, a_2)$ of the duopolists to be:[2]

$$U_1(a_1, a_2) = \begin{cases} \min\{a_1 S_1, a_1 Q(a_1)\} & \text{if } a_1 < a_2 \\[2mm] \min\{a_1 S_1, a_1 Q(a_1) S_1/(S_1+S_2)\} & \text{if } a_1 = a_2 \text{ and } S_2 \geqslant \dfrac{Q(a_1) S_2}{(S_1+S_2)} \\[2mm] a_1 Q(a_1) - S_2 & \text{if } a_1 = a_2 \text{ and } S_2 < \dfrac{Q(a_2) S_2}{(S_1+S_2)} \\[2mm] \max\{0, a_1 Q(a_1) [Q(a_2) - S_2]/Q(a_2)\} & \text{if } a_1 > a_2, \end{cases} \quad (2.1)$$

---

1   The Bertrand–Edgeworth model has been much studied. See e.g. Chamberlin (1956), Shubik (1955), Beckmann (1965) and d'Aspremont and Gabszewicz (1980). The original references are Bertrand (1883) and Edgeworth (1925).

2   When $a_1 = a_2$, firm 1 serves the minimum of S_1 and $Q(a_1) S_1/(S_1 + S_2)$ customers as long as firm 2 is not capacity constrained (i.e. as long as $S_2 \geqslant Q(a_1) S_2/(S_1 + S_2)$). If firm

and

$$
U_2(a_1, a_2) = \begin{cases}
\min\{a_2 S_2, a_2 Q(a_2)\} & \text{if } a_2 < a_1 \\[2mm]
\min\{a_2 S_2, a_2 Q(a_2) S_2/(S_1 + S_2)\} & \text{if } a_2 = a_1 \text{ and } S_1 \geq \dfrac{Q(a_2) S_1}{(S_1 + S_2)} \\[2mm]
a_2 Q(a_2) - S_1 & \text{if } a_2 = a_1 \text{ and } S_1 < \dfrac{Q(a_1) S_1}{(S_1 + S_2)} \\[2mm]
\max\{0, a_2 Q(a_2) [Q(a_1) - S_1]/Q(a_1)\} & \text{if } a_2 > a_1.
\end{cases} \tag{2.2}
$$

It is well known that this duopoly market may not possess a Nash equilibrium in pure strategies; (see, e.g. Chamberlin 1956; d'Aspremont and Gabszewicz 1980).[3] We now confirm that the market always possesses an equilibrium in mixed strategies.

Define the diagonal of the product of the strategy sets:

$$
A^*(1) = A^*(2) = \{(a_1, a_2) \in [\bar{a}, \bar{\bar{a}}]^2 \,|\, a_1 = a_2\}. \tag{2.3}
$$

From (2.1) and (2.2) it is immediate that the discontinuities in $U_i(a)$ are restricted to $A^*(i) - \{(\bar{a}, \bar{a}), (\bar{\bar{a}}, \bar{\bar{a}})\}$. Furthermore, it is simple to confirm that by lowering its price from a position where $\bar{\bar{a}} > a_1 = a_2 > \bar{a}$, a firm discontinuously *increases* its profit. Therefore $U_i(a_1, a_2)$ is everywhere left lower semi-continuous in a_i, and hence weakly lower semi-continuous. Obviously U_i is bounded. Finally, $U_1 + U_2$ is continuous, because discontinuous shifts in clientele from one firm to another occur only where both firms derive the

---

2 *is* capacity constrained, then firm 1 supplies the remainder of the market. When $a_1 > a_2$, if $Q(a_2) < S_2$ then clearly $U_1 = 0$. If, however, $Q(a_2) > S_2$, then the fraction of consumers that are served by firm 2 is $\alpha = S_2/Q(a_2)$. Thus $(1 - \alpha)$ is the proportion of consumers not served by 2. Total sales by firm 1 amount to $(1 - \alpha) Q(a_1)$.

3 There cannot be an equilibrium with $a_1 < a_2$, since, if $Q(a_1) > S_1$, firm 1 will wish to raise its price and, if $Q(a_1) \leq S_1$, firm 2 will wish to lower its price. Similarly, no equilibrium is possible with $a_2 > a_1$. There cannot be an equilibrium with $a_1 = a_2 > \bar{a}$ (the competitive price), since both firms have the incentive to lower their prices slightly. Consider now the case where $\bar{a} > 0$. If $Q(a)$ is inelastic at $\bar{a}$ then $a_1 = a_2 = \bar{a}$ cannot be an equilibrium because either firm can increase its profit by raising its price slightly above $\bar{a}$ if the other firm were to charge $\bar{a}$. In this case an equilibrium does not exist. One may argue that non-existence of an equilibrium in pure strategies is due to the fact that a firm's payoff function is not quasi-concave in its own price. To see this consider a slight modification of the above model. Suppose that there is a positive number η, such that if the firms choose prices *within* a distance of η of each other both receive zero profits; but if their price difference exceeds or is equal to η their profit functions are as in (1) and (2). It is easy to check that if η is small enough the model does not have an equilibrium in pure strategies if market demand is inelastic at $\bar{a}$. However, the payoff functions of this modified game are both upper semi-continuous and graph continuous (Definitions (2), and (3) in chapter 1). From Theorem 3 of chapter 1 we may conclude that the failure of the modified game to possess an equilibrium in pure strategies is due to the fact that a firm's profit function is not quasi-concave in its own price.

same profit per customer. We may therefore use Theorem 5 (chapter 1) to conclude:

Theorem 1. *Consider the price-setting duopoly game* $[(A_i, U_i): i = 1, 2]$, *where* $A_i = [\bar{a}, \bar{\bar{a}}]$, *with* $\bar{a} \geq 0$, *and* $U_i: A_1 \times A_2 \to R^1$ *is defined by* (2.1) *and* (2.2). *The game has a mixed-strategy equilibrium.*

There has been some interest in the symmetric version of the Bertrand–Edgeworth model (see, e.g. Beckmann 1965), to which we now turn. Thus, let $S_1 = S_2$. It is well known that under those parametric conditions (e.g. $S_i > Q(0)$ for $i = 1, 2$) where the duopoly game does have a pure-strategy equilibrium, the equilibrium is unique, and consists of firms choosing the competitive price $\bar{a}$. We now proceed to confirm that under all parametric conditions the symmetric version of the game possesses a symmetric mixed-strategy equilibrium such that the equilibrium probability measure is atomless at all prices in excess of $\bar{a}$.

We have already noted that $A^{**}(i) = A^*(i) - \{(\bar{a}, \bar{a}), (\bar{\bar{a}}, \bar{\bar{a}})\}$. Thus $A_i^{**}(i) = (\bar{a}, \bar{\bar{a}})$. We have also noted above that for all $\tilde{a} \in (\bar{a}, \bar{\bar{a}})$, $\lim_{a_1 \to \tilde{a}} \inf U_1(a_1, \tilde{a}) > U_1(\tilde{a}, \tilde{a})$ and $\lim_{a_2 \to \tilde{a}} \inf U_2(\tilde{a}, a_2) > U_2(\tilde{a}, \tilde{a})$. Thus the game satisfies property (α^*). We may therefore appeal to Theorem 6 in chapter 1 to assert

Theorem 2. *The symmetric version of the Bertrand–Edgeworth duopoly game possesses a symmetric mixed-strategy Nash equilibrium* (μ^*, μ^*), *such that* μ^* *is atomless in the open interval* $(\bar{a}, \bar{\bar{a}})$.[4]

We can easily establish a bit more about the nature of symmetric equilibrium in the Bertrand–Edgeworth model. Define

$$R(a) = aQ(a)$$

$$R^*(a) = \min\{aS_1, R(a)\}$$

$$R^{**}(a) = \max_{\bar{a} \leq a} R^*(\tilde{a}).$$

Corollary.[5] *If* μ^* *is an equilibrium strategy of a symmetric equilibrium in the symmetric Bertrand–Edgeworth game, there exist* a' *and* a'' *with* $\bar{a} \leq a' < a'' \leq \bar{\bar{a}}$ *such that the support of* μ^* *is*

$$T = [a', a''] \cap \{a \mid R^{**}(a) = R^*(a) \text{ and if } a \in (\bar{a}, \bar{\bar{a}}),$$

$$R^{**} \text{ is increasing either from the left or right at } a\}.$$

Proof. Let $a' = \inf \operatorname{supp} \mu^*$ and $a'' = \sup \operatorname{supp} \mu^*$. Define T as in the statement of the Corollary. Consider a such that $R^*(a) < R^{**}(a)$. Choose $\tilde{a} < a$

---

4 This theorem also helps explain why the technique, used by Beckmann (1965), of expressing the equilibrium conditions as a differential equation actually works.

5 We are indebted to Martin Hellwig for drawing our attention to an error in an earlier version of the proof of this Corollary.

such that $R^{**}(\tilde{a}) = R^*(\tilde{a})$. Then, $R^*(\tilde{a}) > R^*(a)$. Because $\tilde{a}S_1 < aS_1$ we know that $R(\tilde{a}) > R(a)$ and $\tilde{a}S_1 > R(a)$. We have, therefore,

$$\int U_1(\tilde{a}, a_2) \, d\mu^*(a_2) > \int U_1(a, a_2) \, d\mu^*(a_2).$$

We conclude that $a \notin \operatorname{supp} \mu^*$.

Next, consider a such that $a \in (\bar{a}, \bar{\bar{a}}), R^{**}(a) = R^*(a)$, and R^{**} is constant at a. If $a \in \operatorname{supp} \mu^*$, then because μ^* has no atoms in $(\bar{a}, \bar{\bar{a}})$ there exist a^0 and a^{00} such that $a^0 < a^{00}, a \in [a^0, a^{00}] \subseteq \operatorname{supp} \mu^*$. Because R^{**} is constant at a, we may assume that R^{**} is constant on $[a^0, a^{00}]$. Furthermore, from the above argument, $R^{**} = R^*$ on $[a^0, a^{00}]$. Therefore, in particular $R^*(a^0) = R^*(a^{00})$. Then $R(a^0) > R(a^{00})$, and so

$$\int U_1(a^0, a_2) \, d\mu^*(a_2) > \int U_1(a^{00}, a_2) \, d\mu^*(a_2).$$

Thus $a \notin \operatorname{supp} \mu^*$, after all.

Finally, consider $a \in T$. If $a \notin \operatorname{supp} \mu^*$ there exist a^0 and a^{00} such that $a \in (a^0, a^{00})$ and $[a^0, a^{00}] \cap \operatorname{supp} \mu^* = \{a^0, a^{00}\}$. Because R^{**} is non-decreasing everywhere, and, in particular strictly increasing either from the left or right at a, $R^{**}(a^0) < R^{**}(a^{00})$. Therefore, because $\{a^0, a^{00}\} \subseteq \operatorname{supp} \mu^*$, $R^*(a^0) < R^*(a^{00})$. Furthermore, because $(a^0, a^{00}) \cap \operatorname{supp} \mu^* = \phi$ the probability firm 2's price is greater than a^0 is the same as that it is greater than a^{00}. Therefore,

$$\int U_1(a^0, a_2) \, d\mu^*(a_2) < \int U_1(a^{00}, a_2) \, d\mu^*(a_2),$$

a contradiction. We conclude that $a \in \operatorname{supp} \mu^*$.   ‖

We may now confirm that $\bar{a} < a'$ when a pure strategy equilibrium does not exist. Now a pure strategy equilibrium does not exist if market demand is inelastic at $\bar{a}$. For in this case if, say, firm 2 chooses $\bar{a}$, firm 1 gains by raising its price marginally above $\bar{a}$. This immediately implies that at a symmetric mixed-strategy equilibrium $\bar{a}$ is not in the support of the equilibrium strategy. Finally, one notes that a firm makes zero profit at $\bar{\bar{a}}$. An argument similar to the one above then demonstrates that $a'' < \bar{\bar{a}}$.

2.3   The Hotelling Model of Price Competition

The model concerns a market for differentiated products. Consumers are distributed uniformly along the unit interval $[0, 1]$.[6] There are two firms

6 We assume a uniform distribution for expository ease. Any non-atomic distribution can be assumed.

$(i = 1, 2)$ located at the points x_1 and x_2 (with $x_2 > x_1$). They costlessly produce products that are identical except for their location. The firms choose mill prices, and the cost of transporting a unit of the commodity is c (> 0) per unit distance. Each consumer purchases precisely one unit of the commodity from the cheapest source (i.e. the firm minimizing mill price plus transport cost), so long as his payment does not exceed his reservation price V (> 0). Otherwise he does without the product. We may then restrict each of the two firms to choose its (mill) price from the range $[0, V]$. Let $a_i \in A_i = [0, V]$ denote the ith firm's (mill) price. Then the profit functions of the two firms can be expressed as:

$$U_1(a_1, a_2) = \begin{cases} 0 \quad \text{if } a_1 > a_2 + c(x_2 - x_1) \\ a_1 \min \{x_1, (V - a_1)/c\} + a_1 \min \{1 - x_1, (V - a_1)/c\} \\ \qquad \text{if } a_1 < a_2 - c(x_2 - x_1) \\ a_1 \min \{x_1, (V - a_1)/c\} + (a_1/2c) \min \{(a_2 - a_1) + c(x_2 - x_1), \\ \qquad 2(V - a_1)\} \quad \text{if } |a_1 - a_2| \leqslant c(x_2 - x_1) \end{cases} \quad (2.4)$$

and

$$U_2(a_1, a_2) = \begin{cases} 0 \quad \text{if } a_2 > a_1 + c(x_2 - x_1) \\ a_2 \min \{x_2, (V - a_2)/c\} + a_2 \min \{1 - x_2, (V - a_2)/c\} \\ \qquad \text{if } a_2 < a_1 - c(x_2 - x_1) \\ a_2 \min \{1 - x_2, (V - a_2)/c\} + (a_2/2c) \min \{c(x_2 - x_1) - (a_2 - a_1), \\ \qquad 2(V - a_2)\} \quad \text{if } |a_1 - a_2| \leqslant c(x_2 - x_1). \end{cases} \quad (2.5)$$

For the problem to be interesting we must suppose that $V > c(x_2 - x_1)/2$. Otherwise the potential market areas of the two firms will not intersect, and there will be no room for competition – the essence of the investigation. In fact, for simplicity of exposition we assume the stronger condition that $V > c$. Define

$$A^*(1) = A^*(2) = \{(a_1, a_2) \in [0, V]^2 \| a_1 - a_2 | = c(x_2 - x_1)\}. \quad (2.6)$$

In figure 2.1 $A^*(1)$ ($= A^*(2)$) is depicted by the two straight lines in the square $[0, V]^2$. Let $A^{**}(i)$ denote the discontinuity set of $U_i(a)$. From (2.4) and (2.5) we conclude that $A^{**}(i) \subseteq A^*(i) = A^*(2)$ for $i = 1, 2$.

One can show that this game does not possess pure-strategy equilibria at all location points, (x_1, x_2).[7] We demonstrate, however, that an equilibrium exists for any pair of locations if firms choose price distributions.

7 See d'Aspremont et al. (1979). To see this, one argues first that if an equilibrium exists, say (a_1^*, a_2^*), then it must be the case that $|a_1^* - a_2^*| \leqslant c(x_2 - x_1)$, and so both serve the market. (If $|a_1^* - a_2^*| > c(x_2 - x_1)$, the firm charging the higher price makes zero profit, and can gain by lowering its price sufficiently.) But if, say, firm 1 sets $a_1 = a_2^* - c(x_2 - x_1) - \epsilon$ (where ϵ is positive and 'small') it captures the entire market. If the firms are located near each other then firm 1 does better by charging this than a_1^*.

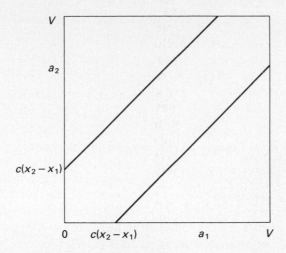

Figure 2.1

One may first verify from (2.4) and (2.5) that although $U_1 + U_2$ is not continuous, it is upper semi-continuous. (For $a_2 > a_1 + c(x_2 - x_1)$, all customers buy at price a_1, whereas at $a_2 = a_1 + c(x_2 - x_1)$, some customers buy at a_2. Thus, total profit jumps up. Similarly, profit jumps up moving from $a_1 > a_2 + c(x_2 - x_1)$ to $a_1 = a_2 + c(x_2 - x_1)$). Note as well that U_1 is bounded and that for all $a_1 \in A_1^{**}(1)$,

$$\lim_{a_1 \to \bar{a}_i} \inf U_1(a_1, a_2) \geqslant U_1(\bar{a}_1, a_2) \quad \text{for all } a_2 \in A_{-1}^{**}(\bar{a}_1)$$

and likewise for $i = 2$. That is, $U_i(a_i, a_{-i})$ is weakly lower semi-continuous in a_i. We may therefore appeal to Theorem 5 in chapter 1 and assert

Theorem 3. *The two-firm Hotelling model of price competition has a mixed-strategy equilibrium for any pair of product qualities.*

Remark 1. The Hotelling model is a symmetric game if either $x_1 = x_2$ or $x_1 = 1 - x_2$. For the first case, i.e. when firms are located at the same point, there is a unique pure-strategy equilibrium, and it is given by $a_1 = a_2 = 0$. This is the competitive outcome. Notice that with $x_1 = x_2$, $A^*(1)$ $(= A^*(2))$ in (2.6) is in fact the diagonal. But from (2.4) and (2.5) it is clear that $(0, 0)$ is *not* a point of discontinuity of U_i. Thus $0 \notin A_1^{**}(1) = A_2^{**}(2)$. It follows that the competitive outcome is consistent with Theorem 6 in chapter 1.

Remark 2. It should be clear that our analysis and results extend immediately to a market with three or more firms. They also extend to the case where firms' 'locations' are points in spaces of two or more dimensions. This second extension, however, is less interesting from the point of view of this paper, since in two or more dimensions, the discontinuities of the one-dimensional model vanish. Therefore, in more than one dimension the standard Glicksberg and Fan existence theorems apply (see Theorem 1 in chapter 1).

3 PRODUCT COMPETITION

In the previous section we assumed that firms competed in prices and that their locations were fixed. In this section we look at the opposite case, where the product price is fixed and firms compete in the characteristics of the product they offer.

Consider a product consisting of m characteristics. The feasible set of characteristics is assumed to be a non-empty, compact, subset of R^m, which we denote by $\bar{A}$. Consumers differ in their preferences over characteristics and it is supposed that there is a continuum of consumer types. A consumer whose favourite vector of characteristics is $x \in \bar{\bar{A}}$ is labelled as type x, and we assume a non-atomic distribution of consumers over $\bar{\bar{A}}$, which we denote by the (Borel) measure ρ.

There are N firms $(i, j = 1, \ldots, N)$, which produce the commodity cost-lessly. The product price is fixed in advance and is the same for all firms. A firm chooses the vector of characteristics it will offer. It can offer at most one vector. Each consumer purchases at most one unit of the product from the firm nearest the consumer's favourite vector. To be precise, the realized utility level (net of payment for the product) of consumer of type $x \in \bar{\bar{A}}$ from consuming a unit of the product with characteristic $a \in \bar{\bar{A}}$ is:

$$W(x, a) = V - c \| a - x \|, \quad \text{where } V, c > 0. \tag{2.7}$$

For simplicity we assume that $V > c \sup_{x \in \bar{A}} \sup_{a \in \bar{A}} \| a - x \|$, so that each consumer purchases precisely one unit.

Let a_i be firm i's location in the feasible set of characteristics $\bar{A}$. Now define

$$B_i(a) \equiv B_i(a_i, a_{-i}) \equiv \{ x \in \bar{\bar{A}} \mid \| x - a_i \| \leqslant \| x - a_j \| \ \forall j \neq i \}. \tag{2.8}$$

If no other firm coincides with i in its choice of location, then $B_i(a)$, firm i's market region, is the set of consumers who purchase from i. However, if n firms $(0 \leqslant n \leqslant N - 1)$, other than i, are located at a_i, then each of these $(n + 1)$ congruent firms has a $1/(n + 1)$ share of $B_i(a)$. Therefore, the profit function of firm i is:

$$U_i(a_i, a_{-i}) = (1 + n)^{-1} \int_{B_i(a)} d\rho(x), \tag{2.9}$$

where $(1 + n)$ is the number of firms located at a_i.

'Firms are profit maximizing, and their strategies are locations. The market is thus represented by the game $[(\bar{A}, U_i); i = 1, \ldots, N]$ where U_i is given by (2.9). Notice that the game is *symmetric*. Eaton and Lipsey (1975) noted that if $m = 1$, $\bar{A} = [0, 1]$, $N = 3$ and ρ is uniform, then the game does not possess a Nash equilibrium in pure strategies.[8] In an accompanying paper, Shaked (1975) proved an identical result for the case where $m = 2$, $\bar{A}$ is the unit circle, $N = 3$ and ρ is uniform.

The payoff function (2.9) violates two hypotheses of the classical pure-strategy existence theorems (see Theorem 1 in chapter 1): namely continuity, and quasi-concavity in a_i. A slight modification of the payoff function suggests, however, that the decisive factor in the non-existence of equilibrium is the failure of the *second* rather than the first hypothesis. In particular, suppose that for given $\epsilon > 0$ we redefine a firm's profit to be zero if it is within ϵ of any other firm but suppose that otherwise the profit function is (2.9). It is a straightforward matter to check that such a modified payoff function satisfies all the hypotheses of Theorem 2 in chapter 1, except the required quasi-concavity. Therefore, the 'blame' for the non-existence of equilibrium in pure strategies in this modified model – and therefore by extension, in the unmodified model – can be assigned to the violation of quasi-concavity.

We now prove that the location game $[(\bar{A}, U_i): i = 1, \ldots, N]$ we have defined in (2.7)–(2.9) possesses a symmetric mixed-strategy equilibrium where, for $N \geqslant 3$ the equilibrium mixed strategy is atomless. To do this we merely confirm that the game satisfies the hypotheses of Theorem 6* in chapter 1. Define

$$A^*(i) \equiv \{(a_i, a_{-i}) \in \bar{\bar{A}}^N \mid \exists j \neq i, a_i = a_j\}. \tag{2.10}$$

It is immediate from (2.9) that the discontinuities of U_i are confined to a subset of $A^*(i)$. Notice further that U_i is bounded and that the game is constant-sum. If ν is the uniform distribution on the unit circle (for $m = 1$, ν places probability one-half on each of 1 and -1), then for all (a_i, a_{-i})

$$\int_{B^m} \liminf_{\theta \to 0} U_i(a_i + \theta e, a_{-i}) \, d\nu(e)$$

$$= \int_{B^m} \liminf_{\theta \to 0} \left[\int_{B_i(a_i + \theta e, a_{-i})} d\rho(x) \right] d\nu(e)$$

---

8 This is easy to check. If all firms coincide at a point, any one can increase its profit by moving slightly away in some direction. But if they do not coincide, the outer flank firms can gain by moving closer to the firm in the middle. Hence there is no equilibrium configuration of locations. Eaton and Lipsey demonstrate, however, that for any value of N other than three, an equilibrium in pure strategies exists in the one-dimensional case.

$$= \begin{cases} \displaystyle\int\!\!\int_{B_i(a)} d\rho(x), & \text{if } n = 0 \\[2em] \dfrac{1}{2}\displaystyle\int_{B_i(a)} d\rho(x), & \text{if } n > 0 \end{cases}$$

$$\geqslant \frac{1}{n+1}\int_{B_i(a)} d\rho(x) = U_i(a_i, a_{-i}),$$

where n is the number of firms other than i located at a_i and the inequality is strict if $n \geqslant 2$. Therefore U_i satisfies property (α^*). (The preceding argument applies to a_i in the interior of $\bar{\bar{A}}$. If a_i lies on boundary, the distribution ν must be modified accordingly.)

Let $A^{**}(i)$ $(\subseteq A^*(i))$ denote the set of discontinuities of U_i. For $N > 2$ note that $A_i^{**}(i) = \bar{\bar{A}}$; that is, any location by a firm is a potential point of discontinuity. (This is not true in the case $N = 2$, since for example, if firms locate along a one-dimensional line segment $(m = 1)$, the mid-point is not an element of $A_i^{**}(i)$). We may now state:

Theorem 4. *For $N > 2$, let $\bar{\bar{A}} \subseteq R^m$ $(m \geqslant 1)$ be non-empty, and compact, and let $U_i : \bar{\bar{A}}^N \to R^1$ satisfy (2.9). Then the game $[(\bar{\bar{A}}, U_i): i = 1, \ldots, N]$ possesses a symmetric mixed-strategy Nash equilibrium*

$$\underbrace{(\mu^*, \ldots, \mu^*)}_{N \text{ times}}$$

where μ^* is atomless on $A_i^{**}(i) = \bar{\bar{A}}$.

Remark 1. Shaked (1982) has computed a symmetric mixed-strategy equilibrium for the case $m = 1, \bar{\bar{A}}, = [0, 1], N = 3$ and ν uniform (the example discussed in footnote 8, p. 91). It consists of each firm choosing a uniform distribution on the interval $[\frac{1}{4}, \frac{3}{4}]$ and zero weight on the outer quartiles. Osborne and Pitchik (1982) show that, in this case, there are other equilibria which involve a mixture of pure and mixed strategies.

Remark 2. We have studied the choices of location and price separately, but our analysis carried over to some cases where firms choose both. Suppose that a strategy consists of choosing a price and location simultaneously. Then our arguments can easily be modified to establish the existence of a mixed-strategy equilibrium in this more elaborate model. The model originally considered by Hotelling (1929), however, was one where firms first choose locations and then prices. Because the strategy spaces of this two-stage model are infinite dimensional, our theorems do not immediately apply.

4 INSURANCE MARKETS

We next consider a model of the market for insurance due to Rothschild and Stiglitz (1976) and Wilson (1977). Our formulation relies substantially on Hahn's (1978) analysis of the Rothschild–Stiglitz model.

There is one commodity (money) in this model, and, for each consumer, there are two states of nature: that of having an accident and that of not. Let goods 1 and 2 be money in the 'no accident' and 'accident' states, respectively. Each consumer has a strictly positive initial endowment $w \in R_+^2$ representing his initial allocation of money in the two states. His preferences are represented by a strictly concave von Neumann–Morgenstern utility function u. We normalize u so that $u(w) = 0$. For convenience we suppose that w and u are the same for all individuals.

Consumers fall into two classes according to their accident proneness. High risk consumers have accidents with probability p_H and low risks with p_L, where $p_L < p_H$. A consumer knows which risk class he belongs to. Therefore, u and p_J ($J = L$ or H) determine his preferences over goods 1 and 2. Clearly, the preferences of a high risk consumer differ from those of a low risk. Indeed, at any consumption pair, the marginal rate of substitution between goods 2 and 1 is greater for the low risk consumer (see figure 2.2). Let us assume a (large) fixed population n of consumers, of whom n_L are low risks and n_H are high risks.

There are two firms (insurance companies).[9] Firms sell insurance contracts which are vectors $c = (c_1, c_2) \in R^2$. One interprets c_1 as the insurance premium and c_2 as the accident benefit net of premium. Each consumer can purchase at most one insurance contract. Consumers of a given risk class buy from the firm offering the most desirable contract for them. (Of course, they will buy that contract only if they prefer it to their initial endowment.) If the two firms offer equally desirable contracts for a given risk class, the consumers in that class divide themselves equally between them.

Firms are expected profit maximizers – their revenues are premia and costs are claim payments – and they regard different consumers' chances of having an accident as independent. They know u, p_H, p_L, n_H and n_L, but cannot tell to which class any given consumer belongs.

A strategy for a firm is to offer a set of contracts. Since there are only two risk classes, it is never necessary for a firm to offer more than two contracts.[10]

9 We could as easily handle more than two.

10 To see this, suppose C is the set of contracts that firm i ($i = 1, 2$) offers. C can be subdivided into C_H, C_L, C_K, the contracts which, given the contracts offered by the other firm, are optimal for high risks, low risks, and neither class, respectively. But since u is strictly concave, there are unique (expected) profit maximizing contracts c^H and c^L within C_H and C_L, respectively. Hence, offering (c^H, c^L) is at least as good as offering C and strictly better if C_H or C_L contain contracts other than c^H and c^L.

Therefore we shall only consider strategies consisting of pairs of contracts (c^H, c^L), where without loss of generality we adopt the convention that high risk consumers find c^H at least as desirable as c^L, and low risks find c^L at least as desirable as c^H.

For $J = H, L$ and contract $c = (c_1, c_2)$, let $V_J(c)$ denote the expected utility of c for a consumer of class J. That is,

$$V_J(c) = p_J u(w_2 + c_2) + (1 - p_J) u(w_1 - c_1).$$

Let $\pi_J(c)$ be the expected profit from the sale of contract c to a consumer of risk class J. Then

$$\pi_J(c) = -p_J c_2 + (1 - p_J) c_1.$$

Suppose that firm 1 offers the contract pair $a_1 = (c^H(1), c^L(1))$ and firm 2, $a_2 = (c^H(2), c^L(2))$. Firm 1's expected profit from risk class J customers is therefore

$$\pi_1^J(a_1, a_2) = \begin{cases} n_J \pi_J(c^J(1)), & \text{if } V_J(c^J(1)) > V_J(c^J(2)) \\ (1/2)\, n_J \pi_J(c^J(1)), & \text{if } V_J(c^J(1)) = V_J(c^J(2)) \\ 0 & \text{otherwise.} \end{cases}$$

Naturally, π_2^J is defined symmetrically. Firm i's total expected profit is therefore,

$$U_i(a_1, a_2) = \pi_i^H(a_1, a_2) + \pi_i^L(a_1, a_2).$$

Consider the contract pair $a^* = (c^{*H}, c^{*L})$ satisfying $w_2 + c_2^{*H} = w_1 - c_1^{*H}$ (i.e. high risks are perfectly insured); $\pi_H(c^{*H}) = \pi_L(c^{*L}) = 0$ (i.e. each of the two risk classes generates zero expected profit); and $V_H(c^{*H}) = V_H(c^{*L})$, (i.e. high risk customers are indifferent between the low risk contract and their own). (See figure 2.2.) We shall call a^* the 'Rothschild–Stiglitz–Wilson' (R–S–W) contract pair. It is easy to see that, if a pure strategy equilibrium exists, both firms must offer a^*. First, no contract can earn positive profit because if, say, firm 1 offered such a contract, firm 2 could offer a contract with slightly better terms for high or low risks (whichever is the profitable class), thereby getting nearly all firm 1's profit for itself. (This is the 'Bertrand'-like feature of the R–S–W model.) Second, among high risk contracts that earn zero profit, the most desirable from the customers' viewpoint is c^{*H}. Therefore c^{*H} is the only high risk contract not subject to the 'undercutting' argument that ruled out positive profits. Finally, the most favourable zero-profit contract for low risks that has the property that high risks do not prefer it to their own is c^{*L}.

However, a^* may not be an equilibrium contract because if there is a sufficiently high proportion of low risks in the population, there exists a 'pooling' contract c^{**} that earns positive profit overall (i.e. $\pi_H(c^{**}) + \pi_L(c^{**}) > 0$), and which both high and low risks prefer to a^*. (See figure 2.2.)[11] We shall show below that nonetheless, a mixed-strategy equilibrium always exists.

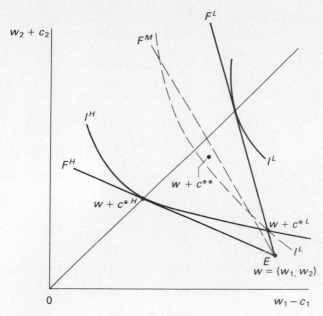

Figure 2.2 I^H is a high-risk indifference curve and I^L is a low-risk indifference curve. EF^H denotes the 'fair-odds' line for high risks (the locus $\pi_H = 0$), and EF^L denotes the 'fair-odds' line for low risks. EF^M is the 'zero-profit' pooling line. $(c*^H, c*^L)$ is the R–S–W contract pair. $c**$ is a pooling contract. The figure depicts a case where a pure-strategy equilibrium does not exist.

11 One can argue, as we did when commenting on the Bertrand–Edgeworth problem in footnote 3, p. 85, that the reason for the non-existence of an equilibrium in pure strategies in the R–S–W model can be traced to the fact that a firm's payoff is not quasi-concave in its own strategy. To see this modify the R–S–W model slightly by introducing 'minimal sensibility' on the part of customers. Suppose that there exist positive numbers η_H and η_L such that if contracts C_1 and C_2 are offered and C_1 is purchased by high risk customers then C_2 is also purchased by them if and only if

$$-\eta_H < V_H(C_2) - V_H(C_1) \leqslant \eta_H,$$

and, likewise, if C_1 is purchased by low risk customers then C_2 is also purchased by them if and only if

$$-\eta_L \leqslant V_L(C_2) - V_L(C_1) < \eta_L.$$

One can now verify that with this modification the expected profit functions of insurance firms are upper semi-continuous. (See Dasgupta and Maskin (1977) for details.) They are of course graph continuous even in the original R–S–W model. But if η_H and η_L are small enough an equilibrium in pure strategies does not exist. We may therefore conclude from Theorem 2 in chapter 1 that the reason for the non-existence of an equilibrium in pure strategies in this modified model is the fact that the expected profit function of a firm is not quasi-concave in its own strategy.

To place the insurance problem within the framework of our general existence theorem, we shall identify a contract c with the utility pair $(V_H(c), V_L(c))$. This identification is legitimate, since the mapping $c \to (V_H(c), V_L(c))$ is one-to-one. A strategy thus consists of offering a quadruple (V_H, V_L, V'_H, V'_L), where, by the convention we have adopted, $V_H \geqslant V'_H$ and $V'_L \geqslant V_L$. That is, (V_H, V_L) corresponds to the high risk contract and (V'_H, V'_L) to the low risk contract. We can therefore confine attention to the compact set

$$V = \{(V_H, V_L) \mid \exists c \text{ with } (V_H(c), V_L(c)) = (V_H, V_L),$$

$$\pi_L(c) \geqslant 0, \max\{V_L, V_H\} \geqslant 0\},$$

since any other contract either earns negative profit or is never purchased. Thus we can take firm i's strategy space to be

$$A_i = \{(V_H, V_L, V'_H, V'_L) \mid \{(V_H, V_L), (V'_H, V'_L)\} \subseteq V, V'_L \geqslant V_L \text{ and } V_H \geqslant V'_H\}.$$

We can now state,

Theorem 5. *The insurance market game has a symmetric equilibrium* (μ^*, μ^*). *Furthermore, for all* $(c^H, c^L) \neq (c^{*H}, c^{*L})$, *with* $\pi_H(c^H) = \pi_L(c^L) = 0$, $\mu^*(c^H, c^L) = 0$.

Proof. We must verify that the hypotheses of Theorem 6* in chapter 1 are satisfied. However, as we have defined the payoff functions, the sum $U_1 + U_2$ is not continuous, nor even upper semi-continuous. This is because the discontinuities in firms' payoffs entail a shift of clientele from one firm's contracts to the other's, and so, if the contracts are not equally profitable, total profit changes discontinuously.[12] We, therefore, slightly modify the payoff functions to restore upper semi-continuity. After establishing the existence of equilibrium with these modified payoff functions, we show that such an equilibrium applies to the original payoffs.

Observe first that discontinuities in firm i's payoff function are confined to the set

$$A^*(i) = \{(a_1, a_2) \in A_1 \times A_2 \mid V_H(1) = V_H(2) \text{ or } V'_L(1) = V'_H(2)$$

where

$$a_i = (V_H(i), V_L(i), V'_H(i), V'_L(i))\}.$$

For $(a_1, a_2) \in A^*(1)$ and $i = 1, 2$, define

$$\bar{U}_i(a_1, a_2) = \lim_{\epsilon \to 0} \sup_{\substack{\|a'_1 - a_1\| < \epsilon \\ \|a'_2 - a_2\| < \epsilon}} U_1(a'_1, a'_2).$$

---

12 We are grateful to David Salant, who reminded us of this point, and therefore helped correct an error in a previous version.

Take

$$U_i^*(a_1, a_2) = \begin{cases} \bar{U}_i(a_1, a_2), & \text{if } (a_1, a_2) \in A^*(1) \text{ and } a_1 \neq a_2 \\ U_i(a_1, a_2), & \text{otherwise.} \end{cases}$$

Clearly U_i^* is bounded. To see that $U_1^* + U_2^*$ is upper semi-continuous, consider a sequence $\{(a_1^n, a_2^n)\}$ converging to (a_1, a_2). If $(a_1, a_2) \notin A^*(1)$ then U_1^* and U_2^* are continuous at (a_1, a_2). If $a_1 = a_2$ then $U_1^* + U_2^*$ is continuous at (a_1, a_2) because the discontinuities in U_1 and U_2 simply entail shifting profit from one firm to another. If $(a_1, a_2) \in A^*(1)$ and $a_1 \neq a_2$, then U_1^* is upper semi-continuous at (a_1, a_2) by construction. Therefore $U_1^* + U_2^*$ is upper semi-continuous. Observe that the discontinuities in firm 1's payoff function, U_1^*, are confined to $A^*(1)$, which meets the requirements of Theorem 2 on the form of the discontinuity set. Consider a point $(a_1, a_2) \in A^*(1)$. Let $a_1 = (c^H(1), c^L(1))$. Suppose that $V_H(1) = V_H(2)$. (The argument is similar if $V_L'(1) = V_L'(2)$.) If $\pi_H(c^H(1)) > 0$, then U_1 and hence U_1^* is right lower semi-continuous in the $V_H(1)$ component at (a_1, a_2). If $\pi_H(c^H(1)) \leq 0$, then U_1^* is left lower semi-continuous in that component.

Now

$$A_1^{**}(1) = \{(c^H, c^L) \in A_1^*(1) \mid \pi_H(c^H) \neq 0 \text{ or } \pi_L(c^L) \neq 0\}.$$

Consider $(c^H, c^L) \in A_1^{**}(1)$. If, say, $\pi^H(c^H) < 0$, then for every $(\hat{c}^H, \hat{c}^L)$ such that $(c^H, c^L, \hat{c}^H, \hat{c}^L) \in A_1^{**}(1)$ U_1^* is left lower semi-continuous in V_H. Moreover, when $(\hat{c}^H, \hat{c}^L) = (c^H, c^L)$, U_1, and hence U_1^* fails to be left upper semi-continuous in V_H. Similar conclusions can be reached when $\pi_H(c^H) > 0$ or $\pi_L(c^L) \neq 0$. Therefore property (α^*) of Theorem 6* in chapter 1 holds. From this theorem, we conclude that there exists a symmetric equilibrium (μ^*, μ^*) for the payoff functions U_1^* and U_2^*, where μ^* is atomless on $A_i^{**}(i)$. Because μ^* is atomless and U_i and U_i^* differ only on A_i^{**},

$$\int U_1(\cdot, a_2) \, d\mu^*(a_2) = \int U_1^*(\cdot, a_2) \, d\mu^*(a_2).$$

Therefore (μ^*, μ^*) is an equilibrium for U_1 and U_2 as well.

To see that $\mu^*(\bar{c}^H, \bar{c}^L) = 0$, if $\pi_H(\bar{c}^H) = \pi_L(\bar{c}^L) = 0$ but $(\bar{c}^H, \bar{c}^L) \neq (c^{*H}, c^{*L})$, observe that if, say, firm 2 placed positive probability on $(\bar{c}^H, \bar{c}^L)$, where $\bar{c}^H \neq c^{*H}$, firm 1 could obtain a positive expected profit by choosing $(\hat{c}^H, \bar{c}^L)$ where $\pi_H(\hat{c}^H) > 0$ but $V_H(\hat{c}^H) > V_H(\bar{c}^L)$, contradicting the supposition that a zero-profit contract pair is part of an equilibrium strategy. ∥

Appealing to Dasgupta and Maskin (1977), Appendix, we can say more about the nature of mixed-strategy equilibrium.[13] First, as in pure-strategy

13 Lemma 8 in the Appendix of Dasgupta and Maskin (1977) is false. The remaining Lemmas are correct and it is these that we are summarizing below in the text.

equilibrium, firms earn zero expected profit. Second, any high risk contract offered provides full insurance and either loses money or breaks even. That is, if (μ_1^*, μ_2^*) is an equilibrium, $\mu_i^* \{(c^H, c^L) \mid \pi_H(c^H) \leqslant 0$ and $w_2 + c_2^H = w_1 - c_1^H\} = 1$, for $i = 1, 2$. Third, any low risk contract offered provides less than full insurance and either makes money or breaks even. That is $\mu_i^* \{(c^H, c^L) \mid \pi_L(c^L) \geqslant 0$ and $w_2 + c_2^L < w_1 - c_1^L\} = 1$, $i = 1, 2$. Finally, high risk customers are indifferent between any high risk–low risk pair offered: $\mu_i^* \{(c^H, c^L) \mid V_H(c^H) = V_H(c^L)\} = 1, i = 1, 2.$[14]

5 CLASSIFICATION

Because they take prices as given, agents in the Arrow–Debreu theory of resource allocation have payoff functions that are continuous (see Arrow and Debreu 1954). Therefore it is no accident that the discontinuities that we have reviewed arise in models of imperfect competition.

One conclusion we can draw from our work, however, is that these discontinuities are *inessential* – not only in the sense that they do not prevent the existence of mixed-strategy equilibrium – but, more importantly, that the discontinuous games can be approximated arbitrarily closely by games to which the classical existence theorems (Theorem 3 of chapter 1) apply. In the Introduction to chapter 1 we mentioned one form of approximation, namely the selection of a finite set of strategies (to which Nash's (1951) theorem then applies). Indeed, our method of proving Theorems 5* and 6* in chapter 1 is through successively finer finite approximations. Alternatively, we would have retained the infinite strategy spaces, but introduced *exogenous* uncertainty in such a way that agents' *expected* payoffs are continuous. (For an application of this device to patent race games, see Dasgupta and Stiglitz (1980).) If the uncertainty is 'small' the game is an approximation to the original discontinuous game. By analogy with our 'finite' arguments one can show that as the uncertainty diminishes a subsequence of mixed-strategy equilibria in these smoothed games converges to a mixed-strategy equilibrium in the discontinuous game. Therefore in this alternative sense the equilibria of the discontinuous games are 'robust'.

The economic games we have studied can be classified according to the extent that there are 'winners' and 'losers'. One should note that in all the examples, except for Hotelling's location model, a firm can always increase its market share by moving in a single consistent direction. Thus, under price competition firms increase their market share by cutting prices. In extreme cases, such as the Rothschild–Stiglitz–Wilson game, a firm can capture the entire market by undercutting its rivals infinitesimally. Such models are pure

14 Rosenthal and Weiss (1983) have explicitly computed a symmetric equilibrium in mixed strategies for a particular specification of preferences in the R–S–W model of insurance.

'winner-loser' games, or *contests*, in the sense that the winner takes all by outdoing its rivals. Other examples of such games are wars of attrition (Riley 1980), patent races (Dasgupta and Stiglitz 1980) and auctions where the higher bid wins (e.g. Dasgupta 1982). In the symmetric versions of pure winner-loser games symmetric equilibria invariably involve a zero expected payoff for each player (where zero is the utility level of a non-participating players).[15] Some models that we have examined, namely the Bertrand-Edgeworth and Hotelling price competition models, share with contests the property that undercutting increases market share; however, these are not pure winner-loser games because the firm either cannot physically accommodate all customers (as in Bertrand-Edgeworth) or else has inherent monopoly power over some portion of the market (as in Hotelling). Even the symmetric equilibria of such games need not entail zero expected payoffs.

By contrast, Hotelling's spatial location model is not a contest at all. It has no winners and losers and the direction of increasing market share depends on the actions of other firms. If, say, in the case of three firms on a line the firm in the middle moves in either direction it encroaches on the market area of the firm it is moving towards, but at the same time loses clientele to the third firm, and these effects counter-balance.

The fact that, in contests, and partial contests (like Bertrand-Edgeworth), there is a favoured direction of movement – and hence a distinguished point at the extremity of this direction – helps us understand the nature of equilibrium to such games. In particular, it helps explain why symmetric equilibrium may involve atoms at such distinguished points. For example, symmetric equilibrium in the insurance game may have an atom at the Rothschild-Stiglitz-Wilson contract. Similarly the pure Bertrand game has all firms setting the competitive price.[16] Viewed in the light of Theorem 6* in chapter 1 these atoms are possible because at the distinguished point firms' payoff functions may not be discontinuous, since 'undercutting' is no longer possible.

REFERENCES

Arrow, K. J. and Debreu, G. 1954: Existence of equilibrium for a competitive economy. *Econometrica*, 22, 265–89.
d'Aspremont, C. and Gabszewicz, J.-J. 1980: On quasi-monopolies. *CORE Discussion Paper 8011*. Université Catholique de Louvain.
d'Aspremont, C., Gabszewicz, J.-J. and Thisse, J. 1979: On Hotelling's 'stability of competition'. *Econometrica*, 47 (5), 1145–50.

15 Many winner-loser games have asymmetric equilibria that do not have the zero-expected-payoff property. See e.g. Riley (1980) and Maskin and Riley (1982).

16 By contrast, in the spatial location model with three or more firms no point is distinguished, and so *symmetric* equilibrium entails no atoms.

Beckman, M. J. 1965: Edgeworth–Bertrand duopoly revisited. In Henn, R. (ed.), *Operations Research–Verfahren, III.* Meisenheim: Sonderdruck, Verlag, Anton Hein, 55–68.

Bertrand, J. 1883: Review of Cournot's 'Rechercher sur la theorie mathematique de la richesse'. *Journal des Savants*, 499–508.

Chamberlin, E. 1956: *The Theory of Monopolistic Competition.* Cambridge: Harvard University Press.

Dasgupta, P. 1982: The theory of technological competition. *ICERD Discussion Paper*. London School of Economics.

Dasgupta, P. and Maskin, E. 1977: The existence of equilibrium: continuity and mixed strategies. *IMSSS Technical Report No. 252*. Stanford University.

Dasgupta, P. and Stiglitz, J. E. 1980: Uncertainty, industrial structure and the speed of R & D. *Bell Journal of Economics* (Spring), 1–28.

Eaton, C. and Lipsey, R. 1975: The principle of minimum differentiation reconsidered: some new developments in the theory of spatial competition. *Review of Economic Studies*, 42, 27–50.

Edgeworth, F. M. 1925: *Papers Relating to Political Economy I.* London: Macmillan.

Hahn, F. H. 1978: On equilibrium with market-dependent information. In H. Albach, E. Helmstädter and E. Henn (eds), *Quantitative Wirtschaftsforschung*. Bonn.

Hotelling, H. 1929: The stability of competition. *Economic Journal*, 39, 41–57.

Maskin, E. and Riley, J. 1982: *On the Uniqueness of Equilibrium in Sealed Bid and Open Auctions*. Mimeo, University of Cambridge.

Nash, J. 1951: Non-cooperative games. *Annals of Mathematics*, 54, 266–95.

Osborne, M. J. and Pitchik, C. (1982. Equilibria for a three-person location problem. *Discussion paper No. 123*. Department of Economics, Columbia University.

Riley, J. 1980: Strong evolutionary equilibria and the war of attrition. *Journal of Theoretical Biology*, 82, 383–400.

Rosenthal, R. and Weiss, A. 1983: *Mixed Strategy Equilibria in Markets with Asymmetric Information*. Mimeo.

Rothschild, M. and Stiglitz, J. E. 1976: Equilibrium in competitive insurance markets: an essay on the economics of imperfect information. *Quarterly Journal of Economics*, 90, 629–49.

Shaked, A. 1975: Non-existence of equilibrium for the 2-dimensional 3-firms location problem. *Review of Economic Studies*, 42, 51–6.

Shaked, A. 1982: Existence and computation of mixed strategy Nash equilibrium for 3-firms location problem. *Journal of Industrial Economics*, 31, 93–6.

Shubik, M. 1955: A comparison of treatments of a duopoly problem; Part II. *Econometrica*, 23, 417–31.

Wilson, C. 1977: A model of insurance markets with incomplete information. *Journal of Economic Theory*, 16, 167–207.

II

IMPERFECT COMPETITION

3

On the Rate of Convergence of Oligopoly Equilibria in Large Markets: An Example

P. Dasgupta and Y. Ushio

In this note we explore the rate of convergence of Cournot–Nash equilibria with free entry and those with an entry-deterring monopolist in a replicated market where the market demand function is linear and firms face linear cost curves.

1   THE MODEL

We consider the market for a homogeneous good, the inverse demand function for which is given by the linear expression

$$p(Q) = A - Q/B, \quad A, B > 0, \tag{3.1}$$

where Q denotes the total quantity of the commodity, and p the market price.

There is an infinite number of potential firms, all facing the same cost curve, and it is supposed that the average cost curve is downward sloping. To be precise, if X is the output of a firm, the cost it incurs is assumed to be given by the linear expression

$$C(X) = \alpha + \beta X \quad \text{if } X > 0,$$

$$= 0 \quad \text{if } X = 0 \text{ where } \alpha, \beta > 0. \tag{3.2}$$

Interest in (3.2), which comprises a set-up cost (α), and a constant marginal cost (β), lies in the fact that it implies that the efficient size of a firm is infinite, a case emphasized by Sraffa (1926) in his classic article.

2   COURNOT–NASH EQUILIBRIA WITH FREE ENTRY

Suppose there is free entry by firms into the industry. What we wish to do for the main part in this note is to explore the existence and characteristics of symmetric Cournot-Nash equilibria in this industry as the market is replicated indefinitely: that is, as $B \to \infty$. The advantage afforded by (3.1) and (3.2) is that we are able to compute such equilibria explicitly.[1]

We begin by analysing symmetric Cournot-Nash equilibria for the case where the number of active firms is exogenously given. To have a non-trivial problem we suppose throughout that $A > \beta$. Let n be a positive integer.

Definition 1. A symmetric Cournot-Nash equilibrium with n firms in an industry characterized by (3.1) and (3.2) is an n-tuple of output levels $(\bar{X}, \ldots, \bar{X})$ such that

$$[A - n\bar{X}/B]\bar{X} - \beta\bar{X} - \alpha \geqslant [A - ((n-1)\bar{X} + X)/B]X - \beta X - \alpha$$

$$\text{for all } X \geqslant 0.$$

For reasons that will become clear subsequently, define

$$n^* \equiv [(A - \beta)/\sqrt{\alpha/B} - 1]. \tag{3.3}$$

where $[x]$ denotes the greatest positive integer not in excess of the number x. We suppose in what follows that $n^* \geqslant 1$. Then routine arguments imply

Proposition 1. Consider an industry characterized by (3.1) and (3.2) and n firms. If $n \leqslant n^*$, then a symmetric Cournot-Nash equilibrium exists and it is characterized by each of the n firms producing $\bar{X}$, where

$$\bar{X} = B(A - \beta)/(1 + n). \tag{3.4}$$

We now consider the case where there is free entry into the industry.

Definition 2. A symmetric Cournot-Nash equilibrium with free entry into an industry characterized by (3.1) and (3.2) is a positive integer, $\bar{n}$, and an $\bar{n}$-tuple of output levels $(\bar{X}, \ldots, \bar{X})$, such that

$$[A - \bar{n}\bar{X}/B]\bar{X} - \beta\bar{X} - \alpha \geqslant [A - ((\bar{n}-1)\bar{X} + X)/B]X - \beta X - \alpha$$

for all $X \geqslant 0$, and

$$[A - (\bar{n}\bar{X} + X)/B]X - \beta X - \alpha \leqslant 0 \quad \text{for all } X \geqslant 0.$$

For an extended discussion of this concept, see Novshek (1980), Novshek and Sonnenschein (1978), Dasgupta and Stiglitz (1980) and several of the articles in the *Journal of Economic Theory, Symposium* (April 1980).

By using a mild variant of the argument employed by Novshek (1980) (see Ushio 1981), one may establish

---

1 Since this paper was drafted we have discovered that Guesnerie and Hart (1985) have, independently, analysed the model discussed here. We expect this example has been analysed by yet others. We have found it useful for teaching purposes and suspect that others will too.

Proposition 2. *Consider a market characterized by* (3.1) *and* (3.2). *Let* $\bar{n} = n^*$, *where* n^* *is defined by* (3.3). *Then, there exists a* $\hat{B}$ (> 0) *such that for all* $B \geqslant \hat{B}$, $\bar{n}$ *firms, each producing output* $\bar{X} = B(A - \beta)/(1 + \bar{n})$, (*see* (3.4)), *comprises a symmetric Cournot-Nash equilibrium with free entry. Furthermore, profit per firm at this equilibrium tends to zero as B tends to infinity.*

Proposition 2 enables us to compute the rate of convergence of this equilibrium as $B \rightarrow \infty$. For notice that for every replication we choose the number of active firms from (3.3) and use (3.4) to compute equilibrium output per firm. For large B, we have from (3.3) that

$$\bar{n} \simeq (A - \beta)/\sqrt{\alpha/B} - 1. \tag{3.5}$$

Using Proposition 2, (3.4) and (3.5) we have

$$\bar{X} \simeq \sqrt{\alpha B}, \tag{3.6}$$

and so

$$\bar{n}\bar{X} \simeq B[(A - \beta) - \sqrt{\alpha/B}]. \tag{3.7}$$

Next, if we denote by $\bar{m} = (p(\bar{n}\bar{X}) - \beta)/\beta$ the index of the degree of monopoly in the industry, then on using (3.7) in (3.1) we conclude that

$$\bar{m} \simeq (\sqrt{\alpha/B})/\beta. \tag{3.8}$$

Finally, routine computations show that for large B the welfare loss ΔW due to oligopoly is

$$\Delta W \simeq (A - \beta)\sqrt{\alpha B},$$

and therefore welfare loss per capita is

$$\Delta W/B \simeq (A - \beta)\sqrt{\alpha/B}. \tag{3.9}$$

We have therefore proved

Proposition 3. *Consider a market characterized by* (3.1) *and* (3.2). *Then, as* $B \rightarrow \infty$, *the symmetric Cournot-Nash equilibrium with free entry described in Proposition 2 has the asymptotic properties,* $\bar{n} \sim \sqrt{B}$, $\bar{X} \sim \sqrt{B}$, $\bar{m} \sim 1/\sqrt{B}$ *and* $\Delta W/B \sim 1/\sqrt{B}$.[2,3]

Proposition 2 identifies a specific selection procedure: for each $B \geqslant \bar{B}$ it considers the largest number of firms consistent with a symmetric Cournot-

---

2 A corresponding result can be proved if instead of replicating the market one allows α to tend to zero. It is readily checked that (3.5)-(3.9) will continue to characterize the sequence obtained via the selection procedure in Proposition 2.

3 If the average cost functions are U-shaped, as in Novshek (1980), then $\bar{n} \sim B\bar{X} \sim$ constant, $\bar{m} \sim 1/B$, and $\Delta W/B \sim 1/\sqrt{B}$.

Nash equilibrium. It should be clear that for large B there exist more than one symmetric Cournot–Nash equilibrium with free entry. Ushio (1983) has proved that the number of such equilibria tends to infinity as B tends to infinity. For an exploration of the asymptotic properties of this set for this and more general markets, see Ushio (1983).

3   ENTRY-DETERRING MONOPOLIST

It is worthwhile comparing Cournot–Nash equilibria with free entry with the outcome that would emerge were a monopolist to pursue an entry-deterring output policy in the industry under study. Thus define

$$Z \equiv \min \{X | (A - (X + Y)/B) Y \leqslant \alpha + \beta Y \quad \text{for all } Y \geqslant 0\}.$$

Then Z is the minimum 'entry-deterring' output level for the monopolist. Routine computations now show that for $B \geqslant 4\alpha/(A - \beta)^2$

$$Z = (A - \beta) B - 2\sqrt{\alpha B}. \tag{3.10}$$

For large B, Z is obviously the profit maximizing output level for the entry-deterring monopolist. Consequently such a monopolist's maximum profit level $\pi(Z)$ is, for large B,

$$\pi(Z) \simeq 2\sqrt{\alpha B}(A - \beta).$$

A simple calculation yields, on using (3.10), that for large B, welfare loss written as $\Delta \tilde{W}$ is $\Delta \tilde{W} \simeq 2\alpha$, and therefore per capita welfare loss $\Delta \tilde{W}/B \simeq 2\alpha/B$. It follows that an entry-deterring monopolist pursues an approximately optimal output policy if the market is large.

We conclude that unbounded increasing returns to scale in production does not, on its own, provide an argument for supposing that an industry is vastly inefficient.

REFERENCES

Dasgupta, P. and Stiglitz, J. E. 1980: Industrial structure and the nature of innovative activity, *Economic Journal*, **90**, 266–93.

Guesnerie, R. and Hart, O. 1985: Notes on the rate of convergence of Cournot–Nash equilibria. Mimeo. Cambridge: University of Cambridge.

Novshek, W. 1980: Cournot equilibrium with free entry. *Review of Economic Studies*, **47**, 473–86.

Novshek, W. and Sonnenschein, H. 1978: Cournot and Walras equilibrium. *Journal of Economic Theory*, **19**, 223–66.

Sraffa, P. 1926: The laws of returns under competitive conditions. *Economic Journal*, **36**, 535–50.

Ushio, Y. 1983: *Cournot–Nash equilibrium in large markets: The case of declining average cost curves*. Mimeo. London: School of Economics.

4

Natural Oligopolies

A. Shaked and J. Sutton

In a market where firms offer products which differ in quality, an upper bound may exist to the number of firms which can co-exist at a non-cooperative price equilibrium. We fully characterize the conditions under which this possibility arises.

1 BACKGROUND

The present paper is concerned with the analysis of price competition in markets where consumers purchase a single unit of some good, the alternative brands of which differ in quality. The defining characteristic of this kind of product differentiation is that, were any two of the goods in question offered at the same price, then all consumers would agree in choosing the same one, i.e. that of 'higher quality'.

Little attention has been paid to the analysis of competition in this 'vertical differentiation' case, in contrast to the widely studied case of 'horizontal differentiation' where the defining characteristic is that consumers would differ as to their most preferred choice if all the goods in question were offered at the same price. The standard paradigm is that of the 'locational' and associated models. In such models, the number of firms in the industry increases indefinitely as the fixed costs associated with entry decline, or, equivalently, as the size of the economy expands. That this can happen, depends in turn on the fact that the market can support an arbitrarily large number of firms, each with a positive market share and a price in excess of unit variable cost. This property is of fundamental importance: for, as firms become more closely spaced, price competition between them implies that prices approach the level of unit variable costs. It is this 'Chamberlain' configuration which forms the basis of the notion of 'perfect monopolistic competition' (Lancaster 1979).

This paper was presented at the 'Agglomeration in Space' meeting (Habay-la-Neuve, Belgium, May 1982) organized with the financial support of the Fonds National de la Recherche Scientifique of Belgium. We would like to acknowledge the help of two referees, whose comments prompted a considerable improvement in the exposition of these results.

The central question posed in the present paper is whether this property will be available in the 'vertical differentiation' case. In a large class of cases, it turns out not to hold; in such cases, no passage to an atomistic, competitive, structure will be possible. However low the level of fixed costs, and independently of any considerations as to firms' choices of product, the nature of price competition in itself ensures that only a limited number of firms can survive at equilibrium.

2　INTRODUCTION

We will be concerned, in what follows, with elaborating a condition which is necessary and sufficient to allow an arbitrarily large number of firms to co-exist with positive market shares, and prices exceeding unit variable costs, at a Nash equilibrium in prices. It may be helpful to begin, in the present section, by setting out this condition in a quite informal manner.

Suppose a consumer with income Y purchases *one unit* of a product of quality u, at price $p(u)$, thereby achieving a level of utility given by, say, the function

$$u \cdot (Y - p(u)).$$

Let each of a number of firms produce one product of some quality u subject to constant unit variable cost, $c(u)$. We consider a hypothetical situation in which a number of products are offered at a price equal to their respective levels of unit variable cost. (The relevance of this case lies in the fact that some firms may not be able to achieve positive sales at a price which covers variable cost, and it is this which limits the number of firms surviving at equilibrium.)

Figure 4.1 shows the function $uc(u)$. Take a line of slope Y_1 through the point $(u, uc(u))$. Then the vertical intercept $AB = u \cdot (Y_1 - c(u))$ represents the utility attained by a consumer of income Y_1 in purchasing a product of quality u at price $c(u)$. Again referring to figure 4.1, the consumer of income Y_1 is indifferent between u at price $c(u)$ at v at price $c(v)$. Finally, we illustrate the optimal quality choice for a consumer of income Y_2, who can purchase any quality at unit variable cost, as the point of tangency q (chosen to maximize the associated intercept).

We are now in a position to identify a fundamental dichotomy which forms the basis of our subsequent analysis. Let consumer incomes lie in some range $[a, b]$ and suppose unit variable cost rises only slowly with quality. Then, if two products are made available at unit variable cost, all consumers will agree in preferring the higher quality product, i.e. all consumers rank the products in the same order. On the other hand, consider the cost function shown in figure 4.2(i); here, we illustrate an example in which $uc(u)$ is convex,

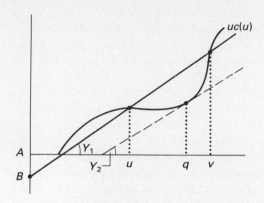

Figure 4.1

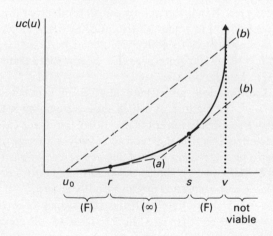

Figure 4.2(i)

and we identify two points of tangency *r* and *s* where the slope of the curve coincides with our extreme income values *a* and *b*. Here, if any set of products lying in the interval below *r* is made available at unit variable cost, all consumers will agree in ranking them in increasing order of quality; and for a set of qualities drawn from the interval above *s*, and sold at unit variable cost, consumers will agree in ranking them in decreasing order of quality. In the intermediate quality range, however, consumers will differ in their ranking of products, at unit variable cost. Now this is reminiscent of the 'location' paradigm noted above, and we shall show in the sequel that the basic property alluded to earlier continues to hold good here – an unbounded number of firms may co-exist with positive market shares and prices exceeding unit variable cost, at equilibrium.

Now, in this 'location-like' situation, the manner in which an arbitrarily large number of firms may be entered, is straightforward: for, within a certain interval, we can always insert an additional firm (product) *between* two existing firms, without precipitating the exit of any other firm.

A second, and quite distinct, kind of situation may arise, however, which is also consistent with the co-existence of an unbounded number of competing firms. While many subcases of this possibility arise, all are quite analogous, and a clear illustration of the mechanism involved is provided by the following example. Suppose costs were zero; and suppose further that the range of incomes extends downwards to zero. In this case, an unbounded number of products may be entered: for no product can have zero profits at equilibrium unless some higher quality product sells for price zero (remember the consumer of income zero is indifferent between all products at price zero, so any product can otherwise find some positive price at which it can earn positive profits). But it now suffices to notice that the highest quality product in the sequence will *not* be sold at price zero; for clearly there exists some price at which it can earn positive profits.

Hence in this situation, an infinite number of products may again be entered – but now, the method by which they are entered is by introducing new products of successively lower quality at the end of the existing range.

What characterizes this situation, and all analogous subcases, is the presence of a consumer – here the consumer of income zero – who is (locally) indifferent between alternative products, at unit variable cost, i.e. the derivative of his utility score with respect to product quality is zero.

The condition which we develop below is designed to exclude these two types of situation. Where that condition is satisfied, all consumers will be agreed in ranking the products in the same strict order, at unit variable cost. When this is so, it follows that one firm could set a price which would drive the remaining firms out of the market. This will not in general occur at equilibrium, however. (For an elementary example, see Jaskold Gabszewicz et al. 1981b). What we show is that, in this case, *there will exist an upper bound independent of product qualities, to the number of firms which can co-exist with positive market shares and prices exceeding unit variable costs, at a Nash equilibrium in prices*.

It is worth stressing immediately that this property is extremely strong: the bound we define depends only on the pattern of tastes and income distribution and is independent of the qualities of the various products offered.

The mechanism through which the result comes about, is that whatever the set of products entered, competition between certain 'surviving' products drives their prices down to a level where every consumer prefers either to make no purchase, or to buy one of these surviving goods *at its equilibrium price*, rather than switch to any of the excluded products, *at any price sufficient to cover unit variable cost*.

The implications of this 'finiteness property' are far-reaching; for, if the technology is such that unit variable cost rises only slowly with quality, so that the 'finiteness property' holds everywhere, then *irrespective of the manner in which product quality is chosen by firms*, the familiar 'limiting process' by which we might arrive at a competitive outcome cannot occur. The number of firms which can co-exist at equilibrium is no longer limited by the level of fixed costs, as in the familiar case, but is instead determined by the upper bound which we identify below. This means, in turn, that the effect of a further reduction in fixed costs, or an increase in the extent of the market, will, once that bound is attained, have no effect on the equilibrium number of firms in the industry.

It is this configuration, in which the finiteness property holds over the relevant quality range, which we label a *natural oligopoly*.

The 'finiteness' property has already been demonstrated for a special case in which all costs are zero, by Jaskold Gabszewicz and Thisse (1980). The aim of the present paper is to provide a necessary and sufficient condition for such an outcome, where costs are present.

Finally, we emphasize that we shall not be concerned here with the question of optimal quality choice by firms; the 'finiteness' property is independent of such considerations. The range of qualities available on the market will, in general, of course depend *inter alia* on the relation between *fixed costs* (including R & D), and product quality. (We have elsewhere examined this problem of quality choice (Shaked and Sutton 1982a, b; 1983).) Here, however, we will take qualities as given and all such costs as sunk costs; and so we will be concerned only with variable cost.[1]

The structure of the paper is as follows. Section 3 presents the model, and in Section 4 we examine price equilibrium. In Section 5 we present a necessary and sufficient condition for 'finiteness'; Section 6 is devoted to a discussion of the results.

3 THE MODEL

A number of firms produce distinct, substitute, goods. We label their respective products by an index $k = 1, \ldots, n$, where firm k sells product k at price

---

1 Labour, materials, and divisible capital equipment. It is of course *long run* unit variable costs which are relevant.

p_k. (We take the goods to be distinct, here, since if two or more goods are identical, then all have price equal to unit variable cost, at a Nash equilibrium in prices, by the usual Bertrand argument. The case where some firms produce an identical quality level is considered in the proof of Proposition 3 below.)

Assume a continuum of consumers identical in tastes but differing in income; incomes are uniformly distributed over some range, $0 < a \leqslant t \leqslant b$.

Consumers make indivisible and mutually exclusive purchases from among our n substitute goods, in the sense that any consumer either makes no purchase, or else buys exactly one unit from one of the n firms. We denote by $U(t, k)$ the utility achieved by consuming one unit of product k and t units of 'other things' (the latter may be thought of as a Hicksian 'composite commodity', measured as a continuous variable), and by $U(t, 0)$ the utility derived from consuming t units of income only.

Assume that the utility function takes the form

$$U(t, k) = u_k \cdot t \quad (k = 1, \ldots, n) \tag{4.1}$$

and

$$U(t, 0) = u_0 \cdot t$$

with $0 < u_0 < u_1 < \ldots < u_n$ (i.e. the products are labelled in increasing order of quality).

(The particular forms of the utility function, and income distribution, used here, play no crucial part in what follows. See Section 6 below.) Let

$$r_{k-1, k} = \frac{u_k}{u_k - u_{k-1}}$$

(whence $r_{k-1,k} > 1$). Then we may define the income level t_k such that a consumer with this income will be indifferent between good k at price p_k and good $k - 1$ at price p_{k-1}, by setting

$$u_{k-1} \cdot (t_k - p_{k-1}) = u_k \cdot (t_k - p_k)$$

to obtain

$$\begin{aligned} t_k &= p_{k-1}(1 - r_{k-1,k}) + p_k r_{k-1,k} \\ &= p_{k-1} + (p_k - p_{k-1}) \cdot r_{k-1,k} \end{aligned} \tag{4.2}$$

and

$$t_1 = p_1 r_{0,1}.$$

It is immediate from inspection of our utility function that a consumer with income above t_k will strictly prefer the higher quality good k, and conversely: the function (4.1) is designed to capture the property that richer consumers are willing to pay more for a higher quality product.

Given any set of prices, then, certain firms have positive market shares bounded by marginal consumers (income levels), firm k selling to consumers of income t_k to t_{k+1} (t_k to b for firm n); the market shares of the higher quality firms corresponding to higher income bands. We shall find it convenient below to identify, sometimes, the set of firms with positive market shares; it is important to remember that a firm may be 'just' excluded in the sense that $t_k = t_{k-1}$ so that it has market share zero: here an infinitesimal fall in its price, or an infinitesimal rise in the price set by either of this firm's neighbours, will cause its market share to become positive.

Let $c(u)$ represent the level of unit variable cost as a function of the quality of the product; it is assumed independent of the level of output. We will assume that $c(u)$ is continuously differentiable (but see Section 6 below). We will write $c(u_k)$ as c_k in what follows.

The profit of any firm k now becomes, for $k = 1, \ldots, n-1$,

$$\pi_k = (p_k - c_k)(t_{k+1} - t_k), \qquad p_k \geqslant c_k,$$

$$\pi_k = 0 \qquad\qquad\qquad \text{otherwise.}$$

From this we may deduce a necessary condition for profit maximization.

For firm k we require

$$(t_{k+1} - t_k) - (p_k - c_k)(r_{k, k+1} + r_{k-1, k} - 1) \leqslant 0,$$

which is the requirement that an *increase* in k's price reduces profit. The corresponding inequality required to ensure that a *reduction* in k's price reduces profits splits into a number of cases according as k's nearest neighbour from above, and/or from below, has market share zero.

4   PRICE EQUILIBRIUM

We seek a non-cooperative price equilibrium (Nash equilibrium), namely: a vector of prices $p_n^*, p_{n-1}^*, \ldots, p_1^*$, such that, for all k, given the prices set by the remaining firms, p_k^* is the profit maximizing price for firm k.

We begin by establishing the existence of such an equilibrium:

Lemma 1. *For any given products $u_1, u_2, \ldots, u_n$ and corresponding prices $p_1, p_2, \ldots, p_{k-1}, p_{k+1}, \ldots, p_n$, for all k, the profit of the kth firm is a single peaked function of its price.*

Proof. Note that for p_k sufficiently high the sales of firm k are zero; similarly, for $p_k = c_k$ revenue equals zero. We establish that for intermediate values of p_k, profit π_k is a single peaked function of p_k.

We note that the market share of firm k is sandwiched between that of two neighbouring firms, $k-1$ and $k+1$. As its price falls, it will at some point squeeze out one or both of these neighbouring firms, thus acquiring a new 'neighbour'.

Consider the function

$$\pi_k = (p_k - c_k)(t_{k+1} - t_k)$$

which is formally defined for all p_k, and which coincides with the profit of firm k over that range of p_k such that firm k has a positive market share bounded by $(k-1)$ and $(k+1)$. We first show that any turning point of π_k is a maximum, i.e. π_k is single peaked. For, differentiating with respect to p_k we have

$$\pi'_k = (p_k - c_k)(1 - r_{k,k+1} - r_{k-1,k}) + t_{k+1} - t_k,$$
$$\pi''_k = 2(1 - r_{k,k+1} - r_{k-1,k}) < 0. \tag{4.3}$$

Suppose now that p_k falls so far as to drive one of its neighbours, $k-1$ say, out of the market. Then its new neighbours are $k-2, k+1$. Again, the profit function $\hat{\pi}_k$ for k sandwiched between $k-2, k+1$, is a single peaked function of p_k. Moreover, at the price at which the market share of $k-1$ becomes zero, i.e. $t_k = t_{k-1}$, we shall show that

$$\hat{\pi}'_k > \pi'_k$$

so that if π_k is increasing at this point then *a fortiori* $\hat{\pi}_k$ is increasing. From this it follows that the profit function is globally single peaked.

To show that $\hat{\pi}'_k > \pi'_k$ we compare π'_k as defined by (4.3) with

$$\hat{\pi}'_k = (p_k - c_k)(1 - r_{k,k+1} - r_{k-2,k}) + t_{k+1} - t_{k-2}$$

and using $t_k = t_{k-1}$, and since (by inspection of the definitions of $r_{k-1,k}$) we have $r_{k-2,k} < r_{k-1,k}$, our result follows. *QED*

From this we obtain the following proposition.

Proposition 1. *For any set of products* $1, \ldots, n$ *a non-cooperative price equilibrium* $p_1, \ldots, p_n$ *exists.*

Proof. This follows immediately by appealing to the fact that each firm's profit function is quasi-concave by virtue of Lemma 1 (Friedman 1977, p. 152). *QED*

5   THE FINITENESS PROPERTY

We proceed by defining the following property:

Definition 1. An interval $[\underline{u}, \bar{u}]$ of qualities possesses the *finiteness property* if there exists a number K such that, at any Nash equilibrium involving a number of products drawn from this interval, at most K enjoy positive market shares and prices exceeding unit variable cost.

Remark. K will depend on the range $[a, b]$ of consumer incomes.

We note that if this property does not hold, then it follows that for all N, there exists a sequence of at least N products co-existing with positive market shares, and prices exceeding unit variable cost, at a Nash equilibrium in prices.

We now turn to the condition required to ensure this 'finiteness' property.

We begin by defining a function $t(u, v)$, which is the income level at which a consumer is indifferent between goods u and v, where both are available at unit variable cost. Setting

$$u(t - c(u)) = v(t - c(v))$$

we have

$$t(u, v) = \frac{vc(v) - uc(u)}{v - u} = c(v)\, r_{uc} + c(u)\,(1 - r_{uc})$$

where $r_{uc} = v/(v - u)$.

Consumers of income above $t(u, v)$ strictly prefer the higher quality good; and conversely.

We begin by deleting from our interval $[\underline{u}, \bar{u}]$ any products for which $t(u_0, u) > b$; such products will not be viable in that even the richest consumer will prefer to make no purchase, rather than buy such a good, even at cost. In general this deletion will leave a number of closed subintervals of quality.

We now state a condition which will be shown, in Propositions 2 and 3 below, to be necessary and sufficient for the finiteness property to hold on any such subinterval, whence it follows immediately that it is necessary and sufficient for finiteness on $[\underline{u}, \bar{u}]$.

We define the function $t(u, u)$,

$$t(u, u) = \lim_{v \to u} t(u, v).$$

Since $c(u)$ is differentiable, and

$$t(u, u) = c(u) + uc'(u),$$

it follows that $t(u, u)$ is well defined.

Now $t(u, u)$ may be interpreted directly, as follows. If all goods are made available at unit variable cost, then a consumer of income $t(u, u)$ attains *either* a maximum, *or* a minimum, of utility, by choosing u. To see this, consider the problem

$$\max u(Y - c(u))$$

Imperfect competition

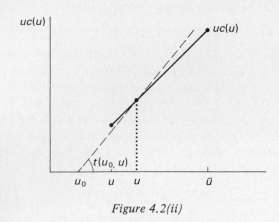

Figure 4.2(ii)

which leads to the first order condition (figure 4.1)

$$Y = (uc(u))' = uc'(u) + c(u) = t(u, u).$$

Our condition for finiteness is that no such consumer is present; to exclude such cases we require that *either* (a) $t(u, u) \notin [a, b]$, *so that all such consumers lie outside our range of incomes, or* (b) $t(u, u) < t(u_0, u)$, *so that any such consumer strictly prefers to make no purchase, rather than buy u*. (The latter case is illustrated in figure 4.2(ii).) Combining these two cases we obtain the following condition.

Condition (F). $t(u, u) \notin [\max(a, t(u_0, u)); b]$.

Remark 1. Condition (F) implies that for all (u, v), $t(u, v) \notin [\max(a, t(u_0, u)); b]$.

This latter condition excludes the appearance of any consumer indifferent between two goods u and v, at unit variable cost. That it follows from (F) is immediate from inspection of figure 4.1. (We might of course replace $t(u_0, u)$ here by $t(u_0, v)$, for if a consumer prefers u_0 to u, and is indifferent between u and v, he prefers u_0 to v also.)

Remark 2. Since $t(u, v)$ is continuous, it follows that $t(u, v)$ is uniformly (in u, v) bounded away from its corresponding interval $[\max(a, t(u_0, u)); b]$.

Remark 3. We here note two cases which will be of interest below.

For any two goods u and v, with $v > u$: (i) If $t(u, v) < \max(a, t(u_0, u))$, then any consumer willing to buy u at cost (in the sense of preferring this to making no purchase) will certainly prefer to buy v rather than u, if both are made available at cost. (ii) If $t(u, v) > b$, then any consumer willing to buy v at cost, will prefer to buy u rather than v if both goods are made available at cost.

In the Introduction, we note that there are two ways in which the 'finiteness' property may fail to hold; we can now interpret the restriction imposed by Condition (F) in terms of these two possibilities.

The first way in which Condition (F) may be violated is by the appearance of some $u \in (\underline{u}, \bar{u})$, such that a consumer of some income $t \in (a, b)$ attains a *maximum* of utility by consuming u, all products being available at unit variable cost. This case violates the requirement that all consumers rank products in the same order at cost; it is analogous to the familiar 'location' models, in that consumers with income above (below) t will prefer a quality above (below) u.

The remaining cases in which Condition (F) is violated are all analogous to the case noted in the Introduction, in which costs are zero, while the range of incomes extends to zero. These include the possibility that, for some $u \in (\underline{u}, \bar{u})$, a consumer of some income $t \in (a, b)$ attains a *minimum* of utility. (The analogy of this case to that in which the range of incomes extends to zero is developed in the proof of Proposition 3 below.) They also include a number of boundary cases; for example, where a consumer of income $t = a$ attains maximum utility at $u = \underline{u}$.

We now turn to our central results, showing that Condition (F) is necessary and sufficient for finiteness.

Proposition 2 (Sufficiency). *Condition (F) implies the finiteness property.*

Proof. First note, by virtue of the continuity of $t(u, v)$, and the differentiability of $c(u)$, that (F) implies that either $t(u, v) > b$ for all (u, v) or $t(u, v) < \max(a, t(u_0, u))$. (Note Remark 1 above.) In the former case, unit variable cost rises so steeply with quality that all consumers rank products (at cost) in decreasing order of quality; while in the latter case $c(u)$ is 'sufficiently flat', and all consumers rank products (at cost) in increasing order of quality.

We here establish the result for the latter case; the proof for the former case being similar.

We establish the result by showing that there exists some $\epsilon > 0$ such that the market share of any good, whose price exceeds unit variable cost, is greater than ϵ.

We first note what happens if two or more goods have the same quality level. Then, by the familiar Bertrand argument, they have price equal to unit variable cost at equilibrium. Moreover, it then follows immediately from Condition (F) that all products of lower quality have a zero market share. Now if the highest quality level is offered by two or more firms, our result therefore follows. Otherwise, denote the highest quality level produced by more than one firm as u_s, where we set $u_s = u_0$ in the case where all products are distinct.

Consider any good $k, k > 1$, which has a price exceeding unit variable cost, and for which $t_k > a$. Then the first order condition for profit maximization by firm k implies

$$t_{k+1} - t_k \geqslant (p_k - c_k)(r_{k-1,k} + r_{k,k+1} - 1).$$

Clearly

$$t_k > \max(a, t(u_0, u_{k-1}), t(u_s, u_{k-1})) = m, \quad \text{say.}$$

(Note $t_k > a$, and since the consumer of income t_k prefers good $k - 1$ at price $p_{k-1} \geqslant c_{k-1}$ to the zero good, we have $t_k > t(u_0, u_{k-1})$. Similarly, $t_k > t(u_0, u_s)$.) Hence

$$t_k = p_k r_{k-1,k} + p_{k-1}(1 - r_{k-1,k}) > m$$

or (remembering $r_{k-1,k} > 1$),

$$(p_k - c_k) r_{k-1,k} \geqslant m + p_{k-1}(r_{k-1,k} - 1) - c_k r_{k-1,k}$$

$$\geqslant m + c_{k-1}(r_{k-1,k} - 1) - c_k r_{k-1,k} = m - t(u_{k-1}, u_k).$$

But bearing in mind the first order conditions above, we have that the market share

$$(t_{k+1} - t_k) > (p_k - c_k) r_{k-1,k} \geqslant m - t(u_{k-1}, u_k)$$

$$> \max(a, t(u_0, u_{k-1})) - t(u_{k-1}, u_k).$$

By virtue of Remarks 1 and 2 above, this last expression is bounded away from zero, uniformly in u, from which our result follows.   *QED*

Proposition 3 (Necessity): *If Condition (F) is violated, then the finiteness property does not hold.*

Proof. As we noted above, we may divide instances in which (F) is violated into two cases according as: (i) $t(u, u)$ maximizes his utility by choosing u (at cost) or (ii) $t(u, u)$ minimizes his utility by choosing u (at cost).

Now in both of these cases the same construction can be used to show how any number of products can be entered in the neighbourhood of u; the essential property used is that there exists a consumer who is locally indifferent between a certain range of goods.

Each of these cases includes a number of subcases; we deal with one subcase, namely, $t(u, u) \in (a, b)$ and $u \in (\underline{u}, \bar{u})$ and $t(u_0, u) < t(u, u)$. The remaining 'boundary' cases can be dealt with in an obvious manner.

Case (i). Here the proof is immediate. We have some interval of qualities for which $t(q, q) \in (\max(a, t(u_0, q)), b)$ at each point q (from the differentiability of $uc(u)$ at q (figure 4.1)).

Thus each quality in this interval is preferred, at cost, to any alternative, by consumers of some income level (as in 'location' models).

Hence, given any sequence of products $u_1, \ldots, u_n$ in this neighbourhood, each good k certainly enjoys a positive market share at equilibrium. Thus any number of distinct products can co-exist with positive market shares and prices exceeding variable cost, and the finiteness property does not hold.

Case (*ii*). This case is more complicated; to show that there are n qualities which can co-exist we need to choose these qualities close to u. The construction of such a set of qualities is carried out in the Appendix.

Here we illustrate the intuition underlying this construction by describing a limiting case, as follows. Suppose there exists a consumer who is indifferent between an interval of qualities (i.e. $uc(u)$ is linear over this interval). Then consider any finite sequence $u_1, \ldots, u_n$ of qualities in this interval.

A product within this sequence will not be driven out of the market unless the seller of some higher quality product in the sequence sets price equal to cost. It suffices then to show that the top quality u_n is not sold at cost. But this is immediate, for this product can certainly earn positive profits by selling at a price exceeding cost.

This argument is of course analogous to that of the zero cost case, with $a = 0$, alluded to above. (As $t(u, u)$ is in the interior of the relevant interval, u_n can be sold to a richer consumer at a price above cost.)

The proof in the Appendix shows how this kind of argument extends to the case of a turning point of $uc(u)$ and thus establishes that the finiteness property does not hold. *QED*

6 DISCUSSION

The condition we have developed above is necessary and sufficient for the finiteness property. That condition refers to the relationship between consumers' willingness to pay for quality improvements, and the change in unit *variable* cost associated with those improvements; thus it involves the interplay of technology and tastes.

The 'finiteness' condition is likely to hold in those industries where the main burden of quality improvement takes the form of R & D, or other fixed costs. Unit variable costs, on the other hand, being the sole costs relevant to our present concerns, may rise only slowly with increases in quality. Indeed, insofar as product innovation is often accompanied by concomitant process innovation, unit variable costs may even fall.

It is this situation, where the 'finiteness' property holds along the relevant interval of qualities, which we have labelled a 'natural oligopoly'.

The finiteness condition does not *in itself* exclude an infinite number of firms; it is consistent with the presence of an arbitrarily large number of firms each selling an identical product at a price equal to unit variable cost, and a bounded number of firms offering a range of distinct, higher, qualities, at prices exceeding unit variable cost.

The implications of our present results are most clearly seen in the context of a model in which firms first incur some *arbitrarily small* fixed cost in entering the industry; then choose the qualities of their respective products, and then compete in price. Here, the presence of any fixed cost, however small, excludes the viability of firms whose prices are not strictly greater than unit variable cost at equilibrium. We have, in Shaked and Sutton (1982a), characterized a perfect equilibrium[2] in this three stage game (entry; choice of quality; choice of price). The outcome is that, given a large number of entrants, only a bounded number (there, two) will choose to enter; they will produce distinct products, and both will earn strictly positive profits at equilibrium. Further reductions in fixed costs, or an expansion in the size of the economy (once our bound is attained), have no effect on the equilibrium number of firms in the industry.

We remark, finally, on a number of directions in which certain assumptions of the present model may be relaxed:

Linearity of Utility Functions; Uniform Income Distribution

The special forms of the utility function and income distribution used here do not play a critical role, and our results may be extended to a wider class of function. (For a full treatment of existence, and finiteness, in the zero cost case, see Jaskold Gabszewicz et al. (1981a).)

Identical Consumers

The assumption that consumers be identical can be relaxed, once some ranking of consumers in order of their willingness to pay is available.

Smoothness of the Cost Function

The analysis extends readily to the case in which $c(u)$ is kinked. In fact a new possible case of 'finiteness' arises here, in that $c(u)$ may be 'flat' up to some point, and 'steep' thereafter, so that the finiteness property holds (consider the first and third zones in figure 4.2(i) joined at a kink). Consumers will now rank products (at cost) in increasing order of quality to the left of the kink, but in decreasing order to the right.

Multi-product Firms

The restriction that each firm produces a single product can be relaxed. If we allow firms to produce a number of products, the finiteness property still

2 See Selten 1975.

holds, in that a bound will exist to the number of *firms* which can enjoy positive market shares at a Nash equilibrium in prices.

APPENDIX

We here provide the construction referred to in the proof of Proposition 3 of the text. We show that where (F) is violated, then for any n, we can choose n distinct qualities sufficiently close to the point u at which (F) fails, such that all coexist with positive market share at a Nash equilibrium in prices. This proof covers both the cases, (i) and (ii), referred to in Proposition 3; while a direct proof for case (i) is possible, the present construction is needed for case (ii). The fact that the present construction covers both cases demonstrates clearly that what enables an infinite number of products to co-exist is the presence of a consumer who is locally (in quality) indifferent between products of differing qualities, where each is made available at cost.

The strategy of our construction is as follows: Choosing n qualities in a particular manner we write down the system of first order conditions which define equilibrium, and we show that a choice of qualities which are 'sufficiently close' ensures that all have a positive market share at equilibrium.

Let u denote the quality at which (F) is violated. Choose $u_n = u$ and $u_k - u_{k-1} = \epsilon$. Note from the definition of $t_1, \ldots, t_k$, that we can express $p_k r_{k-1,k}$ as a function of $t_1, \ldots, t_k$, namely,

$$p_k r_{k-1,k} = t_k + \ldots + t_2 + t_1 \alpha$$

where $\alpha = (u_1 - u_0)/\epsilon$. Similarly, we can express $c_k r_{k-1,k}$ as:

$$c_k r_{k-1,k} = t(u_{k-1}, u_k) + \ldots + t(u_1, u_2) + t(u_0, u_1) \alpha.$$

To simplify the equation, we define a new variable

$$s_k = t_k - t(u_{k-1}, u_k).$$

Then the first order conditions (4.3) take the form:

$$\begin{cases} s_2 + t(u_1, u_2) - a = s_1 \alpha. & s_1 \leqslant a - t(u_0, u_1), \\ s_2 + [t(u_1, u_2) - t(u_0, u_1)] = s_1(2 + \alpha), & s_1 \geqslant a - t(u_0, u_1), \end{cases}$$

$$s_{k+1} - s_k + [t(u_k, u_{k+1}) - t(u_{k-1}, u_k)] = 2(s_k + s_{k-1} + \ldots + s_2 + s_1 \alpha)$$
$$(k = 2, \ldots, n-1),$$

$$b - s_n - t(u_{n-1}, u_n) = s_n + s_{n-1} + \ldots + s_2 + s_1 \alpha.$$

(Note that the first order condition for firm 1 depends on whether 1's lower boundary is below a or not, i.e. whether all consumers buy one of the available products, or otherwise. Hence we have two equations for firm 1.)

From the first order condition for firm k, we may deduce that k's market share is

$$M^k = 2(s_k + \ldots + s_2 + s_1\alpha).$$

As $\epsilon \to 0$, the qualities chosen approach u and $\alpha \to \infty$, $t(u_k, u_{k+1}) \to t(u, u)$ for $k = 1, \ldots, n-1$ and $t(u_0, u_1) \to t(u_0, u)$.

We wish to show that in the limit as $\epsilon \to 0$, the market shares of all products are positive.

Since in any solution the s_k are bounded, it must be the case that s_1 approaches zero. Denote $s_1\alpha$ as $\bar{s}_1$, and write the equations for $\epsilon = 0$ (limit equations). Linearity and continuity guarantee that the solution of the limit system is the limit of the solutions. In the limit the relevant equation for firm 1 corresponds to the first of the pair cited above ($s_1 = 0$).

$$s_2 + [t(u, u) - a] = \bar{s}_1,$$

$$s_{k+1} - s_k = 2(s_k + \ldots + s_2 + \bar{s}_1) \qquad\qquad (k = 2, \ldots, n-1),$$

$$[b - t(u, u)] - s_n = s_n + \ldots + s_2 + \bar{s}_1.$$

Note that $b - t(u, u) > 0$ and $t(u, u) - a > 0$. To show that k's market share $M^k = 2(s_k + \ldots + s_2 + \bar{s}_1)$ is positive, we split the system of equations into two subsystems, and introduce the new variable M^k:

$$\text{System (A)} \quad \begin{cases} s_2 + [t(u, u) - a] = \bar{s}_1, \\[4pt] s_3 - s_2 = 2(s_2 + \bar{s}_1), \\[4pt] s_4 - s_3 = 2(s_3 + s_2 + \bar{s}_1), \\[4pt] \quad - \\[4pt] s_k - s_{k-1} = 2(s_{k-1} + \ldots + s_2 + \bar{s}_1), \\[4pt] M^k = 2(s_k + \ldots + s_2 + \bar{s}_1). \end{cases}$$

$$\text{System (B)} \quad \begin{cases} s_{k+1} - s_k = M^k, \\[4pt] s_{k+2} - s_{k+1} = 2s_{k+1} + M^k, \\[4pt] \quad - \\[4pt] s_n - s_{n-1} = 2(s_{n-1} + \ldots + s_{k+1}) + M^k, \\[4pt] b - t(u, u) - s_n = s_n + \ldots + s_{k+1} + M^k/2. \end{cases}$$

We show that the first system (A) defines s_k as an increasing linear function of M^k with a negative value at $M^k = 0$ and that the second system (B) defines s_k as a decreasing linear function with a positive value at $M^k = 0$. The two functions must therefore intersect at a positive M^k.

To verify these assertions, note that in (A) $s_2, s_3, \ldots, s_k, M^k$ are all strictly increasing linear functions of $\bar{s}_1$; hence s^k can be written as an increasing linear function of M^k. To see that $s^k < 0$ when $M^k = 0$, set $M^k = 0$ in the last equation, and substitute this in the preceding equation, to obtain $s_{k-1} = 3s_k$. Continuing backwards, we represent each s_j in turn, for $j \geqslant 2$, as $q^j s_j$, where q^j is some positive constant, and $\bar{s}_1$ as $q^2 s_2 + [t(u, u) - t(u_0, u)]$. Substituting this in the last equation, we have

$$(1 + q^2 + q^3 + \dots q^{k-1}) s_k + [t(u, u) - t(u_0, u)] = 0.$$

Hence $s_k(0) < 0$.

From system **(B)**, beginning from the first equation, we can write s_{k+1}, $\dots, s_n$ as linear functions of s_k, M^k, increasing in both arguments. Substituting this in the last equation, we find s^k as a decreasing function of M^k. This function is positive for $M^k = 0$ for (from the first equation) $s_{k+1} = s_k$, while from the second $s_{k+2} = 3s_k$, etc. All the s_k can be written as the product of a positive constant and s_k, whence from the last equation we have $s_k > 0$.

Hence the solution M^k is positive. This completes our construction.

REFERENCES

Friedman, J. W. 1977: *Oligopoly and the Theory of Games*. Amsterdam: North-Holland.

Gabszewicz, J. J. and Thisse, J.-F. 1980: Entry (and exit) in a differentiated industry. *Journal of Economic Theory*, **22**, 327–38.

Gabszewicz, J. J., Shaked, A., Sutton, J. and Thisse, J.-F. 1981a: Price competition among differentiated products: a detailed study of a Nash equilibrium. *ICERD Discussion Paper No. 37*, London School of Economics.

Gabszewicz, J. J., Shaked, A., Sutton, J. and Thisse, J.-F. 1981b: International trade in differentiated products. *International Economic Review*, **22**, 527–34.

Lancaster, K. 1979: *Variety, Equity and Efficiency*. New York: Columbia University Press.

Selten, R. 1975: Re-examination of the perfectness concept for equilibrium points in extensive games. *International Journal of Game Theory*, **4**, 25–55.

Shaked, A. and Sutton, J. 1982a: Relaxing price competition through product differentiation. *Review of Economic Studies*, **49**, 3–14 (chapter 5 in this volume).

Shaked, A. and Sutton, J. 1982b: Natural oligopolies and the gains from trade. *ICERD Discussion Paper No. 48*, London School of Economics.

Shaked, A. and Sutton, J. 1983: Natural oligopolies and international trade. In H. Kierzkowski (ed.), *Monopolistic Competition and International Trade*. Oxford: Oxford University Press.

5

Relaxing Price Competition Through Product Differentiation

A. Shaked and J. Sutton

The notion of a perfect equilibrium in a multi-stage game is used to characterize industry equilibrium under monopolistic competition, where products are differentiated by quality.

Central to the problem of providing adequate foundations for the analysis of monopolistic competition, is the problem of describing market equilibria in which firms choose both the specification of their respective products, and their prices. The present paper is concerned with a – very particular – model of such a market equilibrium. In this equilibrium, exactly two potential entrants will choose to enter the industry; they will choose to produce differentiated products; and both will make positive profits.

1   THE EQUILIBRIUM CONCEPT

Our present analysis is based on a three stage non-cooperative game. In the first stage, firms choose whether or not to enter the industry. At the end of the first stage, each firm observes which firms have entered, and which have not. In the second stage each firm chooses the quality of its product. Then, having observed its rivals' qualities, in the final stage of the game, each firm chooses its price. This three-stage process is intended to capture the notion that the price can in practice be varied at will, but a change in the specification of a product involves modification of the appropriate production facilities; while entry to the industry requires construction of a plant.

The strategies of firms specify actions to be taken in each of the three stages.

Thus a (pure) strategy takes one of two forms, 'do not enter', or else 'enter; choose a level of quality, dependent on the number of firms who have entered; and set price, dependent both on the number of entrants and on the quality of their respective products'.

The payoffs will be defined in terms of a model of consumer choice between the alternative products, in Section 2 below. They will be identified with the profit earned by the firm, less a 'cost of entry' of $\epsilon > 0$, for those who enter; and zero for non-entrants.

We may now define the solution concept. As in any non-cooperative game, we might investigate the set of Nash equilibria. Here, as is often the case, that set may be very large. We therefore introduce the now familiar concept of a perfect equilibrium (Selten 1975).

An n-tuple of strategies is a perfect equilibrium in this three-stage game, if, after any stage, that part of the firms' strategies pertaining to the game consisting of those stages which remain, form a Nash equilibrium in that game.

It follows immediately from this that, after any stage, that part of the firms' strategies pertaining to the game consisting of those stages which remain, in fact form a perfect equilibrium in that game.

Thus, for example, when firms have decided whether to enter, and have chosen their qualities, we require that their price strategies are a Nash equilibrium, i.e. a non-cooperative price equilibrium, in the single remaining stage of the game.

To study such a perfect equilibrium, we begin, therefore, by analysing the final stage of the game – being the choice of price, given the number of entrants and the qualities of their respective products (Section 2). We will then proceed, in Section 3, to examine the choice of quality by firms, and in Section 4 we consider the entry decision. Section 5 contains a summary of the argument, and develops some conclusions.

2   PRICE COMPETITION

Consider a number of firms producing distinct, substitute goods.[1] We label their respective products by an index $k = 1, \ldots, n$ where firm k sells product k at price p_k.

Assume a continuum of consumers identical in tastes but differing in income; incomes are uniformly distributed, namely the density equals unity on some support $0 < a \leqslant t \leqslant b$.

Consumers make indivisible and mutually exclusive purchases from among these n goods, in the sense that a consumer either makes no purchase, or else buys exactly one unit from one of the n firms.[2] We denote by $U(t, k)$ the

1 The model of consumer choice over alternative products described here follows Jaskold Gabszewicz and Thisse (1979, 1980). These authors analyse a non-cooperative price equilibrium between firms, the quality of whose products is fixed exogenously. This corresponds to the last stage of our present three-stage process.

2 Thus our consumer buys *either* this product, or that. Contrast Dixit and Stiglitz (1977).

utility achieved by consuming one unit of product k and t units of 'income' (the latter may be thought of as a Hicksian 'composite commodity', measured as a continuous variable); and by $U(t, 0)$ the utility derived from consuming t units of income only.

Assume that the utility function takes the form

$$U(t, k) = u_k \cdot t \tag{5.1}$$

with $u_0 < u_1 < \ldots < u_n$ (i.e. the products are labelled in increasing order of quality).

Let

$$C_k = \frac{u_k}{u_k - u_{k-1}}$$

(whence $C_k > 1$). Then we may define the income level t_k such that a consumer with income t_k is indifferent between good k at price p_k and good $k - 1$ at price p_{k-1}, namely

$$U(t_k - p_k, k) = U(t_k - p_{k-1}, k - 1)$$

whence

$$t_1 = p_1 C_1$$

and

$$t_k = p_{k-1}(1 - C_k) + p_k C_k. \tag{5.2}$$

This is easily checked by reference to (5.1).

Now it follows immediately on inspection of (5.1) that consumers with income $t > t_k$ strictly prefer good k at price p_k to good $k - 1$ at p_{k-1}, and conversely; whence consumers are partitioned into segments corresponding to the successive market shares of rival firms.

Assuming zero costs the profit (revenue) of the kth firm is:

$$R_1 = \begin{cases} p_1(t_2 - a) & t_1 \leqslant a \\ p_1(t_2 - t_1) & t_1 \geqslant a \end{cases}$$

$$R_k = p_k(t_{k+1} - t_k), \quad 1 < k < n \tag{5.3}$$

$$R_n = p_n(b - t_n).$$

Now, at equilibrium (if it exists), it follows trivially that the top quality product will enjoy a positive market share; moreover if any product has zero market share, so also do all lower quality products.

Now where n products co-exist at equilibrium (i.e. each of these n goods has a positive market share) the first order necessary conditions for profit (revenue) maximization take the form, for $k = 1$,

$$t_2 - a - p_1(C_2 - 1) = 0 \qquad t_1 \leqslant a$$

$$t_2 - t_1 - p_1[(C_2 - 1) + C_1] = 0 \qquad t_1 \geqslant a$$

for $k = 2, \ldots, n - 1$,

$$t_{k+1} - t_k - p_k[(C_{k+1} - 1) + C_k] = 0 \qquad\qquad (5.4)$$

for $k = n$,

$$b - t_n - p_n C_n = 0.$$

We may now proceed to establish:

Lemma 1. *Let $b < 4a$. Then for any Nash equilibrium involving the distinct goods $n, n - 1, \ldots, 1$ at most two products (the top two) have a positive market share at equilibrium.*

Proof. Assume that there exists a Nash equilibrium in which three or more products have a positive market share at equilibrium. From inspection of the necessary conditions for profit maximization (5.4), and remembering $C_k > 1$, it follows that, for $k > 1$, and $k = n$, respectively, by rewriting the first order conditions and using the definition of t_k,

$$t_{k+1} - 2t_k - p_k(C_{k+1} - 1) - p_{k-1}(C_k - 1) = 0;$$

$$b - 2t_n - p_{n-1}(C_n - 1) = 0$$

whence

$$b > 2t_n, \qquad t_{k+1} > 2t_k$$

whence

$$4t_{n-1} < b.$$

Now by assumption $b < 4a$, so that $t_{n-1} < a$, i.e. the top two firms cover the market. Thus equilibrium involves at most two products.   ‖

The idea here is that price competition between 'high quality' products drives their prices down to a level at which not even the poorest consumer would prefer to buy certain lower quality products even at price zero. Clearly, the number of products which can survive at equilibrium depends on the distribution of income. Lemma 1 provides a restriction, that $b < 4a$, which is sufficient to limit this number to *at most* two; we shall in fact be concerned with this case in what follows.

It will be convenient at this point, then, to cite the special form of the revenue functions and the first order conditions for the case where $n = 2$, i.e. where exactly two firms enjoy a positive market share.

We define

$$V = \frac{u_2 - u_0}{u_2 - u_1} = \frac{C_2 - 1}{C_1} + 1 \tag{5.5}$$

being a measure of the relative qualities of goods 1 and 2, and the residual good 0.

Applying equation (5.2) we have here that

$$p_1 = \frac{t_1}{C_1} \quad \text{and} \quad p_2 = \frac{t_2 + t_1(V - 1)}{C_2} \tag{5.6}$$

Using equations (5.5), (5.6) we may re-write the first order conditions for profit maximization in terms of t_1, t_2, V, namely

firm 1:

$$\begin{aligned} t_2 &= a + t_1(V - 1) & t_1 &\leqslant a \\ t_2 &= t_1(V + 1) & t_1 &\geqslant a \end{aligned} \tag{5.7}$$

firm 2:

$$b - 2t_2 = t_1(V - 1). \tag{5.8}$$

We identify three regions as illustrated in figure 5.1. For a certain range of p_2 chosen by firm 2, the optimal reply of firm 1 leads to an outcome (t_1, t_2) in region II, i.e. $t_1 = a, aV \leqslant t_2 \leqslant a(V + 1)$. Over this range firm 1 leaves its price constant as p_2 varies; at the price p_1 it chooses, the poorest consumer is just willing to buy good 1. Firm 1 faces a demand schedule which is kinked at this price level (given p_2); and either raising or lowering price reduces

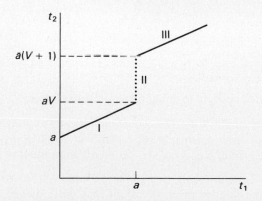

Figure 5.1 The first order conditions for profit maximization by firm 1.

revenue. Thus we have a corner solution, and the equalities of (5.7) are replaced by a pair of inequalities.

Equation (5.8) describes a decreasing function of t_1,

$$t_2 = \tfrac{1}{2}[b - t_1(V-1)].$$

The intersection of (5.7), (5.8) defines the unique equilibrium pair (t_1, t_2), and so the equilibrium pair (p_1, p_2).

Whether the solution lies in region I, II or III depends on where the decreasing function (5.8) cuts the vertical $t_1 = a$, namely

region I if $\qquad\qquad V \geqslant \dfrac{b+a}{3a}$

region II if $\qquad \dfrac{b+a}{3a} \geqslant V \geqslant \dfrac{b-a}{3a}$

region III if $\qquad\qquad V \leqslant \dfrac{b-a}{3a}$

Thus the solution lies in region I when the qualities are 'close', and in region III when the qualities are 'far apart'.

If the solution lies in region III, then $t_1 > a$ and some consumers purchase neither good. If the solution lies in region II then all consumers purchase one or other good – the market is 'covered', and the poorest consumer is indifferent between buying the low quality product 1 or not. In region I the market is again covered, but now the poorest consumer strictly prefers to purchase product 1.

Moreover, we note from equations (5.7), (5.8) that,

in region I:

$$t_1 = \frac{b-2a}{3(V-1)}, \quad t_2 = \frac{b+a}{3} \qquad\qquad (5.9)$$

while

in region II:

$$t_1 = a, \quad t_2 = \tfrac{1}{2}[b - a(V-1)]. \qquad\qquad (5.10)$$

We are now in a position to strengthen our earlier result.

Lemma 2. *Let $2a < b < 4a$. Then of any n firms offering distinct products, exactly two will have positive market shares at equilibrium. Moreover, at equilibrium, the market is covered, i.e. the equilibrium is not in region III.*

Proof. From Lemma 1 only two goods (at most) will survive with positive market shares and positive price. Hence we may write the equations for this case as developed above.

We note from figure 5.1 that the decreasing function (5.8) lies above a for $t_1 = 0$. (Note $t_2(0) = b/2 > a$.)

Hence the two functions (5.7), (5.8) intersect at a point such that $t_1 > 0$, $t_2 > a$, so that the two products co-exist with positive market shares.

To verify that this solution is indeed an equilibrium, it must further be shown that the second order conditions are satisfied, i.e. the revenue function of firm 1, given p_2, is concave, over all p_1; and conversely. This may be verified in a straightforward manner. Moreover, since $b < 4a$, $(b - a)/3a < 1$ and the condition for the solution to be in region III cannot be met (as $V > 1$) so the market is covered. ‖

From this point forward we shall assume that $2a < b < 4a$.

The preceding discussion establishes the existence of a unique price pair which forms a Nash equilibrium in prices, for any two distinct levels of product quality. Moreover, both firms enjoy strictly positive revenue. If on the other hand the firms choose the same level of quality, our use of a non-cooperative price equilibrium ensures that both prices become zero (the Bertrand duopoly case); so that both firms have revenue zero at equilibrium. In either case, the equilibrium vector of payoffs (revenues) is uniquely determined via our preceding discussion.

We now turn to the case where more than two firms enter the industry. Still assuming, as always, that $2a < b < 4a$, we distinguish two cases. If one firm has a quality lower than either of its rivals, it has a zero market share, and so revenue zero, as shown in Lemma 1. If two (or three) firms have an equal lowest quality, then the price of this lowest quality product is zero at equilibrium (again from the usual Bertrand argument). In either case, any firm setting the lowest, or equal lowest, quality, has revenue zero at equilibrium. Thus, the equilibrium vector of payoffs (revenues) of the firms present in the industry is uniquely determined via our preceding characterization.

3   COMPETITION IN QUALITY

We now turn to the preceding stage of the process, in which firms choose quality. Let k denote the number of firms who have entered. We introduce the notation G^k to denote the two-stage game in which quality is first chosen, and then price.

Finding a perfect equilibrium in G^k is equivalent to finding a Nash equilibrium in qualities, the payoffs arising from any vector of qualities being defined by the (unique) equilibrium vector of revenues in the 'choice of price' game of the preceding section.

We suppose for the moment that the number of firms is exactly two, deferring the question of further 'potential entrants' until later.

Each firm chooses a level of quality, being a value u_i, $u_0 < u_i < \bar{u}$, where $\bar{u}$ is an exogenously given upper bound on quality.

We introduce the notation $R(u;v)$ to denote the revenue of a firm whose product is of quality u, its rival's product being of quality v, at a Nash equilibrium in prices.

We will establish the existence of an equilibrium involving differentiated products, as a consequence of two properties of the revenue function $R(u;v)$. The first property, stated in Lemma 3, is that, at equilibrium, the revenue of the firm offering the higher quality product is greater. The second property (Lemma 4) states that the revenue of both firms increases as the quality of the better product improves. The latter property reflects the effect of the lessening of price competition as qualities diverge, and is the key to the existence of an equilibrium with differentiated products in the present analysis. (This runs counter to the classic Hotelling 'Principle of Minimal Differentiation', of course (Hotelling 1928; d'Aspremont et al. 1979).

Lemma 3. *For any two qualities $u > v$, the top quality firm enjoys greater revenue than its rival, i.e.*

$$R(u;v) > R(v;u).$$

Proof. Let the pair of prices p, q for u and v respectively be a Nash equilibrium in prices. Trivially, $p > q$. But one strategy open to the top firm is to set its price equal to q (whereupon the low quality firm has sales zero), and its sales clearly exceed those of its rival in the initial equilibrium. Hence our result follows immediately.   ‖

Lemma 4. *The revenues of both firms increase as the quality of the better product improves, i.e.*

$$R(v;u) \text{ and } R(u;v) \text{ are increasing in } u \text{ for } u \geqslant v.$$

Proof. We establish the result separately for the two cases where the outcome is in region I, and in region II, respectively.

We begin by writing down the revenue of both firms in region I. We have from (5.9) that the revenue of firm 1 is

$$R(u_1;u_2) = p_1(t_2 - a) = \frac{t_1}{C_1}\left(\frac{b - 2a}{3}\right)$$

$$= \left(\frac{b - 2a}{3}\right)^2 \frac{1}{(V-1)\,C_1} = \left(\frac{b - 2a}{3}\right)^2 \frac{u_2 - u_1}{u_1} \qquad (5.11)$$

while the revenue of firm 2 is

$$R(u_2;u_1) = p_2(b - t_2) = \left(\frac{2b - a}{3}\right)^2 \frac{1}{C_2} = \left(\frac{2b - a}{3}\right)^2 \left(\frac{u_2 - u_1}{u_2}\right). \qquad (5.12)$$

Both these expressions increase with u_2, for $u_2 \geqslant u_1$, whence our result follows.

In region II we have from (5.10) that

$$R(u_1; u_2) = p_1(t_2 - a) = \frac{a[b - a(V + 1)]}{2C_1}$$

$$R(u_2; u_1) = p_2(b - t_2) = \frac{[b + a(V - 1)]^2}{4C_2}.$$

That $R(u_1; u_2)$ increases in u_2 follows on noting that V falls as u_2 increases (note C_1 is independent of u_2).

For $R(u_2; u_1)$, we note that, by definition of C_1, C_2, V we have

$$C_2 = C_1(V - 1) + 1$$

whence the logarithmic derivative of $R(u_2; u_1)$ w.r.t. V is

$$\frac{2a}{b + a(V - 1)} - \frac{C_1}{C_1(V - 1) + 1} = \frac{aC_1(V - 1) + 2a - C_1 b}{[b + a(V - 1)][C_1(V - 1) + 1]}$$

where, for region II,

$$\frac{b - a}{3a} \leqslant V \leqslant \frac{b + a}{3a}.$$

The denominator is positive since $V > 1$ so the sign coincides with that of the numerator. We wish to establish therefore, that the numerator is negative; but since it is a linear increasing function of V it suffices to show that it is negative when V takes its maximum value in region II, i.e. $V = (b + a)/3a$.

But here the numerator is

$$C_1\left(\frac{b - 2a}{3}\right) + 2a - C_1 b = 2a - \tfrac{2}{3}C_1(a + b) < 2a(1 - C_1) < 0$$

where we have used the fact that $b > 2a$. Thus $R(u_2; u_1)$ decreases with increasing V, i.e. is increasing in u_2. ||

We now define the 'optimal reply from below' as follows. Let one firm set quality u. Then, of all qualities on the restricted range $[u_0, u]$ we choose that level v which maximizes the revenue $R(v, u)$. Since $R(v; u)$ is continuous in v it follows that for any $u, R(v; u)$ takes a maximum over v in the closed set $[u_0, u]$. Moreover, for $v = u$, $R(v; u) = 0$, while for $u_0 < v < u$, $R(v; u) > 0$; so that the maximum is attained at a quality strictly less than u.

We define the set[3] of optimal replies

---

[3] In fact a lengthy development shows that the optimal reply from below, $\rho(u)$, is unique, but this is not required for our present purposes.

$$\rho(u) = \{v \mid R(v;u) = \max R(s;u); u_0 \leqslant s \leqslant u\}$$

and our preceding remarks imply that $\rho(u) \neq \emptyset$ and $u \notin \rho(u)$ for $u_0 < u$.
We may now establish[4]

Proposition 1. *The game G^2 has a perfect equilibrium in pure strategies; the outcome involves distinct qualities, and both firms earn positive revenue (profits) at equilibrium.*

Proof. We demonstrate the existence of such an equilibrium as follows. Choose a $v \in \rho(\bar{u})$. Then we will show that the pair $(\bar{u}, v)$ is a Nash equilibrium in the 'choice of quality' game, with the payoffs defined as the revenue obtained in the 'choice of price' game of the preceding sections, and so is a perfect equilibrium in G^2.

Let the firm setting $\bar{u}$ be labelled 2, and its rival 1. To show that $(\bar{u}, v)$ is a Nash equilibrium, we note that, given a choice of $\bar{u}$ by firm 2, then the choice of v by firm 1 is optimal, by definition of $\rho(u)$.

To complete our proof we show that, given a choice of v by firm 1, $\bar{u}$ is an optimal choice for firm 2.

We divide the argument into two parts. First note that $\bar{u}$ is preferred to any $u \geqslant v$ by virtue of Lemma 4. Secondly, consider the payoff to firm 2 if it chooses any quality u_2, where $u_0 \leqslant u_2 < v$.

Then we have

$$R(u_2; v) \leqslant R(u_2; \bar{u}) \qquad \text{by Lemma 4.}$$

But

$$R(u_2; \bar{u}) \leqslant R(v; \bar{u}) \qquad \text{as } v \in \rho(\bar{u}).$$

While

$$R(v; \bar{u}) \leqslant R(\bar{u}; v) \qquad \text{by Lemma 3.}$$

Hence

$$R(u_2; v) \leqslant R(\bar{u}; v)$$

and the choice of $\bar{u}$ is indeed optimal for firm 2 as required. ‖

We have thus established that with two firms present, a Nash equilibrium in qualities exists, which is a perfect equilibrium in the two stage game ('choice of quality, choice of price').

---

4 It may be shown indirectly using the Lemma of Roberts and Sonnenschein (1976), that an equilibrium exists in the present model, but the present direct proof is much shorter.

We now consider the outcome if $k > 2$ firms are present. We aim to show here, (a) that the choice of $\bar{u}$ by all firms is a Nash equilibrium,[5] and (b) that for *any* Nash equilibrium, all firms have revenue zero. (Up to this point we have confined our attention to equilibria in pure strategies. In fact the proof of (b) extends trivially to mixed strategies, and we will establish the result in this more general setting below.)

Proposition 2. (a) *The game* $G^k, k > 2$ *has a Nash equilibrium*

$$u_i = \bar{u}, 1 \leqslant i \leqslant k.$$

(b) *For every Nash equilibrium of* G^k *the payoff for each firm is zero.*

Proof. (a) Suppose all firms but one choose $\bar{u}$. Then at least two firms sell an identical product of quality $\bar{u}$; following the familiar Bertrand argument for a non-cooperative price equilibrium between two firms selling an identical product, we have immediately that each of these firms sets price zero. Hence our remaining firm earns payoff zero for any choice $u \leqslant \bar{u}$; for either its price is zero (at $u = \bar{u}$) or its sales are zero (at $u < \bar{u}$). Hence G^k has a Nash equilibrium, $u_i = \bar{u}, 1 < i < k$.

(b) In order to establish this, we show that in every perfect equilibrium at least two firms adopt the pure strategy $\bar{u}$; whence the result follows immediately.

Let μ^i be a probability measure on $[u_0, \bar{u}]$ and let $\{\mu'\}$ be a Nash equilibrium for G^k. Let V_i be the lim inf of the support of μ^i. Assume $V_1 \leqslant V_2 \leqslant \ldots \leqslant V_k$, and furthermore assume that if any of the μ^i has an atom at V_1 then we label the firms so as to denote it (or one such firm) as 1.

First we show that the payoff of 1 is zero. If V_1 is an atom of μ^1 then the pure strategy V_1 yields payoff zero to firm 1 (given $\mu^2, \ldots, \mu^k$); for here the probability is zero that firm 1 offers the (sole) highest quality; or the (sole) second highest quality, product, whence from the analysis of the non-cooperative price equilibrium it earns payoff zero.

If, on the other hand, μ^1 does not have an atom at V_1 then there is a descending sequence of points in the support of μ^1 with limit V_1. The payoff of all these points as pure strategies is the same, but it tends to zero in the limit where quality approaches V_1: for the probability of the limit point V_1 being the (sole) highest quality, or the (sole) second highest quality, is zero (none of the μ^i has an atom at V_1). Thus the payoff to firm 1 is zero.

We may now deduce that at least two firms adopt the pure strategy $\bar{u}$. Suppose firstly that none of the strategies $\mu^1, \ldots, \mu^k$ is the pure strategy $\bar{u}$.

---

5 We repeat that a perfect equilibrium in G^k is equivalent to a Nash equilibrium in qualities, the payoffs arising from any vector of qualities being defined by the (unique) equilibrium values of revenue in the 'choice of price' game.

Then there is a neighbourhood of $\bar{u}$, and an $\epsilon > 0$, such that with probability $\epsilon > 0$ none of the firms $2, \ldots, k$ choose a quality in that neighbourhood. Now we have just shown that the payoff to firm 1 is zero; we now note that μ^1 can not be an optimal strategy, for by choosing the pure strategy $\bar{u}$ firm 1 can now achieve a strictly positive payoff.

Thus at least one of the strategies $\mu^1, \ldots, \mu^k$ is the pure strategy $\bar{u}$. Denote it μ^k. Assume that no firm adopts this strategy. Then there is a neighbourhood of $\bar{u}$, and an $\epsilon > 0$, such that with probability $\epsilon > 0$ none of the firms $2, \ldots, k-1$ choose a quality in this neighbourhood. Firm 1 can thus earn a strictly positive payoff by choosing its quality in this interval.

Hence at least two of the $\mu^1, \ldots, \mu^k$ are the pure strategy $\bar{u}$. Hence all payoffs are zero. ∥

4 ENTRY

We have now shown how, in the present model, only two firms can survive with positive prices, and positive market shares, at equilibrium; and how the entry of further firms leads to a configuration in which the top quality product is available at price zero, while all firms earn zero revenue (profits).

We now consider the analysis of entry to the industry. We introduce a 'small' cost[6] of entry $\epsilon > 0$; our results in fact are independent of the size of ϵ. We define the game G_ϵ^k as the game G^k introduced above, with ϵ subtracted from all payoffs. Let there be n potential entrants; they play the three-stage game E_ϵ^n as follows. At the first stage each firm decides whether to enter or not; according as the number who choose to enter is k, these k firms then play the game G_ϵ^k. Those firms who choose not to enter receive payoff zero.

We establish:

Proposition 3. *For any $\epsilon > 0$ (sufficiently small), and any number $n > 2$ of potential entrants*

(a) *there exists a perfect equilibrium in which two firms enter; and in which they produce distinct products, and have positive revenues (profits).*

(b) *no perfect equilibrium exists in which $k > 2$ firms enter.*

Proof. Corresponding to any pair[7] of firms drawn from n potential entrants, given a decision by these two firms to enter, the payoff to each of the other firms from not entering is zero, while the payoff from entering is

---

6 Trivially, if ϵ is sufficiently large, no firm will enter.

7 Of course *any* pair of firms may enter. Similarly, in the 'choice of quality' stage, we have, corresponding to the equilibrium $(\bar{u}, v)$, its mirror image $(v, \bar{u})$. The question of *which* firm enters, or sets the higher quality, is outside the scope of this type of model.

$-\epsilon$ by virtue of Proposition 2. This establishes (b). Where exactly two firms enter however, each earns a positive payoff (since ϵ is 'small'); and then (a) follows immediately from Proposition 1.   ‖

5 SUMMARY AND CONCLUSIONS

We have here described a perfect equilibrium of a three-stage game in which a number of firms choose firstly, whether to enter an industry; secondly, the quality of their respective products, and thirdly, their prices.

At the final stage of the game, in a non-cooperative price equilibrium, there is an upper bound to the number of firms which enjoy positive market shares, at positive prices (production costs being assumed zero). This reflects the fact that competition between the surviving 'high quality' products drives their prices down to a point at which not even the poorest consumer prefers the (excluded) low quality products even at price zero. This number reflects *inter alia* the utility functions of consumers and the shape of the income distribution. We have here taken a particular form of utility function and assumed a uniform distribution of incomes on $[a, b]$ where $2a < b < 4a$; whence our upper bound is 2. It can be shown by extending our discussion in a natural way, that this upper bound rises as the range of incomes increases.

We establish two results which form the core of the analysis.

(a) We show that where the number of firms equals two, these two firms will choose distinct qualities, and both will enjoy positive profit at equilibrium. The intuitive idea behind this result is that, as their qualities become close, price competition between the increasing similar products reduces the profit of both firms.

(b) We show that if three or more firms are present, competition in choice of quality drives all firms to set the same 'top' level of quality permitted while prices, and so profits, become zero. This reflects the fact that no one of the three firms will now prefer to set its quality lower than that of its two rivals, as it would thereby certainly earn revenue zero at equilibrium.

Combining (a) and (b) and introducing a small cost of entry ϵ, we deduce that *the only perfect equilibrium in the three-stage game is one in which exactly two firms enter; in which they produce distinct products, and earn positive profits at equilibrium.* Moreover, this equilibrium configuration is independent of ϵ.

A natural question concerns the extension of this model to cases where the upper bound on the number of products which can survive exceeds two. This remains an open question; while property (b) generalizes readily, we have not succeeded in generalizing property (a). Our present argument does not generalize in an obvious manner here.

REFERENCES

d'Aspremont, C., Jaskold Gabszewicz, J. and Thisse, J.-F. 1979: On Hotelling's 'stability in competition'. *Econometrica*, **47**, 1145–50.

Dixit, A. and Stiglitz, J. E. 1977: Monopolistic competition and optimum product diversity. *American Economic Review*, **67**, 297–308.

Gabsewicz, J. J. and Thisse, J.-F. 1979: Price competition, quality and income disparities. *Journal of Economic Theory*, **20**, 340–59.

Gabszewicz, J. J. and Thisse, J.-F. 1980: Entry (and exit) in a differentiated industry. *Journal of Economic Theory*, **22**, 327–38.

Hotelling, H. 1928: Stability in competition. *Economic Journal*, **39**, 41–57.

Roberts, J. and Sonnenschein, H. 1976: On the existence of Cournot equilibrium without concave profit functions. *Journal of Economic Theory*, **13**, 112–17.

Selten, R. 1975: Re-examination of the perfectness concept for equilibrium points in extensive games. *International Journal of Game Theory*, **4**, 25–55.

6

The Theory of
Technological Competition

P. Dasgupta

1   THE SCHUMPETERIAN HERITAGE

It is not self-evident that economists ought to engage in the task of explaining the characteristics of technological innovations. It is even less evident that development and inventive activities are related to the structure of economic organizations. Or so it would seem from the near-complete absence of a discussion of such issues in resource allocation theory.[1] So would it seem as well from the sheer volume of effort that has been spent over the past quarter of a century to try to demonstrate that economic forces are a prime architect of technological change.[2] If there is a single driving force behind these empirical investigations it is the writings of Joseph Schumpeter (most especially perhaps his *Capitalism, Socialism and Democracy*. See Schumpeter 1976). Since recent developments in the theory of technological competition have addressed a few of the empirical findings, they reflect this heritage as well.

Economists are prone to having hero-figures. In the economics of technological change Joseph Schumpeter continues to reign as the undisputed Godfather. As with all such personalities there is much discussion about what he actually *meant*. Nevertheless it is clear that the several components of his scheme of thought are not all equally persuasive and some, it can be argued, have been downright detrimental to further developments of the subject. Thus, for example, Rosenberg (1976), chapter 4, has shown how Schumpeter's obsession with the act of *innovation*, and the dominant role he gave to charismatic entrepreneurs at the vanguard of clusters of innovation, has deflected attention from economic aspects of *inventive* and *development*

---

1 Leading graduate texts on microeconomics, such as Malinvaud (1972), Layard and Walters (1978) and Varian (1978), contain absolutely no discussion of these matters.
2 Excellent documentations of this empirical research are in Kamien and Schwartz (1975) and (1982), chapter 3, and Boylan (1977). Rosenberg (ed.) (1971) continues to be the best collection of essays on the subject.

activity. But the Schumpeterian view that there are periodic appearances of clusters of innovation (and this forms an important ingredient in his theory of business cycles) should be distinguished from his beliefs about the influence of the size of firms and the concentration of industries on technological change. And it is the latter which has had much the greater influence on recent thinking. Here too, his influence – or to be more precise, the influence of what economists *thought* he meant – has not been entirely beneficial.[3]

The point is that, like other system-builders, Schumpeter did not write with the utmost clarity. It is easy enough to be beguiled into thinking that one understands the Schumpeterian vision until, that is, one attempts to formalize it. Take for example Schumpeter's claim that monopolistic firms *supply* more innovations than competitive firms.[4] On this he says:

there are superior methods available to the monopolist which either are not available at all to a crowd of competitors or are not available to them readily: for there are advantages which, though not strictly unattainable on the competitive level of enterprise, are as a matter of fact secured only on the monopoly level, for instance, because monopolization may increase the sphere of influence of the better, and decrease the sphere of influence of the inferior, brains, or because the monopoly enjoys a disproportionately higher financial standing. (Schumpeter 1976, p. 101.)

Here Schumpeter seems to be saying that large size has distinct advantages, whereas elsewhere on the same page he recognizes that monopoly and large size are not synonymous. Now, someone interested in the structure of *industries*, but not so much in the internal organization of *firms*, would be justified in treating an assertion about the relationship between the size of firms and their research and development (R & D) opportunities as a *hypothesis*. In this sense Schumpeter's belief that there are increasing returns to scale in R & D both to the size of R & D establishment and to the size of the firm engaged in R & D, *is* a hypothesis.[5] But the same status must not be awarded to claims about the relationship between *monopolistic* firms and their supply of innovations, for such claims ought to be derivable propositions within any theory which purports to embrace the structure of industries.

Here Schumpeter is less than clear. His famous chapter on the process of creative destruction (Schumpeter 1976, chapter 7) suggests strongly that he regarded the *threat* of entry by rival innovators as providing the essential spur

3 For different illustrations of this, see Fisher and Temin (1973) and Dasgupta and Stiglitz (1977, 1980a).

4 His claim that a monopolistic firm will have a greater *demand* for innovations (because its market power enables it to benefit more from innovations) has been shown to be false by Arrow (1962a).

5 Fisher and Temin (1973) provide a powerful critique of a large body of literature that has attempted to test this hypothesis.

to a sitting monopolist to innovate. But I have found no passage in which he asks whether the incentives for innovation would be less or more in a competitive industry if the innovator had guarantee of some form of patent protection. One can argue that recent propositions on pre-emptive patenting provide some partial support for the Schumpeterian view on the relationship between monopoly and the supply of innovations (see Dasgupta and Stiglitz 1980b and Gilbert and Newbery 1982). But these are derived propositions, not hypotheses. (See Section 5 below.)

The lack of clarity in Schumpeter's writings is most conspicuous when one reflects that an entire generation of researchers has interpreted his views on market structure and innovative activity in *causal* terms: *from* market structure *to* innovative activity. Admittedly it has been customary to note in passing that the influence is not unidirectional, but the theoretical literature in which both market structure and innovative activity are endogenous remains sparse.[6] Most theoretical treatments of the subject take industrial structure as a datum. What is possibly more disturbing is that empirical observations on the relationship between innovative activity and the structure of industries have consistently been given a causal interpretation. (See Nelson et al. 1967 and Kamien and Schwartz 1975, 1982 for references. An important exception is the work of Levin and Reiss 1982.) The policy implications of such interpretations are rather obvious. For example, if it is held that industrial concentration is a *reason* for the intensity of innovative activity, then presumably anti-trust legislation will be called into question. The question is whether industrial structure ought to be raw data in a theory of technological competition. Quite obviously, except in the short run, it ought not. It would seem then that innovative activity and industrial structure both in turn depend on such ingredients as technological 'opportunities', demand conditions, the nature of capital markets and the legal structure.[7] At least some of

6 Dasgupta and Stiglitz (1977, 1980a, 1980b, 1981), Levin (1978), Loury (1979) and Futia (1980) are examples of this small literature. Nordhaus (1969) is an important precursor. Scherer (1967a), Barzel (1968) and Kamien and Schwartz (1972, 1978) have suggestive features. But they are not comprehensively explored. von Weizsacker (1980), chapters 8 and 9, contains interesting, elaborate constructions. But he does not model industrial structure explicitly, and in any case, he is for the most part concerned with *biases* in R & D activity in a market economy relative to a socially managed one. Nelson and Winter (1977, 1978) are part of an impressive research programme on Schumpeterian competition. Theirs *is* a somewhat different approach to these issues. But it would appear that *analytical* results are hard to come by in this approach. A serious defect in Futia (1980) and Dasgupta and Stiglitz (1981) is that in order to admit 'realistic' features into their models of competition ad hoc assumptions had to be imposed on what firms attempt to achieve and what they can or cannot do. In what follows I want to avoid ad hoc assumptions (such as the precise form of bounded rationality) very strongly.

7 J. K. Galbraith has consistently emphasized that demand conditions are significantly influenced by expenditures on persuasion. (See e.g. Galbraith 1974.) This can be accom-

the empirical explorations have tested hypotheses about such dependence. It is of considerable interest to know whether simple theoretical considerations can accommodate such empirical findings. In the following section I shall present a set of such empirical findings. The remainder of the paper will be devoted to an examination of theoretical constructions that can cope with them. To be explicit, in Section 3 I review a model of *process* innovation and look at the nature of a particular form of technological competition. In Section 4 I discuss the issue of imitative research briefly. A central feature of the models in these two sections is that firms make their moves *simultaneously*. In Section 4, therefore, I consider situations where it is natural to have firms move *sequentially*. The issue of pre-emptive patenting, which is the subject of this section, is best discussed in this way. One of my purposes is to locate conditions under which a sitting monopolist pre-empts on *all* potential patents. I shall be able to report only some limited results on this question. But they are suggestive. Finally, in Section 6 I attempt to classify models of technological competition. I argue that an essential distinction is based on whether the game describing the form of technological competition is *continous* or *discontinuous*. This depends, quite obviously, on the form of rewards to innovators under the social organization in question, in particular, whether or not the competition is in the form of *tournaments*. The models developed in Sections 3 and 5 are examples of these two forms of competition.

2   EMPIRICAL OBSERVATIONS

Before presenting one of his growth theories, Professor Kaldor, in a now classic article, began by listing a set of 'stylized facts' which, he felt, a growth model ought to generate as implications (see Kaldor 1961). I rather doubt that the empirical observations that I shall list below can *all* be elevated to the status of stylized facts; 'academic rumours' would be a more accurate description. In the field of technological change there is often some ambiguity about what hypothesis the investigator has in fact tested (see Fisher and Temin 1973). Moreover, economists attempting to test the same hypothesis have in several cases obtained conflicting results (see Kamien and Schwartz 1975, 1982). In addition, one if often forced – due to data limitations – to use vastly imperfect surrogates for variables one wants to measure (e.g. the number of patents as a measure of the output of R & D effort). Unquestion-

---

modated in the models that I shall discuss subsequently. Spence (1980) provides an analysis of advertising as barriers to entry. Levin and Reiss (1982) have used an extended version of the model presented in Section 3.3 below to test the hypothesis that R & D investment and industrial structure are a jointly determined outcome of the competitive process. Their findings provide some support for the view that they are.

ably we are in treacherous terrain. A theorist has to have gall to follow Professor Kaldor's deep footprints even at the best of times. Here it is positively foolhardy. I guess I have to soften my pose by saying that it is no *disgrace* if a theory of technological competition accommodates the empirical observations that I shall list below.[8]

I want to separate the empirical observations into two categories. The first are those that should influence the choice of hypotheses that a model of technological competition is based on. The second are those that the theory should explain.

I begin with the first set:

1   Over a wide range of industries it has been observed that there is a positive association between R & D effort (i.e. research inputs) and innovative output. (See e.g. Comanor 1965, Schmookler 1966, Mansfield 1968 and Comanor and Scherer 1969.)

2   The cost associated with developing something seems to increase more than proportionately with contraction of the period of development. That is, the transformation possibilities between time and cost are convex to the origin. (See Mansfield et al. 1971.)

3   By and large the technological possibilities between R & D inputs and innovative outputs do not display any economies of scale with respect to the size of the firm in which R & D is undertaken. (See Kamien and Schwartz 1975, pp. 8–11 for detailed comments on this observation.)

4   Technological opportunities for making inventions and undertaking innovations are not independent of advances in basic scientific knowledge. Phillips (1966) and Rosenberg (1974) in particular have emphasized the importance of progress in the underlying scientific base for making innovative possibilities easier.

5   Success breeds success. Phillips (1971) in particular has argued that because learning involves costs successful firms possess an advantage over their rivals in enjoying greater possibilities for further successes.

6   A principal goal of R & D activity is the creation of entry barriers. The nature of inventive activity by existing firms defines limits to entry by new firms; that is, research and development can be a major element of interfirm rivalry. (See e.g. Comanor 1964, 1967 and Freeman 1965.)

Observation (1) may appear banal. But it is good to have actual evidence for it. If it were otherwise the *economics* of technological change would be an uninteresting subject; in any event, I would not be writing this paper now.

---

8 Kamien and Schwartz (1982), chapter 3, have an excellent and detailed documentation of these empirical findings and I have gained much from this. Unfortunately they do not do much with them in the remainder of their book.

Observation (2) is interesting, because it suggests that in the construction of formal models one would want to assume some degree of diminishing returns to R & D effort. I hasten to add that this will *not* imply that the theory of technological competition will be similar to the theory of price competition. In particular I shall note subsequently that (2) in itself does *not* rule out significant increasing returns to scale in the relationship between a firm's R & D effort and its *economic* benefits.

Observation (3) has been much discussed and I shall not comment on it. Observation (4) may appear self-evident. It has required emphasis by various authors (in particular Rosenberg 1974) because there are theories that regard basic science today to be so versatile that its progress, or so it is claimed, does not influence the *direction* of R & D activity (see Schmookler 1966). Observation (5) is interesting because it provides a direct reason for the persistence of monopoly. It is related to Professor Arrow's notion of learning-by-doing (see Arrow 1962b). I shall look at the implications of this when I come to discuss the issue of pre-emptive patenting in Section 5.

Observation (6) is of great importance. It provides a central distinctive characteristic of technological competition. One would clearly want a model of technological competition to blend with conventional price competition if the possibilities of entry barriers through R & D activity are negligible. In Section 3 I shall review a model of technological competition which has precisely this feature.

I now come to the second list of empirical observations:

1*   A considerable body of research evidence suggests that larger firms do *not* engage in greater R & D activity *relative* to their size than smaller firms. (See Kamien and Schwartz 1975, pp. 16–18 for an assessment of this.)

2*   There is a positive association between the degree of concentration in an industry and innovative activity within it, so long as concentration is not too great. That is, measures of R & D input relative to industry sales achieve their maximum at 'moderate' levels of concentration (see Scherer 1967b). It has also been suggested (see Comanor 1967) that concentration is associated with innovative activity in those cases where technological and innovative opportunities are weak.

3*   Industries facing greater technological and innovative opportunities tend to be more concentrated (see Scherer 1967b).

4*   Growth in demand for the products of an industry stimulates R & D activity within it (see Schmookler 1966).

5*   There is some evidence that past R & D successes lead to greater current R & D effort on the part of successful firms. It has been argued that from this one might expect these firms to produce further innovations and thus widen the gap between themselves and their rivals (see Grabowski 1968).

6*   Research activity appears to be strongest in industries where entry barriers are neither too high nor too low; that is, it is strongest in industries where, say, rapid imitation is not possible but where entry has not been effectively foreclosed (Comanor 1967).

7*   Recent work by Professor Zvi Griliches and his associates suggests that there is a positive relationship between a firm's R & D activity and its stock market value (see e.g. Pakes 1984).

8*   Imitative research is a pervasive phenomenon. Mansfield, Schwartz and Wagner (1981) have reported that 60 per cent of the patented innovations in a sample of 48 industries studied by them were imitated within four years.

Observations (1*) and (3), though related, are nowhere near to being the same. Even if one uses (3) as an ingredient in a model one would still need to check if those firms that *become* larger in the process of technological competition spend more on R & D relative to their size. Observation (2*) has been much discussed in the literature and it has been customary to impute a *causal* explanation to it. I shall come back and comment on this interpretation in the next section. The latter half of (2*) and (3*) have had several interpretations. For example, Comanor (1967) interprets 'innovative opportunities' as the ease with which firms can engage in product differentiation. There are others, and I shall provide a natural one for the model that I discuss in the next section.

Observation (4*), chiefly associated with the works of Jacob Schmookler, has been widely discussed (see e.g. Rosenberg 1976 and Dasgupta and Stiglitz 1981). It provides the basis for a demand-led view of technological change and is, quite naturally, appealing to economists.

Observations (5) and (5*) are clearly related, in that (5) may be used as an immediate explanation for (5*). I shall attempt to probe this issue with some care when discussing pre-emptive patenting in Section 5. Observation (6*) may appear to be really rather obvious and readily explainable. Nevertheless it merits theoretical clarification. Observation (7*) is interesting and can be addressed properly only in a model with an explicit stock market. I shall not do that here. Instead I shall use the crude device of regarding a firm's profit level as a surrogate for its stock market value. Observation (8*) has long been suspected of being true through casual empiricism. But it is only recently that systematic work has been done on the matter. Mansfield et al. (1981) have chided theorists for not incorporating technological imitation into their models, without bothering to ask what it is that the theorists they cite were *trying* to do.

A theoretical model does not become more virtuous by having additional complexities thrown in. I take it that the idea is *not* to have more and more 'real' features of the world introduced into the same model. The model would then not illuminate. It seems to me that the thing that has plagued theoretical work in the economics of technological competition is precisely a denial of this. For example, it is patently the case that the outcome of inventive and development activity is uncertain and that R & D decisions are not of the 'once and for all' variety; that is, a firm phases its R & D programme over time.[9] In fact much' has been made of this. The question is whether it is ridiculous to ignore either or both. The answer, quite obviously, is to what end the model is constructed. One can hardly avoid introducing uncertainty if, say, it is the relationship between firm size and choice of the degree of risk-taking in R & D strategy that is under investigation. But no significant additional insight is obtained if results are restricted to those relating, say, the *expected* date of R & D completion to other variables, when the same kind of relation has been obtained in a model devoid of uncertainty.

A slight unease about such methodological issues is reflected as well in the recent monograph by Kamien and Schwartz (1982), where they catalogue modern *approaches* to theories of market structure and innovation according to whether they are *decision* theoretic or *game* theoretic. It transpires that by the former they mean investigations that study a firm's response to an exogenously given (or evolving) market environment and by the latter those which allow firms to interact strategically. But these are not different *approaches* at all. The former simply asks a more restricted set of questions. To say they are different approaches is rather like saying that the chapter on the competitive firm in, say, Debreu (1959) is a different approach to a study of price taking behaviour from the chapter on competitive equilibrium in the same book.

I emphasize these rather obvious methodological points because it is my intention in the remainder of this paper to discuss theoretical constructs that can accommodate the empirical observations that I have listed, and I want *only* to consider the most 'economic' constructs that will do the work for me. An appeal to Occam's dictum is particularly important here. That the models which follow are 'simplistic' and do not capture many 'real world' features is not a confession, it is an assertion.

3   NON-TOURNAMENT FORMS OF TECHNOLOGICAL COMPETITION

3.1   Preliminaries

The construction I shall discuss in this section has been presented in detail in Dasgupta and Stiglitz (1980a), Section II. Here I want to have the model face

---

9 Examples of models incorporating both features are Dasgupta, Heal and Majumdar (1977), Kamien and Schwartz (1978) and Reinganum (1981a). Models containing the latter feature are ofteh called 'dynamic' which, in economics, invariably carries approbation.

the empirical observations listed in the previous section. The model is timeless and devoid of uncertainty. I study a market for a homogeneous product and I assume away income effects. Technological competition takes the form of *process innovation*.[10] I imagine that firms cannot manufacture the product without engaging in R & D activity, but that technological opportunities and the patent structure are such that if a firm spends x on R & D it can manufacture the commodity at unit cost $c(x)$, where $c(x)$ is twice continuously differentiable, is declining in x, and displays diminishing returns to R & D expenditure; that is, $c(0) = \infty$, $c'(x) < 0$ and $c''(x) > 0$. The model therefore captures the features embodied in observations (1)-(3).[11]

Let $p(Q)$ be the market demand function, where Q is total output of the commodity in question. I assume it to be twice continuously differentiable and downward sloping. Often I shall specialize and consider the iso-elastic forms:

$$p(Q) = \sigma Q^{-\epsilon}, \qquad \sigma, \epsilon > 0; \tag{3.1}$$

and

$$c(x) = \beta x^{-\alpha}, \qquad \beta, \alpha > 0. \tag{3.2}$$

3.2 Exogenously Given Entry Barriers

To fix ideas I begin with the case where there are precisely n firms in the industry – which in this case means that it is only these n firms that can engage in R & D and final production. Firms are indexed by i and j ($i, j = 1, \ldots, n$), and x_i (≥ 0) and Q_i (≥ 0) denote respectively the R & D expenditure and output level of firm i. All firms by hypothesis choose their R & D expenditure and output levels *simultaneously*. It follows that profit earned by i, which I denote by π_i, is of the form:

$$\pi_i = \left(p\left(\sum_{j \neq i} Q_j + Q_i \right) - c(x_i) \right) Q_i - x_i \tag{3.3}$$

10 The model can easily be adapted to a market for (potentially) differentiated products where firms are engaged in *product* innovation. Since the model becomes a tiny bit more complicated I refrain from adapting it here.

11 We can allow for spillover in the acquisition of knowledge by having the R & D expenditures of *other* firms influence unit cost of production of a given firm. The implications of such a modified model are precisely the ones one would expect from a model of incomplete appropriability of knowledge. I do not therefore present this extension. (For such extensions see Leung 1982 and Levin and Reiss 1982.) In any event, the issue of *imitative* research is more delicate, and requires an explicit intertemporal formulation. I discuss this briefly in the next section.

I am interested in a non-cooperative outcome. It is then natural to look at Nash–Cournot equilibria. Since the game is symmetric (output is homogeneous and firms face the same innovation opportunities, $c(x)$) we look for a symmetric equilibrium (i.e. where all firms pick the same strategy). I am not only interested in an existence theorem, I want also to be able to characterize equilibria so as to confront the model with the empirical observations. Towards this we specialize and suppose that $p(Q)$ and $c(x)$ satisfy equations (3.1) and (3.2) respectively. It is then a simple matter to prove:

Theorem 1. If $p(Q)$ and $c(x)$ satisfy (3.1) and (3.2) respectively and if n is a positive integer, then a symmetric Nash–Cournot equilibrium amongst n firms exists if

$$\text{(i) } \epsilon < n \leqslant \epsilon(1 + \alpha)/\alpha \quad \text{and (ii) } \epsilon(1 + \alpha)/\alpha > 1. \tag{3.4}$$

Proof. See Dasgupta and Stiglitz (1980a), Appendix 1.[12] ‖

In fact one can explicitly compute symmetric Nash–Cournot equilibrium which, as it happens, is unique. Routine calculations show that if $p(Q)$ and $c(x)$ satisfy (3.1) and (3.2) respectively and if we denote R & D expenditure and output level of the representative firm at the symmetric equilibrium by x^* and Q^*/n respectively, then:

$$x^* = [\sigma(\alpha/n)^\epsilon \beta^{\epsilon-1}(1 - \epsilon/n)]^{1/(\epsilon - \alpha(1-\epsilon))} \tag{3.5}$$

and

$$Q^*/n = (1/\alpha\beta)\,[\sigma(\alpha/n)^\epsilon \beta^{\epsilon-1}(1 - \epsilon/n)]^{(1+\alpha)/(\epsilon - \alpha(1-\epsilon))} \tag{3.6}$$

Notice that $x^*(n + 1) < x^*(n)$ and $Q^*(n + 1) > Q^*(n)$; that is, if *inter-firm rivalry* is increased, equilibrium R & D effort per firm decreases, but market output increases (see also Loury 1979).[13]

The central limitation of this construct, for my purposes here, is that industrial structure is not explained; it is not endogenous. That is, the number of firms in the industry is given in advance of the analysis. But I need this model to confront observation (7*) of the previous section for reasons that will become clear subsequently.

---

12 As there is an extensive discussion of the theorem in Dasgupta and Stiglitz (1980a) I shall not elaborate on it here. Condition (ii) in fact guarantees that a firm's *profit* level, as a function of its R & D expenditure, faces diminishing returns at large levels of R & D expenditure.

13 However, one should note that $(n + 1)x^*(n + 1) > nx^*(n)$. The model captures in a sharp form the wastes of duplication of R & D under technological competition. A socially managed industry in this model would, of course, have only *one* R & D laboratory.

I want to see the relationship between a firm's profit level and the level of its R & D activity. Both are endogenous to the construct of course. So I shall have to vary some parameter of the model and see if equilibrium values of the two move in the same direction.

Using (3.1), (3.2), (3.5) and (3.6) in equation (3.3) it is a routine matter to check that:

$$\pi_i^* = [((\epsilon(1 + \alpha) - n\alpha)/\alpha)/(n - \epsilon)] \, [\sigma(\alpha/n)^\epsilon \beta^{\epsilon-1}(1 - \epsilon/n)]^{1/(\epsilon - \alpha(1-c))} \quad (3.7)$$

(where π_i^* denotes the *equilibrium* level of profit). Obviously I want to assume that $\epsilon(1 + \alpha) > n\alpha$ (see condition (i) of (3.4)). Thus $\pi_i^* = \pi^* > 0$ in (3.7).

From (3.5) and (3.7) we obtain:

Corollary 1.1. If the conditions of Theorem 1 are satisfied $\partial x^*/\partial \sigma$, $\partial \pi^*/\partial \sigma > 0$; $\partial x^*/\partial \beta$, $\partial \pi^*/\partial \beta \gtreqqless 0$ as $\epsilon \gtreqqless 1$; and $x^*(n) > x^*(n + 1)$, $\pi^*(n) > \pi^*(n + 1)$. That is, in a cross-section study of industries differing solely by σ (the size of the market) *or* β (the underlying scientific base; see observation (4)), *or* n (the number of firms), one would find a positive association between a firm's R & D activity and its profit level (see (7*)). However, there is no causal direction in this relationship.

3.3 Endogenous Entry Barriers

I come now to the central issue I wish to look at in this section, the implications for the theory of technological competition when industrial structure is endogenous; that is, when the number of firms in the industry is *not* a datum. I suppose that there is a very large number of *potential* firms. The number of active firms is determined within the model. It is simplest to assume that the decision of whether or not to enter and decisions on how much to spend on R & D and how much to produce are made simultaneously by all firms.[14] It is clear from equation (3.3) that R & D expenditure is a form of *fixed cost* and it is a strategic variable. It creates entry barriers for rival firms by enabling a firm to produce the commodity at low unit cost (see observation (6)).

---

14 It is an easy enough matter to sequence the decisions by having firms first decide on whether or not to enter and then decide on R & D expenditure and output levels simultaneously. As regards the features I wish to highlight here (subgame) perfect equilibria in such a model are no different from the equilibria I shall be studying in the text. It is a great deal more complicated to characterize (subgame) perfect equilibria if firms first decide whether or not to enter and then decide on R & D expenditures and then on output levels. I do not know if perfect equilibria in such a model have the features I wish to highlight below.

The obvious equilibrium notion is the Nash–Cournot one. I state it formally as:

Definition.[15] $(n^*, (x_1^*, Q_1^*), \ldots, (x_i^*, Q_i^*), \ldots, (x_{n^*}^*, Q_{n^*}^*))$ is an equilibrium (with free legal entry) if for $i = 1, \ldots, n^*$,

$$\left(p \left(\sum_{j \neq i} Q_j^* + Q_i^* \right) - c(x_i^*) \right) Q_i^* - x_i^* \geqslant \left(p \left(\sum_{j \neq i} Q_j^* + Q_i \right) - c(x_i) \right) Q_i - x_i$$

$$\text{for all } x_i, Q_i \geqslant 0, \qquad (3.8)$$

and

$$\left(p \left(\sum_{i=1}^{n^*} Q_i^* + Q \right) - c(x) \right) Q - x \leqslant 0 \quad \text{for all } x, Q \geqslant 0. \qquad (3.9)$$

As before I am interested not only in an existence theorem but also in the characteristics of equilibria. Towards this I specialize and suppose that $p(Q)$ and $c(x)$ satisfy (3.1) and (3.2). Then one has the following theorem:

Theorem 2. If $p(Q)$ and $c(x)$ satisfy (3.1) and (3.2) respectively there then exists $\bar{\alpha}(\epsilon, \beta, \sigma)$ (> 0) such that if $0 < \alpha \leqslant \bar{\alpha}(\epsilon, \beta, \sigma)$, there is a symmetric Nash–Cournot equilibrium with free entry.

Proof. Mild variations on the arguments in Novshek (1980) and Dasgupta and Stiglitz (1980a).

Looking at equation (3.2) one notes that α is the elasticity of the invention possibility curve. The smaller is α the less are 'innovational opportunities'. Therefore I shall use α as the index of 'innovational opportunities' in the industry. Theorem 2 says that a symmetric equilibrium under technological competition with free legal entry exists if innovational opportunities are not excessive. But the problem is that even symmetric equilibrium need not be unique. I therefore take a hint from condition (i) in Theorem 1 and consider the following selection mechanism (see Dasgupta and Stiglitz (1980a), Appendix 2). Write by $[y]$ as the largest positive integer not in excess of the real number y. Now consider the number $\epsilon(1 + \alpha)/\alpha$, (see condition (i) in Theorem 1). If we choose $n = [\epsilon(1 + \alpha)/\alpha]$, then $\epsilon(1 + \alpha)/n\alpha \simeq 1$ if α is small enough. Theorems 1 and 2, and equation (3.7) imply that if α is small enough a symmetric equilibrium with free entry exists and that the equilibrium profit

---

15 For discussions of this equilibrium concept, see Novshek (1980), Dasgupta and Stiglitz (1980a), von Weizsacker (1980), Chapter 4 and the Symposium on large economies in the *Journal of Economic Theory* (August 1980). Dasgupta and Ushio (1981) and Guesnerie and Hart (1981) consider a special case of this model by eschewing R & D activity: they assume that there exists $\bar{x}$ (> 0) such that $c(x) = \infty$ if $0 \leqslant x < \bar{x}$ and $c(x) = \beta > 0$ if $x \geqslant \bar{x}$.

level per firm is negligible if the number of active firms selected is $[\epsilon(1+\alpha)/\alpha]$. It follows that provided α is small enough we can suppose that profit per firm in equilibrium is negligible. I assume this. If we use an asterisk to denote eqilibrium values of economic variables, it is a routine matter to show that:

$$\epsilon/n^* = n^*x^*/p(Q^*)\,Q^*, \tag{3.10}$$

$$n^*x^*/p(Q^*)\,Q^* = \alpha/(1+\alpha), \tag{3.11}$$

and

$$p(Q^*)/c(x^*) = 1 + \alpha \tag{3.12}$$

(See Dasgupta and Stiglitz 1980a, Section II.)

In fact one can easily solve these equilibrium conditions and express n^*, x^* and Q^* explicitly as:

$$n^* = \epsilon(1+\alpha)/\alpha \tag{3.13}$$

$$x^* = [\sigma\alpha^{2\epsilon}\beta^{\epsilon-1}\epsilon^{-\epsilon}(1+\alpha)^{-(1+\epsilon)}]^{1/(\epsilon-\alpha(1-\epsilon))} \tag{3.14}$$

and

$$Q^* = [\epsilon(1+\alpha)/\alpha^2\beta]\,[\sigma\alpha^{2\epsilon}\beta^{\epsilon-1}\epsilon^{-\epsilon}(1+\alpha)^{-(1+\epsilon)}]^{(1+\alpha)/(\epsilon-\alpha(1-\epsilon))} \tag{3.15}$$

I now proceed to analyse this equilibrium in the light of the empirical observations that I listed in Section 2.

First, notice from equation (3.13) that n^* does not depend on σ and β.[16] From equation (3.10) we may therefore conclude with

Corollary 2.1. In a cross-section study of industries differing solely by way of σ (the size of the market) and β (the underlying scientific base), firms will be found to spend the same amount on R & D relative to their size; that is, $n^*x^*/p(Q^*)\,Q^*$ is independent of σ and β. (See (1*).)

I come now to (2*). Since the equilibrium being studied is symmetric any declining function of n^* can be used as a measure of industrial concentration. Here of course concentration is endogenous. I take the index of industrial concentration to be $1/n^*$. Note that the equilibrium conditions that I am studying are valid only if α is small; that is, if 'innovative opportunities' are weak. From (3.13) we conclude that equilibrium concentration is 'low'. We now note equation (3.10) to obtain

Corollary 2.2. In a cross-section study of industries characterized by the same ϵ but differing α one would observe a positive linear relationship between industrial concentration $(1/n^*)$ and R & D expenditure as a fraction

16 This is clearly a mathematical artifact, depending severely on the parametrization (3.1) and (3.2). Since nothing much would be gained by moving away from this parametrization and *then* locating conditions under which the following corollaries hold, I refrain from doing this.

of sales $(n^*x^*/p(Q^*)\,Q^*)$, and this relation holds only if innovative opportunities are weak. (See (2^*).) But no causality should be imputed to this relationship, since both are simultaneously determined.

We may next quickly confirm from equation (3.13) the following corollary.

Corollary 2.3. $\partial n^*/\partial\alpha < 0$, and so industries facing greater innovative opportunities are more concentrated. (See (3^*).)

Next, equations (3.13) and (3.14) imply

Corollary 2.4. $\partial n^*/\partial\sigma = 0$ and $\partial x^*/\partial\sigma > 0$. Therefore an increase in the size of the product market leads to an increase in equilibrium R & D activity per firm, as well as R & D activity for the industry as a whole. (See (4^*).) (Notice that the $c(x)$ function can be given the more conventional interpretation of a menu of technologies characterized by less or more 'specialization' in production. The result, $\partial x^*/\partial\sigma > 0$, can then be used to substantiate the classical claim that the division of labour varies with the size of the market and that, in particular, the greater the size of the market, the greater is the division of labour.)

Observation (5^*) obviously cannot be accommodated by the model under discussion, not so much because it demands an explicit intertemporal structure, as much as the fact that it demands that we distinguish among firms. A model in which firms are *ex-ante* identical cannot obviously broach (5^*). I shall look at (5^*) in Section 5.

It is obvious that, as it stands, (6^*) can be given several interpretations. Comanor (1967) was among other things concerned with the spill-over of knowledge acquired through R & D and the possibilities of imitative research. Since I have prohibited any spill-over of knowledge in the model I cannot discuss this interpretation. But Comanor (1967) was also concerned with barriers to entry created by innovative opportunities. For the model under study the parameter which reflects the possibilities for the creation of entry barriers is α, the elasticity of the innovative locus. I remind the reader that the zero-profit approximation which we have maintained so far is valid only if α is 'small', that is, if innovative opportunities are 'small'. From equations (3.13) and (3.14) we note that $x^* \to 0$ and $n^* \to \infty$ as $\alpha \to 0$, but that $n^*x^* \to 0$ as $\alpha \to 0$. In addition, equation (3.12) tells us that $p(Q^*)/c(x^*) \to 1$ as $\alpha \to 0$, and so we have

Corollary 2.5. If innovative opportunities are weak, so that barriers to entry are weak then the weaker are innovative opportunities the smaller is R & D effort in the industry. In particular, if innovative opportunities are vanishingly small technological competition is vanishingly small and we would expect price competition to prevail; that is equilibrium under technological competition tends to a Walrasian equilibrium. (See (6^*).)[17]

17 Tandon (1982) has investigated the welfare losses under oligopoly when α is not negligible.

It should now be clear why I was forced to look at (7*) by way of the model of Section 3.2. For computational ease I have assumed α to be small enough in this section for equilibrium profit per firm to be 'negligible'. Quite obviously I cannot test (7*) in such a context.

4 IMITATION

Imitative innovation would appear to be pervasive. The valuable recent work by Mansfield, Schwartz and Wagner (1981) suggests that, as one might expect, imitators usually *do* save on innovation costs (in a sample of 48 new products they found that on average the ratio of imitation cost to innovation cost was 0.65). But, of course, by definition the imitator *follows*, and so does not enjoy the profits that the innovator makes in the interim period. It is not unusual to hear the opinion that some firms are congenital imitators while others are leaders. There may well be something in this, though it would be an error to think that from the *economic* point of view imitative research has less to commend it (see Rosenberg 1976, chapter 4).[18] From the analytical point of view it seems therefore that a preliminary question of some importance is whether it is possible that it is strategically convenient for one firm to be the innovator and for another to be the imitator even when the two are *ex-ante* similar. The answer must undoubtedly be 'yes', for we are familiar with such phenomena in what are called 'games of coordination' (also called 'mixed-motive' games; see Schelling 1960).

Thus consider a game characterized by two firms, each of which has two choices: innovate *now* (*N*) or *later* (*L*). Suppose the payoff matrix of the game is the one given in the accompanying diagram:

$i = 2$ \ $i = 1$	L	N
L	(8, 8)	(5, 10)
N	(10, 5)	(4, 4)

The game is symmetric; implying that neither firm has an advantage. It has two pure-strategy Nash equilibria, (N, L) and (L, N). At such a Nash equili-

---

18 Contrast this with Schumpeter's obsession with the periodic emergence of the daring and charismatic leader who innovates, only to be followed by a cluster of further innovations by others (see Schumpeter 1939). Dasgupta and Stiglitz (1981) construct a model in which periodicity of innovations is explained by sunk-costs involved in R & D. It is an implication of the model that a competitive industry is characterized by overly frequent but 'small' innovations as compared to a socially managed industry.

brium, one is the innovator (N) and the other the imitator (L). Moreover, each firm has a preferred equilibrium.[19] It remains to construct a simple economic model which gives flesh to this payoff matrix.[20]

Assume, as in the foregoing game, that there are two firms ($i = 1, 2$). A firm can adopt a new technology either now ($t = 0$) or at date T (> 0). The present value of expenditures involved in being an innovator is a constant, C^* (> 0); that of being an imitator is C^{**} (with $0 < C^{**} < C^*$). So long as neither has innovated each earns profits at the rate $\pi_0 (> 0)$. So long as one firm has adopted, but not the other, the innovator earns profits at the rate π_1 (> 0) and the other at the rate π_2 (> 0). After both have adopted each earns profits at the rate π_3 (> 0). Naturally one wants to assume that $\pi_1 > \pi_0 > \pi_2$.[21] The capital market is assumed perfectly competitive, and the rate of interest is a constant r (> 0). Each firm is interested in the present value of its profits.[22] A firm's strategy is its date of adoption of the new technology. By hypothesis a firm can choose either $t = 0$ or $t = T$. Let $V_1(t_1, t_2)$ be the present value of profits earned by firm 1 if firm i chooses t_i ($i = 1, 2$). The game is symmetric. Therefore $V_1(t_1, t_2) = V_2(t_2, t_1)$. Finally, we may compute the payoff matrix explicitly as:

$$\left.\begin{aligned}
V_1(0, 0) &= \pi_3 \int_0^\infty e^{-rt}\, dt - C^* \\[2em]
V_1(0, T) &= \pi_1 \int_0^T e^{-rt}\, dt + \pi_3 \int_T^\infty e^{-rt}\, dt - C^* \\[2em]
V_1(T, 0) &= \pi_2 \int_0^T e^{-rt}\, dt + \pi_3 \int_T^\infty e^{-rt}\, dt - C^{**} \\[2em]
V_1(T, T) &= \pi_0 \int_0^T e^{-rt}\, dt + \pi_3 \int_T^\infty e^{-rt}\, dt - C^*.
\end{aligned}\right\} \qquad (4.1)$$

19 There is also a symmetric mixed-strategy Nash equilibrium, where each firm chooses L with probability 1/3. But even at this equilibrium there is a chance of 4/9 that the two will not innovate simultaneously.

20 That is, in what follows I restrict myself to an economic game in which players face binary choice. This is for expositional ease only. I shall return to infinite games in Section 5 since I want to highlight the discontinuous structure of patent races under certainty. If cast as an infinite game a model of imitation will also be discontinuous. I want to avoid the issue of discontinuity in this section.

21 Reinganum (1981b) discusses an infinite economic game which can be suitably modified to capture the idea of imitative possibilities. I am restricting myself to this finite (binary choice) game for expositional ease.

22 I am, of course, side-stepping important features of capital markets. In an interesting paper Bhattacharya and Ritter (1982) have analysed a model in which firms are required to finance R & D from external sources and to improve the borrowing terms they must disclose technological information directly useful to their rivals.

We have supposed that $\pi_1 > \pi_0 > \pi_2$. From (4.1) it is then simple to check that if

$$(\pi_0 - \pi_2)\, e^{-rT} > r(C^* - C^{**}) > (\pi_3 - \pi_2)\, e^{-rT}$$

the payoff matrix of this game has the same form as the one in the foregoing table and, in particular, there are two pure-strategy Nash equilibria $(0, T)$ and $(T, 0)$ and a symmetric mixed-strategy equilibrium.

5   PRE-EMPTIVE PATENTING

5.1   Tournaments as Discontinuous Games

The model of technological competition that I analysed in Section 3 has three features worth emphasizing. First, it assumes implicitly that there are a large number of research strategies – strictly speaking an infinite number of research strategies. Each active firm picks a niche for itself amongst them. Stated another way, the model assumes a continuum of possible patents to be won. (In equilibrium of course, only a finite number are awarded.)

Second, the payoff functions of firms are all continuous. Thus in fact the model does not distinguish winners and losers sharply: if a firm alters his action slightly, his net reward changes slightly. Put another way, the reward schedules faced by the competitors are not of the form of a *tournament*, where performance is rewarded on the basis of its *rank* within the set of all realized performances.

Third – and this is not an essential feature – it was assumed that firms moved simultaneously, that is, there was no firm which was distinctive in being allowed to move first.

The essence of patent races is that they *are* races, and the reward structure is such that *ex-post* payoffs are discontinuous. In the absence of uncertainty technological competition in the form of patent races leads to *discontinuous games*. Fortunately, the nature of the discontinuities that patent races suffer from is such that such games *do* possess equilibria, provided competitors choose mixed strategies (see Dasgupta and Maskin 1986a, 1986b).[23]

The essence of a patent race among competitors enjoying complete and perfect information, both about the world and about one another, can be distilled if we analyse the following bidding game: N players $(N \geqslant 2)$ bid for an indivisible object valued by each at V (> 0). All bids are forfeited. The highest bidder wins the object. If there are K $(\leqslant N)$ highest bidders each of these K players wins the object with probability $1/K$.

---

23 Imitation games are also typically discontinuous. We avoided this issue in the previous section by restricting ourselves to a finite game. But it should be emphasized that an essential form of uncertainty is eschewed here, that firms face uncorrelated risks in R & D. See Section 6 on this.

Let a_i $(i = 1, \ldots, N)$ be player i's bid. Then we may as well suppose that $0 \leqslant a_i \leqslant V$. Notice that i's payoff function is discontinuous at the set of points $a_i = \max\{a_j, j \neq i\}$. Suppose the players bid simultaneously. It is then simple to check that the game does not have a Nash equilibrium in pure strategies. But if players mix their bids there is an equilibrium. In particular the symmetric outcome in which each player chooses the cumulative distribution function $(a/V)^{1/(N-1)}$, for $0 \leqslant a \leqslant V$, is a Nash equilibrium. Notice first that in equilibrium each player expects zero net profit; that is, all rents are dissipated if there are N $(\geqslant 2)$ bidders. Notice as well that at this equilibrium each player expects to bid V/N. If we were now to interpret a forfeited bid as sunk-cost in R&D and if firms face the same (deterministic) function relating the date of invention to R&D expenditure and if this function is monotonically decreasing, then we may conclude that the greater is competition (i.e. the larger is N) the more distant is the expected date of invention; that is, the slower is the rate of technological progress. (Note the corresponding result in Section 3.2.)

In what follows I want to study games of this type. I shall vary the number of players and the number of objects to be bid for and vary the players' payoffs with a view to analysing the issue of pre-emptive patenting.

5.2   The Pre-emptive Monopolist: A Single Patent Race

Suppose there are two firms, $i = 1, 2$. Firm 1 is the sitting monopolist, his past success being protected by a patent. The race is for the next patent. If the monopolist wins, his profit is $\bar{V}$. But if firm 2 wins, then profits to the two players 1 and 2 are V^* and V^{**} respectively. Naturally I shall assume that $\bar{V} > V^* + V^{**}$. This is the precise sense in which the monopolist has a greater incentive to win the next patent, and it captures observation 5 in Section 2 in an indirect manner – for it abstracts the idea that a monopolist's payoff, *relative* to its R&D effort, in obtaining the patent exceeds its rivals.

By definition the sitting monopolist is already in the industry. Thus I let the monopolist make the first move. This is followed by a bid from firm 2. The monopolist is therefore a Stackelberg leader.

If the monopolist bids V^{**} (plus a tiny bit, to be precise) he will win the patent. This is because V^{**} is firm 2's reservation price for the patent. If the monopolist bids less than V^{**} he will be beaten in the race and forfeit his bid. His choice therefore boils down to either bidding V^{**} or not bidding at all. If he chooses the former his payoff is $\bar{V} - V^{**}$; if the latter, it is V^*. He will therefore choose the former. This is the pre-emption result in its simplest form.[24]

---

24 See Dasgupta and Stiglitz (1980b) and Gilbert and Newbery (1982). In other contexts pre-emptive behaviour has been discussed by Eaton and Lipsey (1979, 1980) and Dixit (1980) among others.

Notice at once that the patent may be for a technology which is *strictly inferior* to the one which the monopolist holds. The pre-emption argument goes through, but the monopolist will not actually *use* the new patent. His incentive for winning it is simply to prevent his rival from using it. In this case the monopolist will pre-empt and hold a sleeping patent.[25]

Matters are somewhat more complicated if the monopolist faces more than one rival for the new patent. Consider the general case of N $(\geqslant 2)$ rivals, $i = 1, \ldots, N$, who are all identical. I label the monopolist as $i = 0$ and I assume as before that he bids first. At the second move the rivals bid simultaneously. Now suppose the monopolist bids a_0. (Obviously $0 \leqslant a_0 \leqslant V^{**}$.) We have already seen that there is no equilibrium in pure strategies at the second stage of the game if $a_0 < V^{**}$. It is now an easy matter to check that at the second stage there is a symmetric mixed-strategy equilibrium in which *each* of the N rivals, $i = 1, \ldots, N$ chooses the following mixed strategy: 'no bid' with probability $(a_0/V^{**})^{1/(N-1)}$, and for $a_0 \leqslant a \leqslant V^{**}$ the cumulative distribution function $(a/V^{**})^{1/(N-1)}$ (see Section 5.1).

I now return to the monopolist's choice of a_0. The monopolist will obviously win the patent if *all* rivals bid under a_0 which, as we have just seen, means that *each* rival bids nothing (i.e. does not enter the race). The chance of that is $(a_0/V^{**})^{N/(N-1)}$. The monopolist loses if at least one of the rivals bids in excess of a_0. Now, the chance of this happening at the second stage of the game is $1 - (a_0/V^{**})^{N/(N-1)}$. It follows that if the monopolist selects a_0 his expected profit is:

$$(a_0/V^{**})^{N/(N-1)} [\bar{V} - V^*] + V^* - a_0 \tag{5.1}$$

By hypothesis $\bar{V} > V^* + V^{**}$. From (5.1) we may therefore conclude that the monopolist will choose $a_0 = V^{**}$ and thus pre-empt.

5.3 The Pre-emptive Monopolist: Multiple Patent Races

Quite obviously a monopolist cannot guarantee pre-emption if there are uncertainties in invention possibilities, and if these firms' uncertainties are not perfectly correlated. The reason why one wants to study models with no uncertainty in the invention process here is that it enables one to distil the relative incentives that firms may have for entering patent races. The question I want to ask now is whether a sitting monopolist will wish to pre-empt *all* potential discoveries if there are several of them. Presumably not, unless he

---

25 The phenomenon of sleeping patents is very similar to the maintenance of excess capacity as an entry-deterring device which has been analysed by Spence (1977) among others. These models, being timeless, cannot identify situations where 'excess capacity' is maintained only for a finite period. For illustrations where it is strategically convenient to hold an unused patent for only a finite period, see Dasgupta, Gilbert and Stiglitz (1982).

expects increasing returns to his profits in the acquisition of patents. The analysis that follows makes this precise.[26]

For tractability I assume that the monopolist ($i = 1$) faces a single rival $i = 2$. There are N (≥ 1) patents to be won. They are identical in their economic effects. The payoff for the monopolist in winning K ($0 \leq K \leq N$) patents is $\tilde{V}(K)$ and for the rival is $V^{**}(K)$. By assumption

$$\tilde{V}(K + 1) > \tilde{V}(K) > 0 \qquad \text{for } 0 \leq K \leq N - 1, \tag{5.2}$$

$$V^{**}(K + 1) > V^{**}(K) \qquad \text{for } 0 \leq K \leq N - 1, \tag{5.3}$$

$$\tilde{V}(K) > V^{**}(K) \qquad \text{for } 0 \leq K \leq N \tag{5.4}$$

and

$$V^{**}(0) = 0. \tag{5.5}$$

Consider first the case where the rival's payoff is *superadditive*:

$$V^{**}(K)/K \geq V^{**}(J)/J \quad \text{for } J < K. \tag{5.6}$$

If the monopolist intends to win precisely K ($0 \leq K \leq N$) patents in such a situation, he should bid nothing for ($N - K$) and $H(K)$ for *each* of the rest, where

$$H(K) = [V^{**}(N) - V^{**}(N - K)]/K. \tag{5.7}$$

If he does this the payoff to him (in obtaining K patents) is

$$M(K) \equiv \tilde{V}(K) - KH(K)$$

or

$$M(K) = \tilde{V}(K) - V^{**}(N) + V^{**}(N - K) \tag{5.8}$$

The monopolist's problem is to choose K so as to maximize $M(K)$. A *sufficient* condition for complete pre-emption is therefore $M(K + 1) \geq M(K)$ for all K; or

$$\tilde{V}(K + 1) + V^{*}(N - (K + 1)) \geq \tilde{V}(K) + V^{**}(N - K) \quad \text{for all } K \tag{5.9}$$

(5.9) is intuitively appealing, for it says that *total* industry profits are rising with the number of patents captured by the monopolist. But it does not say directly whether the *monopolist* enjoys increasing or decreasing returns in the acquisition of patents. However, note that (5.9) is guaranteed if

$$\tilde{V}(K + 1) - \tilde{V}(K) > \tilde{V}(K) - \tilde{V}(K - 1) \quad \text{for } K \geq 1, \tag{5.10}$$

---

26 In a splendid recent paper Eswaran and Lewis (1982) have addressed this question in the context of firms bidding for oil reserves. Their arguments depend heavily on the characteristics of intertemporal oligopolistic markets for exhaustible resources. It would be good to have results on partial pre-emption for less structured markets. The example in the text is designed to study this.

and

$$\tilde{V}(1) - \tilde{V}(0) \geqslant V^{**}(N) - V^{**}(N-1). \tag{5.11}$$

It follows that (5.6), (5.10) and (5.11) are together sufficient for complete pre-emption.

Suppose instead the other extreme to (5.6), that is, that the rival's payoff is *subadditive*, i.e.

$$V^{**}(K)/K < V^{**}(J)/J, \quad \text{for } J < K. \tag{5.12}$$

This case does not allow us to obtain as clean a set of sufficient conditions for complete pre-emption on the part of the monopolist.

First note that if the monopolist decides to win precisely K patents, then under (5.12) he will bid nothing for $N-K$ of them and $L(K)$ for *each* of the remaining ones, where

$$L(K) = V^{**}(N-K+1) - V^{**}(N-K). \tag{5.13}$$

In this event his payoff $M(K)$ is:

$$M(K) = \tilde{V}(K) - KL(K)$$

or

$$M(K) = \tilde{V}(K) + KV^{**}(N-K) - KV^{**}(N-K+1). \tag{5.14}$$

It follows immediately from (5.14) that a *sufficient* condition for complete pre-emption $(M(K) \geqslant M(K-1)$ for $1 \leqslant K \leqslant N)$ is:

$$\tilde{V}(K) - \tilde{V}(K-1) \geqslant (2K-1)\,[V^{**}(N-K+1) - V^{**}(N-K)]$$

$$\text{for } 1 \leqslant K \leqslant N. \tag{5.15}$$

The conditions linking the monopolist's payoff and that of the rival that have been stressed here are suggestive of the kind of increasing returns in the profitability of inventions that are sufficient for complete pre-emption. It seems to me also that the formulation adopted here for studying patent races is suggestive for another reason. The question can be asked whether it really is advantageous for the monopolist to move first. John Vickers of the University of Oxford has pointed out to me in his comments on this paper that if the monopolist's payoff is superadditive it would win *all* patents at zero cost if the sequence of moves were to be reversed. One concludes then that there may be serious disadvantages in having to move first.

6 A CLASSIFICATION OF TECHNOLOGICAL COMPETITION

Models attempting to capture the phenomenon of technological competition have been of two broad kinds. There are those that are continuous games and there are those that are discontinuous. If this classification appears excessively mathematical it is a deception. The classification is based on the manner in which models postulate the structure of rewards that firms in an industry expect to get if they engage in R & D activity. The economic organization I analysed in Section 3 is one which generates a continuous game. Much technological competition displays this feature. (It has this feature when for example, there is a continuum of potential discoveries to choose from.) The models that I studied in the previous section are discontinuous games. They arise in those social organizations where competition assumes the form of a tournament; that is, roughly speaking, where the 'winner' is clearly identifiable, where the winner 'takes all' and where there is no 'neighbourhood' race for rivals to move to. One can have a tournament when there is only a discrete number of potential discoveries. Patent races are a pristine form of tournaments. They remain so in the face of imitation. Imitation typically dilutes the innovator's profits; it does not alter the fact that competition for the (imperfectly protectable) patent is essentially a tournament. It is for this reason that theorists usually concentrate on patent races where the winner literally 'takes all'. The analysis of Section 4 should clarify this.

But I want now to argue that such discontinuous games that I have presented in Section 5 are really rather spurious. They *hint* at something, but they are also misleading. Tournaments distinguish winners and losers sharply, but on their own they do not make for discontinuous games. One requires in addition the hypothesis that firms face uncertainties that are perfectly correlated.[27] This is really hard to swallow. If they are not then, in general, no firm can be certain of being the winner – no matter how much effort it puts in – unless it can make it unprofitable for rivals to enter the race. Firms in such circumstances will choose probability distributions whose parameters are affected by R & D effort. Typically their *expected* profits (or payoffs) will be continuous functions. The resulting games reflecting technological competition are therefore continuous. (See Loury 1979 and Dasgupta and Stiglitz 1980b.) The theory of pre-emptive patenting should not be taken too literally. It merely highlights relative incentives among firms. The second purpose of this chapter has been to distinguish these two broad classes of models capturing technological competition by means of two sets of examples (Sections 3 and 5).[28] Not surprisingly, they display somewhat different features. My first purpose has been to look at a number of empirical observations on technological competition, and to produce models that can explain them. I re-emphasize that these observations are still the subject of contro-

27 The model analysed in the previous section assumes no environmental uncertainty and so satisfies this condition trivially.

28 I am therefore arguing implicitly that at the analytical level the customary classification consisting of product and process innovations is unilluminating.

versy among applied economists. But many years ago a distinguished physicist advised the world never to trust an experimental result until it is confirmed by theory. So perhaps we should now start believing in them.

REFERENCES

Arrow, K. J. 1962a: Economic Welfare and the Allocation of Resources for Inventions. In R. R. Nelson (ed.) *The Rate and Direction of Inventive Activity*. Princeton, N.J.: University Press. Reprinted in N. Rosenberg (1971).

Arrow, K. J. 1962b: The Economic Implications of Learning by Doing. *Review of Economic Studies*, **29**, 155–73.

Barzel, Y. 1968: Optimal Timing of Innovations. *Review of Economics and Statistics*, **50**, 348–55.

Bhattacharya, S. and Ritter, J. R 1982: Innovation and Communication: Signalling with Partial Disclosure. *Review of Economic Studies*, **49**.

Boylan, M. G. 1977: The Sources of Technological Innovations. In B. Gold (ed.) *Research, Technological Change, and Economic Analysis*. Lexington, Mass.: Lexington Books.

Comanor, W. S. 1964: Research and Competitive Product Differentiation in the Pharmaceutical Industry in the United States. *Economica*, **31**, 372–84.

Comanor, W. S. 1965: Research and Technical Change in the Pharmaceutical Industry. *Review of Economics and Statistics*, **47**, 182–90.

Comanor, W. S. 1967: Market Structure, Product Differentiation and Industrial Research. *Quarterly Journal of Economics*, **81**, 639–57.

Comanor, W. S. and Scherer, F. M. 1969: Patent Statistics as a Measure of Technical Change. *Journal of Political Economy*, **77**, 392–8.

Dasgupta, P., Gilbert, R. and Stiglitz, J. 1982: Invention and Innovation under Alternative Market Structures: the Case of Natural Resources. *Review of Economic Studies*, **49**, 567–82.

Dasgupta, P., Heal, G. and Majumdar, M. 1977. Resource Depletion and Research and Development. In M. Intriligator (ed.) *Frontiers of Quantitative Economics*, vol. IIIB. Amsterdam: North Holland.

Dasgupta, P. and Maskin, E. 1986a: The Existence of Equilibrium in Discontinuous Economic Games, 1: Theory. *Review of Economic Studies*, January 1986 (chapter 1 in this volume).

Dasgupta, P. and Maskin, E. 1986b: The Existence of Equilibrium in Discontinuous Economic Games, 2: Applications. *Review of Economic Studies*, January 1986 (chapter 2 in this volume).

Dasgupta, P. and Stiglitz, J. 1977: Market Structure and Research and Development, Paper presented at the World Congress of the *International Economic Association on Economic Growth and Resources*, Tokyo, August 1977. London School of Economics. Mimeo.

Dasgupta, P. and Stiglitz, J. 1980a: Industrial Structure and the Nature of Innovative Activity. *Economic Journal*, **90**, 266–93.

Dasgupta, P. and Stiglitz, J. 1980b: Uncertainty, Industrial Structure and the Speed of R & D. *Bell Journal of Economics*, Spring, 1–28.

Dasgupta, P. and Stiglitz, J. 1981: Entry, Innovation, Exit: Towards a Dynamic Theory of Oligopolistic Industrial Structure. *European Economic Review*, **15**, 137–58.

Dasgupta, P. and Ushio, Y. 1981: On the Rate of Convergence of Oligopoly Equilibria in Large Markets: An Example. *Economic Letters*, **8**, 13–17 (chapter 3 in this volume).

Debreu, G. 1959: *Theory of Value*. New Haven, Conn.: Yale University Press. Cowles Foundation Monograph.

Dixit, A. 1980: The Role of Investment in Entry Deterrence. *Economic Journal*, **90**, 95–106.

Eaton, B. C. and Lipsey, R. 1979: The Theory of Market Pre-emption: the Persistence of Excess Capacity and Monopoly in a Growing Spatial Market. *Economica*, **46**, 149–58.

Eaton, B. C. and Lipsey, R. 1980: Exit Barriers and Entry Barriers to Entry. *Bell Journal of Economics*, **11**, 721–9.

Eswaran, M. and Lewis, T. R. 1982: Evolution of Market Structure in a Dominant Firm Model with Exhaustible Resources. Department of Economics, University of British Columbia. Mimeo.

Fisher, F. M. and Temin, P. 1973: Returns to Scale in Research and Development: What Does the Schumpeterian Hypothesis Imply? *Journal of Political Economy*, **81**, 56–70.

Freeman, C. 1965: Research and Development in Electronic Capital Goods. *National Institute Economic Review*, **34**, 40–91.

Futia, C. A. 1980: Schumpeterian Competition. *Quarterly Journal of Economics*, **94**, 675–95.

Galbraith, J. K. 1974: *Economics and the Public Purpose*. London: Deutsch.

Gilbert, R. and Newbery, D. 1982: Pre-emptive Patenting and the Persistence of Monopoly. *American Economic Review*, **72**.

Grabowski, H. G. 1968: The Determinants of Industrial Research and Development: A Study of the Chemical, Drug and Petroleum Industries. *Journal of Political Economy*, **76**, 292–306.

Guesnerie, R. and Hart, O. 1981: Notes on the Rate of Convergence of Cournot–Nash Equilibria. University of Cambridge. Mimeo.

Kaldor, N. 1961: Capital Accumulation and Economic Growth. In F. A. Lutz and D. C. Hague (eds) *The Theory of Capital*. London: Macmillan.

Kamien, M. I. and Schwartz, N. L. 1972: Market Structure, Rival's Response, and the Firm's Rate of Product Improvement. *Journal of Industrial Economics*, **20**, 159–72.

Kamien, M. I. and Schwartz, N. L. 1975: Market Structure and Innovation: A Survey. *Journal of Economic Literature*, **13**, 1–37.

Kamien, M. I. and Schwartz, N. L. 1978: Potential Rivalry, Monopoly Profits and the Pace of Inventive Activity. *Review of Economic Studies*, **45**, 547–57.

Kamien, M. I. and Schwartz, N. L. 1982: *Market Structure and Innovation*. Cambridge: Cambridge University Press.

Layard, R. and Walters, A. A. 1978: *Microeconomic Theory*. New York: McGraw-Hill.

Leung, H. M. 1982: Industrial Structure and R & D Spill-Overs. London School of Economics. Mimeo.

Levin, R. C. 1978: Technical Change, Barriers to Entry and Market Structure. *Economica*, **45**, 347–61.

✔Levin, R. C. and Reiss, P. C. 1982: Tests of a Schumpeterian Model of R & D and Market Structure. In Z. Griliches (ed.) *R & D, Patents and Productivity*. Chicago: University of Chicago Press.

Loury, G. 1979: Market Structure and Innovation. *Quarterly Journal of Economics*, **93**, 395–410.

Malinvaud, E. 1972: *Lectures on Microeconomic Theory*. Amsterdam: North Holland.

Mansfield, E. 1968: *Industrial Research and Technological Innovation – An Econometric Analysis*. New York: W. W. Norton.

Mansfield, E. et al. 1971: *Research and Innovation in the Modern Corporation*. New York: W. W. Norton.

Mansfield, E., Schwartz, M. and Wagner, S. 1981: Imitation Costs and Patents: An Empirical Study. *Economic Journal*, **91**, 907–18.

Nelson, R. R., Peck, M. J. and Kalachek, E. D. 1967: *Technology, Economic Growth and Public Policy*. Washington, DC: Brookings Institution.

Nelson, R. R. and Winter, S. G. 1977: Dynamic Competition and Technical Progress. In B. Balassa and R. R. Nelson (eds) *Economic Progress, Private Values and Public Policy: Essays in Honour of William Fellner*. Amsterdam: North Holland.

Nelson, R. R. and Winter, S. G. 1978: Forces Generating and Limiting Concentration under Schumpeterian Competition. *Bell Journal of Economics*, **9**, 524–48.

Nordhaus, W. D. 1969: *Invention, Growth and Welfare*. Cambridge, Mass.: MIT.

Novshek, W. 1980: Nash–Cournot Equilibrium with Entry. *Review of Economic Studies*, **47**, 473–86.

Pakes, A. 1981: Patents, R & D and the Stock Market Rate of Return. NBER Working Paper No. 786.

Phillips, A. 1966: Patents, Potential Competition and Technical Progress. *American Economic Review*, **56**, 301–10.

Phillips, A. 1971: *Technology and Market Structure: A Study of the Aircraft Industry*. Lexington, Mass.: Lexington.

Reinganum, J. F. 1981a: Dynamic Games of Innovation. *Journal of Economic Theory*, **25**, 21–41.

Reinganum, J. F. 1981b: On the Diffusion of New Technology: A Game Theoretic Approach. *Review of Economic Studies*, **48**, 395–406.

Rosenberg, N. (ed.) 1971: *The Economics of Technological Change*. Harmondsworth: Penguin Modern Economic Readings.

Rosenberg, N. 1974: Science, Innovation and Economic Growth. *Economic*

Journal, **84**, 90–108.

Rosenberg, N. 1976: *Perspectives in Technology.* Cambridge: Cambridge University Press.

Scherer, F. M. 1967a: Research and Development Resource Allocation under Rivalry. *Quarterly Journal of Economics,* **81**, 359–94.

Scherer, F. M. 1967b: Market Structure and the Employment of Scientists and Engineers. *American Economic Review,* **57**, 524–31.

Schmookler, J. 1966: *Invention and Economic Growth.* Cambridge, Mass.: Harvard University Press.

Schumpeter, J. 1939: *Business Cycles.* New York: McGraw-Hill.

Schumpeter, J. 1976: *Capitalism, Socialism and Democracy,* 5th edition. London: Allen and Unwin.

Spence, A. M. 1977: Entry, Capacity, Investment and Oligopolistic Pricing. *Bell Journal of Economics,* **8**, 534–44.

Spence, A. M. 1980: Notes on Advertising, Economies of Scale and Entry Barriers. *Quarterly Journal of Economics,* **94**, 493–504.

Tandon, P. 1982: Innovation, Market Structure and Welfare. Department of Economics, Boston University. Mimeo.

Varian, H. 1978: *Microeconomic Analysis.* New York: W. W. Norton.

von Weizsacker, C. C. 1980: *Barriers to Entry: A Theoretical Treatment.* Berlin: Springer-Verlag.

7

Strategic Considerations in Invention and Innovation: The Case of Natural Resources

P. Dasgupta, R. Gilbert and J. E. Stiglitz

Strategic considerations may induce a resource importing country to invent a substitute earlier than it intends to put it to use. There are also circumstances in which it would wish to delay an invention date even if it could obtain it at an earlier date at no extra cost. Similar paradoxical results obtain if resource cartels behave strategically. Setting prices high may be a way of deterring invention. If those engaged in R & D are not resource users, and the cartel has access to similar R & D technology, it will pre-empt rivals. This may not be the case if resource users can also engage in R & D.[1]

1 INTRODUCTION

Cost-benefit studies of research and development (R & D) programmes for alternative energy sources (e.g. National Research Council 1978) typically ignore strategic considerations, in particular the fact that the choice of an R & D programme influences the decisions of resource owners, and thereby the current energy market. In this article we present a framework for analysing such interactions.

Towards this we consider the simplest of technological environments. We suppose that there is a single grade of an exhaustible natural resource and a potential manufacturing process (a 'backstop' technology) which, if developed, will enable a perfect substitute to be produced at constant unit cost. To have an interesting problem we suppose, as is realistic, that unit extraction

1 In preparing this article we have benefited greatly from the comments of Nancy Gallini and the Editors of *Econometrica* and from financial support from the National Science Foundation. Gallini et al. (1982) have independently developed an analysis similar to the one presented in Section 2. Olson (1985) contains a most comprehensive analysis of the problems discussed in this paper and presents considerably sharper conclusions. We are grateful to Mr Olson for his comments on our paper.

cost is less than the unit cost of production with the new technology once development has been completed. We suppose further that the entire resource stock has been cartelized, and that the cartel's market is restricted to a single consumer which we shall refer to as the importing country. We ignore uncertainty entirely, so that we may highlight strategic interactions. In particular, we model the R & D technology as a deterministic function relating capitalized expenditure at the initial date to the date development is completed – the latter date being nearer, the larger is capitalized expenditure.[2]

In the next section we shall analyse optimal R & D programmes for the importing country. For simplicity of exposition we shall suppose there that the importing country's government faces no rivals in R & D, and that it makes the first move; in doing so it takes into account the cartel's response to its R & D strategy. Quite clearly, the nature of the intertemporal equilibria depends on which agents have access to the R & D technology, what is the order of moves, and what kinds of commitments it is possible to undertake. In Section 3, therefore, we comment briefly on the implications of alternative assumptions regarding this.

2   R & D STRATEGY FOR AN IMPORTING COUNTRY

2.1   The Model

The model is partial equilibrium. A foreign cartel is assumed to own the entire stock of an exhaustible natural resource, which is costless to exact. Remaining reserves at date t ($\geqslant 0$) are denoted by S_i, and it is supposed that the initial stock, S_0, is known. The importing country is the sole demander of the resource and the market demand in this country at each date for the flow of the resource is given by the continuously differentiable function $Q = f(p) \geqslant 0$, where p denotes the resource price. It is assumed that $f'(p) < 0$, and we write $p(Q) \equiv f^{-1}(Q)$. We suppose, for expositional ease, that the elasticity of demand is a non-increasing function of output. Write $R(Q) = Qp(Q)$ as the revenue function and $m(Q) \equiv R'(Q)$ for marginal revenue. In what follows we suppose that $R(Q)$ is strictly concave in Q. The social rate of discount in the importing country is taken to be a positive number, r. For simplicity of exposition we take it that the cartel uses r in discounting its profits (rents).

We shall suppose that the government of the importing country finances its R & D expenditure through general taxation. Once development is completed the backstop technology will enable a perfect substitute to be produced

2 This is often called a time–cost curve in the R & D literature. See, e.g. Mansfield et al. (1981).

at unit cost $C (> 0)$. We assume that $p(0) > C$. We also assume that the government will not be engaged in production, but will make the new technology publicly available. Thus, the sector producing the substitute will be perfectly competitive.

We turn finally to the R & D technology. Assume that there is a monotonically decreasing and continuously differentiable function $X(T)$, with $X(T) > 0$ for all $T \geqslant 0$, which has the interpretation that completion of R & D at date T requires a commitment of capitalized expenditure $X(T)$ at date $t = 0$.[3] For expositional simplicity assume $X(0) = \infty$ and $X(\infty) = 0$.

The importing nation's payoff is the present discounted value of the flow of its net social surplus. The government makes the first move by announcing the date development will be completed. By hypothesis the announcement is credible because it is backed by R & D commitment. The cartel makes the second move by announcing its extraction policy. The cartel's payoff is the present discounted value of the flow of profits. The importing nation behaves strategically by taking the cartel's response into account when choosing its R & D policy. Let $U(Q) = \int_0^Q p(Q') dQ'$, and let Y_t denote output of the substitute at t. It follows that equilibrium of this two-move game can be obtained by solving the following constrained optimization problem:

$$\underset{T, Y_t \geqslant 0}{\text{maximize}} \left[\int_0^T U(\tilde{Q}_t(T)) e^{-rt} dt \right.$$

$$\left. + \int_T^\infty [U(\tilde{Q}_t(T) + Y_t) - CY_t] e^{-rt} dt - X(T) - \pi \right]$$

where $\tilde{Q}_t(T)$ maximizes $\qquad\qquad\qquad\qquad$ (7.1)

$$\int_0^T R(Q_t) e^{-rt} dt + \int_T^\infty \min \{R(Q_t), CQ_t\} e^{-rt} dt = \pi$$

$$\text{subject to} \int_0^\infty Q_t dt = S_0, \quad Q_t \geqslant 0.$$

3 This is the simplest possible characterization of an R & D technology. (See Dasgupta and Stiglitz (1980) for this and some generalizations.) It implicitly supposes that T is a deterministic functional of the time path of the flow of R & D expenditures x_t (for $0 \leqslant t \leqslant T$), say $T = F(\{x_t\})$. Then we may define $X(T)$ as:

$$X(T) \equiv \min \int_0^T e^{-rt} x_t dt, \quad \text{subject to} \quad T \geqslant F(\{x_t\}).$$

2.2   Optimal R & D

We first consider the cartel's response, that is, the suboptimization problem in
(7.1). Let $\bar{Q}$ (>0) solve $p(Q) = C$, and let T_3 $(\leqslant \infty)$ denote the date at which
the cartel would exhaust its stock if $T = \infty$. (T_3 is the earliest date of invention for which the cartel is unconstrained. $T_3 < \infty$ if the demand curve has a
choke-off price.) Let $\mu(T)$ denote the multiplier associated with the resource
constraint in (7.1). Routine control theoretic arguments can then be used to
establish that there exists a date T_1 (with $T_3 > T_1 > 0$) and, for each T there
is a date $\tilde{T}$ (with $T_3 > \tilde{T} > T_1$), such that:

$$m(\tilde{Q}_t(T)) = \mu(T)e^{rt} \quad \text{for} \quad 0 \leqslant t < T^*, \tag{7.2}$$

where $T^* = \min\{\max\{T_1, T\}, T_3\}$
($T^* = \min\{T, T_3\}$ if $m(\bar{Q}) < \mu(T)e^{r\min(T, T_1)}$);

$$\tilde{Q}_t(T) = \bar{Q} \quad \text{for} \quad T^* \leqslant t \leqslant \tilde{T}, \tag{7.3}$$

with $\mu(T)e^{r\tilde{T}} = C$;[4] and

$$\tilde{Q}_t(T) = 0 \quad \text{for} \quad t > \tilde{T} \tag{7.4}$$

($\tilde{T}$ is the date of resource exhaustion.)

In words, if $T \leqslant T_1$ marginal revenue rises at the rate r until T_1, at which
date price equals C, after which it remains at C. If $T_1 < T < T_3$ marginal
revenue rises at the rate r until T, at which date price falls discontinuously to
C. (At T there may or may not be any remaining reserves. See below.) If
$T \geqslant T_3$, marginal revenue rises at the rate r until T_3 at which date reserves
are exhausted, and the market is inoperative during (T_3, T).

Hoel (1978) has analysed the cartel's response to our problem for the case
$T = 0$. He has shown that if $-f'(p)p/f(p) > 1$ at $p = C$, there exists $\hat{S}$ such
that if $S_0 > \hat{S}$, then $T_1 > 0$ and $S_{T_1} > 0$. For concreteness we shall assume
that this is so.[5] It is then obvious that the cartel's response is invariant to T
if $0 \leqslant T \leqslant T_1$. From this we may conclude that the importing nation will
choose $T \geqslant T_1$.

Since $S_{T_1} > 0$, it follows by continuity of the state variable that $S_T > 0$
if T is slightly larger than T_1. Condition (7.3) implies then that *for T slightly
larger than* T_1

$$\mu(T)e^{rT} = Ce^{-rS_T/\bar{Q}}, \tag{7.5}$$

---

4 We shall note presently that there exists a date $T_2 (T_1 < T_2 < T_3)$ such that if
$T \geqslant T_2$, then $\tilde{T} = T^*$; that is, if $T \geqslant T_2$, then the cartel does not pursue the extraction
phase characterized by (7.3).

5 The remaining possibilities can similarly be analysed, but we wish to avoid a complete taxonomy here.

and (7.2) implies that

$$S_T = S_0 - \int_0^T m^{-1}(\mu(T) e^{rt}) dt. \tag{7.6}$$

From (7.5) and (7.6) we can therefore conclude that

$$\int_0^T m^{-1}(\mu(T) e^{rt}) dt + (\bar{Q}/r) \log(C/\mu(T)) = S_0 + \bar{Q}T. \tag{7.7}$$

Differentiating (7.7) with respect to T, and writing $q(\cdot) \equiv m^{-1}(\cdot)$, we have

$$\tilde{Q}_T^-(T) + \int_0^T \mu'(T) e^{rt} q'(\mu(T) e^{rt}) dt - (\bar{Q}/r) \mu'(T)/\mu(T) = \bar{Q}, \tag{7.8}$$

where $\tilde{Q}_T^-(T) \equiv \lim_{t \to T-0} \tilde{Q}_t(T)$. But $\tilde{Q}_T^-(T) < \bar{Q}$, from (7.2) and (7.3). Therefore (7.8) implies that $\mu'(T) < 0$. From (7.2) it follows that $d\tilde{Q}_t(T)/dT > 0$, and therefore that $dS_T/dT < 0$. In fact, from (7.5) and (7.6) it follows that there exists a negative number, $-\delta$, such that

$$-\delta > dS_T/dT > -\bar{Q}. \tag{7.9}$$

Since (7.9) implies that dS_T/dT is bounded away from zero, we can conclude that there exists a date T_2, such that $S_T = 0$ if $T \geqslant T_2$, and $S_T > 0$ if $T < T_2$. This means that $\tilde{T} = \min\{T, T_3\} \equiv T^*$ if $T \geqslant T_2$, and $T_2 > \tilde{T} > T$ if $T < T_2$. Furthermore, $\tilde{T}$ is increasing in T in the interval (T_1, T_2).[6]

We have established the somewhat surprising result that $\mu(T)$ - and hence the initial price $p(Q_0(T))$ - is decreasing in T, and $\tilde{Q}_t(T)$ is increasing in T in the interval (T_1, T_2). It is simple to check that $\mu(T)$, and hence $p(Q_0(T))$, is increasing (and therefore $\tilde{Q}_t(T)$ is decreasing) in T if $T_3 \geqslant T > T_2$. (By definition of T_3, $\mu(T)$ and $\tilde{Q}_t(T)$ are invariant to T if $T \geqslant T_3$.) Thus $\mu(T)$ attains its minimum value at $T = T_2$. (See figure 7.1). The intuition behind this result is easy to see. Let $T_1 < T < T_2$. We know that $S_T > 0$. Now suppose that the invention date is delayed slightly, say, to $T + \Delta T$, but suppose that the cartel does not alter its initial price in response to this change. Then, by (7.2) and (7.3) the amount sold by date $T + \Delta T$ would be slightly less than on the initial trajectory. Therefore, the date of exhaustion, $\tilde{T}(T + \Delta T)$, would be slightly later. The present value of the marginal revenue at that date is $Ce^{-r\tilde{T}}$, and this is smaller than it previously was. But by hypothesis, marginal revenue at $t = 0$ remains the same. To restore equality the cartel must lower its initial price slightly, by an amount which is sufficiently small that $\tilde{T}$ remains larger than it originally was.

6 To see this, note that if $T < T_2$, then $\tilde{T} = T + S_T/\bar{Q}$. Thus $d\tilde{T}/dT = 1 + (dS_T/dT)/\bar{Q} > 0$, on using (7.9).

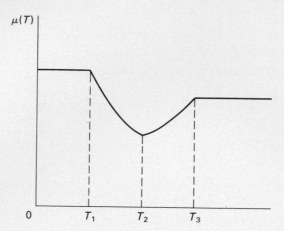

Figure 7.1 $T_3 = \infty$ if demand function does not have choke-off price.

Turning now to the importing country's optimization problem in (7.1) we note first that optimal Y_t is the form: $Y_t = 0$ for $0 \leqslant t \leqslant \tilde{T}$ and $Y_t = \bar{Q}$ for $t > \tilde{T}$ if $T \leqslant T_3$; $Y_t = 0$ for $0 \leqslant t < T$ and $Y_t = \bar{Q}$ for $t \geqslant T$ if $T > T_3$. We note next that if $T < T_2$ there is a lag between the date at which development is completed and the date at which it is brought into line. But if $T \geqslant T_2$ the invention is brought into line the day development is completed. *We now show that, provided that technological possibilities are favourable, it is optimal for the importing country to choose T in the interval (T_1, T_2); that is, it is optimal to complete development of the backstop technology before the cartel plans to exhaust its reserves.* Naturally, advancing the completion date increases R & D costs. Nevertheless, such crash programmes can be optimal precisely because they are a *credible* means of forcing the cartel to pursue a more favourable intertemporal pricing policy.

To confirm this, suppose that optimum $T \leqslant T_3$. Since we know that $T \geqslant T_1$, we may use (7.2) and (7.3) to re-express the importing country's objective as

$$\underset{T \geqslant T_1}{\text{maximize}} \left[\int_0^T V(\tilde{Q}_t(T)) e^{-rt} \, dt + V(\bar{Q}) e^{-rT}/r - X(T) \right], \qquad (7.10)$$

where $V(Q) \equiv U(Q) - p(Q))Q$.

Notice first that even if $X''(T) > 0$, (7.10) is not necessarily concave in T. However, on the assumption that optimum $T \in (T_1, T_3)$ and does not equal T_2, it must satisfy the social cost–benefit rule:

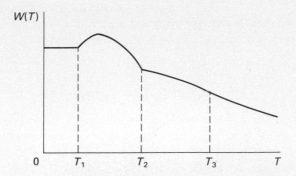

Figure 7.2 $W(T) \equiv \int_0^T V(\bar{Q}_t(T)) e^{-rt} \, dt + V(\bar{Q}) e^{-rT}/r$ if $T \leqslant T_3$; and $W(T) \equiv \int_0^{T_1} V(\bar{Q}_t(T)) e^{-rt} \, dt + \int_{T_3}^T V(0) e^{-rt} \, dt + \int_T^\infty V(\bar{Q}) e^{-rt} \, dt$ if $T \geqslant T_3$.

$$\int_0^T V'(Q_t(T))[d\bar{Q}_t(T)/dT] e^{-rt} \, dt + [V(\tilde{Q}_T^-(T)) - V(\bar{Q})] e^{-rT} = X'(T).[7]$$

$$(7.11)$$

The first term on the left-hand side of (7.11) yields the effect of a delay in the date of R&D completion on social surplus generated in the importing country before that date. We have seen that it is positive if $T_1 < T < T_2$, and is negative if $T_2 < T < T_3$. (For $T \geqslant T_3$ it is zero.) However, each additional moment's delay results in a loss in social benefits due to the fact that market price just before this date exceeds C (i.e. $p(\tilde{Q}_T^-(T)) > C$). The second term on the left-hand side of (7.11) is negative, and measures this loss. The sum of these two effects must equal the R&D expenditure saved because of this delay, which is the right-hand side of (7.11). In figure 7.2 we have drawn the *gross* benefit function of the importing country (the first two terms in (7.10)). We have seen that its slope is negative for $T > T_2$. It is simple to confirm that its slope is negative if T is slightly less than T_2. It follows that by suitably choosing $X(T)$, and therefore the right-hand side of (7.11), we can ensure that optimum T is less than T_2, establishing the result we have emphasized above. But note that the gross benefit function is *positively* sloped in a neighbourhood to the right of T_1. This implies that optimal T is outside this neighbourhood. What this means is that there is a precise sense in which one may have an invention too early. *It pays the importing country*

---

7 If optimum T exceeds T_3 and is finite, it must satisfy the cost–benefit rule:

$$-[V(\bar{Q}) - V(0)] e^{-rT} = X'(T).$$

to delay making the invention until some time after T_1, not only because it saves on R & D costs but also, somewhat paradoxically, because it benefits from a more favourable pricing policy on the part of the cartel. One notes in particular that in this interval a delay in the completion date is beneficial to *both* parties.

2.3   Optimal Taxation and R & D

Suppose that the importing country has an additional control: the taxation of resource imports. If, as we have been assuming so far, the importing country moves first, it can impose a 100 per cent advalorum tax, and thereby appropriate *all* rents from the cartel. If, in addition, demand is iso-elastic (with elasticity greater than unity), marginal revenue is proportional to price, and so the equilibrium outcome is equivalent to the optimum resource extraction and R & D programme in a centrally planned economy. (For an analysis of this last, see Dasgupta et al. 1982.) But if demand is not iso-elastic then, even though all rents can be appropriated by the importing country, it cannot enforce the optimal intertemporal allocation of the exhaustible resource.

The matter is a great deal more complex if the cartel has the first move. The extent to which it can avoid being taxed depends on the means that are at its disposal for making retaliations credible.

3   DETERRENCE AND PRE-EMPTION

The preceding analysis was based on the hypothesis that the government of the importing country had sole access to the R & D technology, and that it made the first move. In this section we briefly discuss the implications of dropping each of these hypotheses.

Begin by dropping the second hypothesis.[8] Suppose the cartel can, at date $t = 0$, commit itself to any sales path over the interval $[0, \hat{T}]$. We take it that $\hat{T} < T_1$, to capture the fact that futures contracts extend only for short periods. Consider the case where the cartel and the importing country move simultaneously.[9] Suppose $T > T_1$. (We shall see that (Nash) equilibrium T exceeds T_1.) Given T, it is simple to calculate the cartel's response: it is the solution of the sub-optimization problem of (7.1). This yields $S_{\hat{T}}(T)$, the remaining reserves at $\hat{T}$. It remains to analyse the importing country's response. From the analysis presented in Section 2.2 we may infer that (Nash) equilibrium T will not be less than T_1. If the cartel does commit itself

8 We revert to the construct of Section 2.2 and suppose that the only control available to the importing country is R & D.

9 The analysis for the case where the cartel moves first can likewise be developed.

to a sales policy during $[0, \hat{T}]$ the importing country cannot influence the cartel's extraction of its remaining reserves in this period, but it can from $\hat{T}$ onwards. It follows that if equilibrium $T \leqslant T_3$ the importing country's problem is:

$$\underset{T \geqslant T_1}{\text{maximize}} \left[\int_{\hat{T}}^{T} V(\tilde{Q}_t(T)) \, e^{-rt} \, dt + V(\bar{Q}) \, e^{-rT}/r - X(T) \right], \quad (7.12)$$

subject to $S_{\hat{T}}$ being available at $\hat{T}$.

The solution of (7.12), assuming it to be unique, yields the reaction function of the importing country. Let T_n be the Nash equilibrium date of invention.[10] It can be shown that if $T_n < (>) T_2$, then T_n is less than (greater than) the optimum date of invention in the model of Section 2.2. But this means that if $T_n < T_2$, the cartel would prefer to follow rather than move simultaneously – or in other words, prefer not to bind itself to any contract for the period $(0, \hat{T})$. In this case the equilibrium outcome would be the same as the one in Section 2.2.

Let us now drop the hypothesis that the importing country has sole access to the R & D technology. To begin with, continue to assume that the *cartel's* R & D technology is vastly inferior to its rivals', so that it does not enter the R & D race. In order to assess the incentives for developing the substitute product two broad categories of agents must be distinguished: resource *users* and R & D firms. By the latter we mean firms that are not resource users themselves. Such a firm is indifferent to the cartel's current pricing policy, except in so far as it influences the size of remaining reserves at the date the firm's R & D programme is completed – the value of the invention to the firm being smaller, presumably, the larger are remaining reserves. Resource *users*, on the other hand, *do* care about the cartel's current extraction policy, as expression (7.10) makes clear. In Section 2.2 we analysed the incentives that a particular type of resource user (an importing country) has for developing a substitute product. Consider now by way of contrast the case where there is a patent race *only* among R & D firms, with the winner taking all. For concreteness, we may suppose that the cartel makes the first move and commits itself to an extraction policy, and that this is followed by R & D competition. If reserves are positive at the date the patent is awarded, the market at the date is one of duopoly. Let $Z(S_T)$ be the present value of profits to the patent winner at T if S_T denotes remaining reserves at T. Suppose that free entry among R & D firms results in zero profit as an equilibrium condition. Then equilibrium T must be the smallest solution of the equation:

$$Z(S_T) \, e^{-rT} = X(T). \quad (7.13)$$

10 It is clear that if $\hat{T} = 0$ the present model reduces to the one in Section 2.2.

It is natural to assume that $Z'(S) < 0$. This and (7.13) imply that, contrary to what is often thought, a high price for a resource today does not imply that the incentives among R & D firms to invent a substitute are high. *R & D deterrence involves the cartel maintaining a high price for its resource.* Indeed, it is a simple matter to confirm that equilibrium in this game involves a higher resource price than would have prevailed in a market where there is no threat of entry by R & D firms. But the welfare effects are ambiguous, since resource price after the invention is lower.

Now suppose that the cartel also has access to the R & D technology, but continue to assume that no resource *user* can engage in R & D. In this case it is easy to see that the cartel will pre-empt its rivals and win the patent.[11] The reason is this. For any given level of remaining reserves the cartel's combined profits from resource sales and substitute production (were it to win the patent) exceeds the sum of the profits accruing to it from resource sales and to the patent winner from substitute production (were the cartel not to win the patent). It follows that given any level of remaining reserves the cartel makes positive profits at all R & D levels for which rivals earn zero profit.

If the cartel can engage in R & D it has two sets of controls to deter rivals: the resource price and R & D expenditure. One might conjecture that the cartel resorts less to the former if pre-emptive patenting is an option. It is a simple matter to confirm this intuition if demand is iso-elastic and the initial stock is 'large'. In such a situation a market in which the cartel can engage in R & D has prices lower at all dates prior to the date of invention. Invention and innovation both occur earlier than in the case where the cartel cannot compete in R & D. Moreover, the dates of R & D completion and innovation do not coincide: there are 'sleeping patents'.

The argument establishing pre-emptive patenting on the part of the cartel does *not* hold if resource *users* also have access to the R & D technology. The cartel's combined profits from resource sales and substitute production do not necessarily exceed the sum of benefits accruing to it from resource sales and the benefits to the patent winner if the winner is a resource user. In particular, the payoff to the resource user from making the invention depends not only on the size of remaining reserves at the date development is completed, but also on the cartel's pricing policy prior to this date.

4 CONCLUSIONS

Strategic considerations are clearly central to the design of R & D policies by resource importing countries and to the determination of extraction policies by resource cartels. Yet national energy studies rarely take them into

---

11 The general argument is given in Dasgupta and Stiglitz (1980).

account. In this article we have attempted to provide a framework for such an analysis. Strategic considerations may induce a resource user (e.g. an importing country) to complete the development of the substitute product at a date earlier than the date at which it intends to introduce it, even though this involves additional R & D expenditure. Concomitant with this are circumstances in which an importing country deliberately delays R & D completion, *even* if it could complete at an earlier date at no extra cost, because such a delay induces the cartel to *lower* its price at all dates prior to R & D completion.

Similar paradoxical results obtain if the resource cartel behaves strategically. The threat of the development of a substitute by R & D firms induces the cartel to *raise* its price and, if the cartel also has access to a similar R & D technology, it pre-empts its rivals, thereby maintaining its monopoly position. This pre-emption argument, however, does not carry over if resource users compete in the R & D race.

REFERENCES

Dasgupta, P., Gilbert, R. and Stiglitz, J. 1982: Invention and innovation under alternative market structures: the case of natural resources. *Review of Economic Studies*, **49**, 567–82.

Dasgupta, P. and Stiglitz, J. 1980: Uncertainty, market structure and the speed of R & D. *Bell Journal of Economics*, **11**, 1–28.

Gallini, N., Lewis, T. and Ware, R. 1982: *Strategic Timing and Pricing of the Substitute in the Cartelized Resource Market*. Mimeo, Department of Economics, University of British Columbia.

Hoel, M. 1978: Resource extraction, substitute production and monopoly. *Journal of Economic Theory*, **19**, 28–37.

Mansfield, E., Schwartz, M. and Wagner, S. 1981: Imitation costs and patents: an empirical study. *Economic Journal*, **91**, 907–18.

National Research Council 1978: *Energy Modelling for an Uncertain Future*. Supporting Paper 2 of *Study of Nuclear and Alternative Energy*, National Academy of Sciences, Washington, D.C.

Olson, T. 1985: *Strategic Development of a Backstop Technology*. Mimeo, Department of Economics, University of Bergen.

III

THE DESIGN OF ORGANIZATIONS

8

On the Revelation Principle under Complete and Incomplete Information

R. Repullo

This paper shows that if a social choice rule f can be implemented in Nash strategies (under complete information) or in Bayesian strategies (under incomplete information) by an indirect mechanism g, (a) there exists a direct mechanism h (i.e. one in which agents report their characteristics) which truthfully implements f in Nash or Bayesian strategies, and (b) under certain conditions there exists a subdirect mechanism k (i.e. one in which agents report their preferences) which truthfully implements f in Nash or Bayesian strategies. The mechanisms h and k, however, do not necessarily implement f in Nash or Bayesian strategies. It is then shown that under certain condition (c) the direct mechanism h, and (d) the subdirect mechanism k not only implement f truthfully in Nash or Bayesian strategies, but also implement f.[1]

1 INTRODUCTION

A social choice rule is a correspondence that selects a set of optimal social states for each possible configuration of agents' preferences over social states. When these preferences are not publicly known, it is assumed that the planner devises a mechanism, that is, a rule which specifies a social state for each vector of strategies chosen by the agents. To determine the strategies chosen in equilibrium, two possible information structures may be considered, namely, complete and incomplete information.

Under complete information it is assumed that each agent not only knows his own preferences but also the preferences of the other agents. A mechanism then defines a game with complete information for which the solution concept proposed is Nash equilibrium.

1 This paper brings together two earlier papers entitled Implementation by Direct Mechanisms under Incomplete Information (*ICERD Theoretical Economics Discussion Paper 83/69*, London School of Economics) and On the Revelation Principle under Complete and Incomplete Information (*CARESS Working Paper #84-18*, University of Pennsylvania). I am grateful to P. Dasgupta, K. Binmore, and A. Postlewaite for helpful discussions.

Under incomplete information, on the other hand, it is assumed that each agent has a characteristic which determines his preferences over social states and his beliefs about the characteristics of the other agents. A mechanism then defines a game with incomplete information for which the solution concept proposed is Bayesian equilibrium.

In this paper we show that any environment with complete information is a special case of an environment with incomplete information.[2] Thus all the results obtained for the latter apply as well to the former, and so we can now restrict our attention to Bayesian implementation.

Formally, a mechanism is said to *implement* a social choice rule in Bayesian strategies if (a) the game defined by the mechanism has at least one Bayesian equilibrium, and (b) the equilibrium outcomes for each vector of characteristics are contained in the corresponding social choice set.

A special kind of mechanisms are those in which the the strategy set for each agent coincides with either the set of his possible characteristics (which we call direct mechanisms) or the set of his possible preferences (which we call subdirect mechanisms). For these mechanisms one may define an alternative notion of implementation: a direct mechanism (or a subdirect mechanism) *truthfully implements* a social choice rule in Bayesian strategies if (a) truth-telling is a Bayesian equilibrium for the game defined by the mechanism, and (b) the truth-telling outcome for each vector of characteristics is contained in the corresponding social choice set.

The distinction between direct and subdirect mechanisms has not been made in the literature. But it turns out to be important when we come to discuss the following paradox. It is well known that for any mechanism that implements a social choice rule in Bayesian strategies there exists a direct mechanism which truthfully implements it in Bayesian strategies. By our previous discussion this result, known as the *revelation principle*, must hold true for implementation in Nash strategies. But surprisingly the revelation principle is not supposed to be true for Nash implementation.[3]

To resolve this paradox we will distinguish between the revelation principle for direct and the revelation principle for subdirect mechanisms. The former guarantees that for any mechanism that implements a social choice rule in Bayesian (or Nash) strategies, there exists a direct mechanism which truthfully implements it in Bayesian (or Nash) strategies. The latter, on the other hand, would guarantee the existence of a subdirect mechanism which truthfully implements the social choice rule in Bayesian (or Nash) strategies. In this paper we show that while the revelation principle for direct mechanisms is always true, the revelation principle for subdirect mechanisms holds true only when a certain condition is satisfied.

---

2 This result was previously noted by Laffont and Maskin (1982), and in the context of economic environments by Postlewaite and Schmeidler (1984).

3 See, however, Laffont and Maskin (1982) and Maskin (1983).

It should be noticed, however, that these results make use of a notion of implementation which is rather weak. In particular, there is nothing that guarantees that agents will always choose to play the truthful equilibrium when alternative untruthful equilibria exist. To illustrate the nature of the problem, in this paper we present an example of a social choice rule that can be implemented in Bayesian strategies by an indirect mechanism. By the revelation principle, there exists a direct mechanism which truthfully implements it in Bayesian strategies. However, this direct mechanism does not implement the given social choice rule, because there is an untruthful equilibrium which for a certain vector of characteristics gives an outcome outside the corresponding social choice set. Furthermore, the truthful equilibrium is shown to be Pareto-dominated by the untruthful equilibrium, so that the former is very unlikely to be chosen by the agents.

Given the problem with the notion of truthful implementation illustrated by this example, we then proceed to state a condition under which the direct and subdirect mechanisms given by the revelation principle not only implement the social choice rule truthfully, but also implement it. The fact that this result, which we call the strong revelation principle, is not true in general implies that for environments with complete or incomplete information it cannot be claimed that there is no loss of generality in restricting attention to direct (or subdirect) mechanisms.

The paper is organized as follows. Section 2 introduces the notation and basic definitions. In Section 3 we discuss the (weak) revelation principle for direct and subdirect mechanisms under incomplete information, and in Section 4 we present the example mentioned above. Section 5 then discusses the strong revelation principle for direct and subdirect mechanisms under incomplete information. In Sections 6 and 7 we extend these results to environments with complete information. Finally, Section 8 contains our concluding remarks.

2 NOTATION AND BASIC DEFINITIONS

Let A denote the set of social states and let $I = \{1, \ldots, n\}$ be the set of agents. Each agent $i \in I$ has a von Neumann–Morgenstern utility function u_i on the set A. Let U_i be the set of all possible utility functions for agent i, normalized so that if $u_i, u_i' \in U_i$ are such that $u_i(\cdot) = a + bu_i'(\cdot)$, with $b > 0$, then $a = 0$ and $b = 1$.

A *social choice rule* (SCR) is a correspondence $f: U \Rightarrow A$ which specifies a non-empty choice set $f(u) \subset A$ for each vector of utility functions $u \in U = \Pi_{i \in I} U_i$.

A *mechanism* (game form) is a function $g: S \to A$ which specifies a social state $g(s) \in A$ for each vector of strategies $s \in S = \Pi_{i \in I} S_i$, where S_i denotes agent i's strategy set.

Given a mechanism g the question arises as to what strategies are going to be chosen by the agents. To answer this question it is essential to specify the information that agents are assumed to have about one another. Two different information structures have been studied in the literature.

Under *complete information* it is assumed that each agent i not only knows his own utility function u_i, but also the utility functions $u_{-i} = (u_1, \ldots, u_{i-1}, u_{i+1}, \ldots, u_n)$ of the other agents. A mechanism g together with a vector of utility functions $u \in U$ then defines a game with complete information.

A *Nash equilibrium* for the game (g, u) is a vector of strategies $s \in S$ such that for all $i \in I$ and $s_i' \in S_i$ we have

$$u_i[g(s_i, s_{-i})] \geqslant u_i[g(s_i', s_{-i})].$$

Let $N(g, u)$ denote the set of Nash equilibria for the game (g, u).

The mechanism g is said to *implement the SCR f in Nash strategies* if for all $u \in U$ we have

   (i) $N(g, u) \neq \emptyset$, and
   (ii) $g(N(g, u)) \subset f(u)$.

Under *incomplete information* it is assumed that each agent i has a characteristic $\theta_i \in \Theta_i$ which summarizes all the information that he may have. In particular, θ_i determines (i) a utility function $v_i(\theta_i) \in U_i$, and (ii) a probability measure $\mu_i(\theta_i)$ on the set $\Theta_{-i} = \Pi_{j \neq i} \Theta_j$. Thus in this framework agents' characteristics determine both preferences over social states and beliefs about the characteristics of the other agents. It is also assumed that the array $B = (\Theta_i, v_i(\cdot), \mu_i(\cdot))_{i \in I}$ is common knowledge to all agents as well as to the planner.[4]

A mechanism g together with the array B defines a game with incomplete information in the sense of Harsanyi (1967–68). A *strategy rule* for agent i in the game (g, B) is a function $\sigma_i = \Theta_i \rightarrow S_i$ which specifies a strategy choice $\sigma_i(\theta_i) \in S_i$ for each possible characteristic $\theta_i \in \Theta_i$. Let $\Sigma_i(g)$ be the set of all strategy rules for agent i in the game defined by the mechanism g, and let $\Sigma(g) = \Pi_{i \in I} \Sigma_i(g)$.

A *Bayesian equilibrium* for the game (g, B) is a vector of strategy rules $\sigma \in \Sigma(g)$ such that for all $i \in I$, $\theta_i \in \Theta_i$, and $s_i \in S_i$ we have

$$\int v_i[g(\sigma_i(\theta_i), \sigma_{-i}(\theta_{-i})) \mid \theta_i] \, d\mu_i(\theta_{-i} \mid \theta_i)$$
$$\geqslant \int v_i[g(s_i, \sigma_{-i}(\theta_{-i})) \mid \theta_i] \, d\mu_i(\theta_{-i} \mid \theta_i),$$

where $v_i(\cdot \mid \theta_i) = v_i(\theta_i)(\cdot)$ and $\mu_i(\cdot \mid \theta_i) = \mu_i(\theta_i)(\cdot)$. Let $B(g) \subset \Sigma(g)$ denote the set of Bayesian equilibria for the game (g, B).

---

4 For an excellent discussion of this approach see Myerson (1983).

The mechanism g is said to *implement the SCR f in Bayesian strategies* if

(i) $B(g) \neq \emptyset$, and
(ii) $g(\sigma(\theta)) \in f(v(\theta))$ for all $\theta \in \Theta = \Pi_{i \in I} \Theta_i$ and $\sigma \in B(g)$,

where $v(\theta) = (v_1(\theta_1), \ldots, v_n(\theta_n))$.

It is important to realize that in this definition of implementation the SCR f is still defined on the set U of agents' utility functions and not on the set Θ of agents' characteristics, and so in this sense our approach differs from the standard approach in the literature. However, there seems to be no good reason why a planner would want to introduce agents' beliefs in the SCR that he wants to implement. Moreover, our approach allows us to unify the treatment of the complete and incomplete information cases because our SCRs are defined prior to the specification of the information that agents are assumed to have about one another.

3 THE WEAK REVELATION PRINCIPLE UNDER INCOMPLETE INFORMATION

In this section we first define the concepts of direct and subdirect mechanisms, and we then introduce an alternative notion of implementation which is available for them, namely truthful implementation in Bayesian strategies. This notion of implementation leads to the statement of the revelation principle for direct and subdirect mechanisms.

A *direct mechanism* is a function $h: \Theta \to A$ which specifies a social state $h(\theta) \in A$ for each vector of characteristics $\theta \in \Theta$. Thus a direct mechanism is a mechanism for which the strategy set S_i for each agent i is the set Θ_i of his possible characteristics.

A *subdirect mechanism* is a function $k: U \to A$ which specifies a social state $k(u) \in A$ for each vector of utility function $u \in U$. Thus a subdirect mechanism is a mechanism for which the strategy set S_i for each agent i is the set U_i of his possible utility functions.

The direct mechanism h *truthfully implements the SCR f in Bayesian strategies* if

(i) $\hat{\sigma} \in B(h)$, and
(ii) $h(\hat{\sigma}(\theta)) \in f(v(\theta))$ for all $\theta \in \Theta$,

where $\hat{\sigma} \in \Sigma(h)$ satisfies $\hat{\sigma}(\theta) = \theta$ for all $\theta \in \Theta$.[5]

The subdirect mechanism k *truthfully implements the SCR f in Bayesian strategies* if

5 That is, agent i with characteristic θ_i truthfully reports his characteristic θ_i.

    (i) $\bar{\sigma} \in B(k)$, and

    (ii) $k(\bar{\sigma}(\theta)) \in f(v(\theta))$ for all $\theta \in \Theta$,

where $\bar{\sigma} \in \Sigma(k)$ satisfies $\bar{\sigma}(\theta) = v(\theta)$ for all $\theta \in \Theta$.[6]

It should be noticed that implementation and truthful implementation are quite different concepts. Indeed, the fact that the direct mechanism h (the subdirect mechanism k) truthfully implements the SCR f does not imply that h (or k) implements f, since there may be untruthful equilibria which yield outcomes outside the social choice set. Also, the fact that the direct mechanism h (the subdirect mechanism k) implements the SCR f does not imply that h (or k) truthfully implements f, since truth-telling may not be a Bayesian equilibrium.

We can now establish the following results.

Theorem 3.1 (weak revelation principle for direct mechanisms). *If g is a mechanism that implements the SCR f in Bayesian strategies, there exists a direct mechanism h which truthfully implements f in Bayesian strategies.*

Proof. See Dasgupta et al. (1979, pp. 206–7). ‖

Theorem 3.2 (weak revelation principle for subdirect mechanisms). *If g is a mechanism that implements the SCR f in Bayesian strategies, and there exists $\sigma \in B(g)$ satisfying*

    (U) *for all $i \in I$ and $\theta_i, \theta_i' \in \Theta_i$ we have $\sigma_i(\theta_i) = \sigma_i(\theta_i')$ whenever $v_i(\theta_i) = v_i(\theta_i')$*

then there exists a subdirect mechanism k which truthfully implements f in Bayesian strategies.

Proof. Let us define $k = g \circ \sigma \circ \gamma$, where $\gamma: U \to \Theta$ is an arbitrary function satisfying $v(\gamma(u)) = u$ for all $u \in U$.[7] Now since g implements f and by construction $v(\gamma(v(\theta))) = v(\theta)$ for all $\theta \in \Theta$ we have

$$k(\bar{\sigma}(\theta)) = k(v(\theta)) = g(\sigma(\gamma(v(\theta)))) \in f(v(\gamma(v(\theta)))) = f(v(\theta))$$

for all $\theta \in \Theta$, so that it remains to show that $\bar{\sigma} \in B(k)$. Suppose not. Then there exists some $i \in I$, $\theta_i \in \Theta_i$, and $u_i \in U_i$ such that

$$\int v_i \left[k(u_i, v_{-i}(\theta_{-i})) \mid \theta_i \right] d\mu_i(\theta_{-i} \mid \theta_i)$$
$$> \int v_i \left[k(v_i(\theta_i), v_{-i}(\theta_{-i})) \mid \theta_i \right] d\mu_i(\theta_{-i} \mid \theta_i).$$

By the definition of k this implies

$$\int v_i \left[g(\sigma_i(\gamma_i(u_i)), \sigma_{-i}(\gamma_{-i}(v_{-i}(\theta_{-i})))) \mid \theta_i \right] d\mu_i(\theta_{-i} \mid \theta_i)$$
$$> \int v_i \left[g(\sigma_i(\gamma_i(v_i(\theta_i))), \sigma_{-i}(\gamma_{-i}(v_{-i}(\theta_{-i})))) \mid \theta_i \right] d\mu_i(\theta_{-i} \mid \theta_i).$$

---

6 That is, agent i with characteristic θ_i truthfully reports his utility function $v_i(\theta_i)$.

7 Notice that this definition implies $\gamma(u) = (\gamma_1(u_1), \dots, \gamma_n(u_n))$ for all $u \in U$.

But by assumption (U) we have $\sigma_i(\theta_i) = \sigma_i(\gamma_i(v_i(\theta_i)))$ for all $i \in I$ and $\theta_i \in \Theta_i$, so we conclude

$$\int v_i \left[g(\sigma_i(\gamma_i(u_i)), \sigma_{-i}(\theta_{-i})) \mid \theta_i \right] d\mu_i(\theta_{-i} \mid \theta_i)$$

$$> \int v_i \left[g(\sigma_i(\theta_i), \sigma_{-i}(\theta_{-i})) \mid \theta_i \right] d\mu_i(\theta_{-i} \mid \theta_i),$$

which contradicts $\sigma \in B(g)$. $\parallel$

Assumption (U) may be shown to be satisfied if in the mechanism g every agent always has a dominant strategy. Thus we have the following result.

Corollary 3.1. *If g is a mechanism that implements the SCR f in Bayesian strategies, and there exists $\sigma \in B(g)$ satisfying*

(DS) *for all $i \in I$, $\theta_i \in \Theta_i$, $s_i \in S_i$, and $s_{-i} \in S_{-i}$ we have*

$$v_i \left[g(\sigma_i(\theta_i), s_{-i}) \mid \theta_i \right] \geqslant v_i \left[g(s_i, s_{-i}) \mid \theta_i \right],$$

then there exists a subdirect mechanism k which truthfully implements f in Bayesian strategies.

Proof. Let us define $\sigma' = \sigma \circ \gamma \circ v$, where $\gamma : U \to \Theta$ is defined as in Theorem 3.2. By assumption (DS) it is clear that $\sigma' \in B(g)$. Moreover, for any $i \in I$ and $\theta_i, \theta_i' \in \Theta_i$ with $v_i(\theta_i) = v_i(\theta_i')$ we have

$$\sigma_i'(\theta_i) = \sigma_i(\gamma_i(v_i(\theta_i))) = \sigma_i(\gamma_i(v_i(\theta_i'))) = \sigma_i'(\theta_i').$$

Hence the result follows from Theorem 3.2. $\parallel$

It is important to realize that, contrary to the assertion in Laffont and Maskin (1982, p. 44), Theorem 3.1 does not imply that the set $B(g)$ of Bayesian equilibria for the mechanism g is isomorphic to the set $B(h)$ of Bayesian equilibria for the direct mechanism h. But this means that, contrary to the claim in Harris and Townsend (1981, p. 35) and Holmstrom and Myerson (1983, p. 1804), one cannot conclude that there is no loss of generality in restricting attention to direct mechanisms. The only thing that the weak revelation principle says is that the direct mechanism h *truthfully* implements the SCR f in Bayesian strategies. But this is a rather weak result since there is nothing that guarantees that agents will always choose to play the truthful Bayesian equilibrium when alternative untruthful equilibria exist. Moreover, these untruthful equilibria need not correspond to some equilibria in the mechanism g, which suggests that h may not implement f in Bayesian strategies. The example in the following section illustrates this possibility.

4 AN EXAMPLE

Suppose that $A = \{a, b, c, d, e, p\}$ and that there are two agents ($i = 1, 2$) with $\Theta_1 = \{\theta_1, \theta_1', \theta_1''\}$ and $\Theta_2 = \{\theta_2, \theta_2', \theta_2''\}$, where the corresponding utility functions are given by

$$u_1 = v_1(\theta_1) = v_1(\theta_1'') = \begin{matrix} a & b & c & d & e & p \\ [8 & 2 & 6 & 7 & 1 & 0] \end{matrix}$$

$$u_1' = v_1(\theta_1') = [2 \quad 4 \quad 6 \quad 1 \quad 3 \quad 0]$$

$$u_2 = v_2(\theta_2) = v_2(\theta_2'') = [8 \quad 2 \quad 6 \quad 1 \quad 7 \quad 0]$$

$$u_2' = v_2(\theta_2') = [2 \quad 4 \quad 6 \quad 3 \quad 1 \quad 0]$$

and the corresponding beliefs are given by

$$\mu_1(\theta_1) = \mu_1(\theta_1') = \begin{matrix} \theta_2 & \theta_2' & \theta_2'' \\ [1/4 & 1/2 & 1/4] \end{matrix} \qquad \mu_2(\theta_2) = \mu_2(\theta_2') = \begin{matrix} \theta_1 & \theta_1' & \theta_1'' \\ [1/4 & 1/2 & 1/4] \end{matrix}$$

$$\mu_1(\theta_1'') = [1/2 \quad 1/2 \quad 0 \,] \qquad\qquad \mu_2(\theta_2'') = [1/2 \quad 1/2 \quad 0 \,].$$

Consider the SCR f defined by

$$f = \begin{matrix} & u_2 & u_2' \\ & \begin{bmatrix} \{a\} & \{b\} \\ \{b\} & \{c\} \end{bmatrix} & \begin{matrix} u_1 \\ u_1'. \end{matrix} \end{matrix}$$

The SCR f can be implemented in Bayesian strategies by the mechanism

$$g = \begin{matrix} & s_2 & s_2' & s_2'' \\ & \begin{bmatrix} a & b & d \\ b & c & e \\ e & d & p \end{bmatrix} & \begin{matrix} s_1 \\ s_1' \\ s_1''. \end{matrix} \end{matrix}$$

In the mechanism g, agent 1 chooses rows as strategies and agent 2 columns. The compute the set of Bayesian equilibria we note first that s_1' is a dominant strategy for agent 1 with characteristic θ_1', and that s_2' is also a dominant strategy for agent 2 with characteristic θ_2'. Then it is easy to check that we have a unique Bayesian equilibrium, namely

$$\sigma_1 = \begin{matrix} \theta_1 & \theta_1' & \theta_1'' \\ [s_1 & s_1' & s_1] \end{matrix} \qquad\qquad \sigma_2 = \begin{matrix} \theta_2 & \theta_2' & \theta_2'' \\ [s_2 & s_2' & s_2] \end{matrix}$$

which satisfies $g(\sigma(\theta)) \in f(v(\theta))$ for all $\theta \in \Theta$. Hence g implements f in Bayesian strategies.

Consider now the direct mechanism

$$h = g \circ \sigma \begin{matrix} & \theta_2 & \theta_2' & \theta_2'' \\ & \begin{bmatrix} a & b & a \\ b & c & b \\ a & b & a \end{bmatrix} & \begin{matrix} \theta_1 \\ \theta_1' \\ \theta_1''. \end{matrix} \end{matrix}$$

By Theorem 3.1 the mechanism h truthfully implements f in Bayesian strategies. However, h does not implement f, because apart from the truthful equilibrium

$$\begin{array}{ccc} \theta_1 & \theta_1' & \theta_1'' \\ \hat{\sigma}_1 = [\theta_1 & \theta_1' & \theta_1''] \end{array} \qquad \begin{array}{ccc} \theta_2 & \theta_2' & \theta_2'' \\ \hat{\sigma}_2 = [\theta_2' & \theta_2' & \theta_2''] \end{array}$$

there is another equilibrium, namely

$$\begin{array}{ccc} \theta_1 & \theta_1' & \theta_1'' \\ \hat{\sigma}_1' = [\theta_1' & \theta_1' & \theta_1'] \end{array} \qquad \begin{array}{ccc} \theta_2 & \theta_2' & \theta_2'' \\ \hat{\sigma}_2' = [\theta_2' & \theta_2' & \theta_2'] \end{array}$$

in which state c obtains when agents' characteristics are θ_1 and θ_2, even though $c \notin f(v_1(\theta_1), v_2(\theta_2))$. Furthermore, it can be checked that the untruthful equilibrium $\hat{\sigma}'$ Pareto-dominates the truthful equilibrium $\hat{\sigma}$,[8] so that the latter is not likely to be chosen by the agents.

Now since $\sigma \in B(g)$ satisfies assumption (U), we can also consider the subdirect mechanism

$$k = g \circ \sigma \circ \gamma = \begin{array}{cc} & u_2 \ u_2' \\ \begin{bmatrix} a & b \\ b & c \end{bmatrix} & \begin{array}{c} u_1 \\ u_1'. \end{array} \end{array}$$

By Theorem 3.2 the mechanism k truthfully implements f in Bayesian strategies. However, as before, k does not implement f, because apart from the truthful equilibrium

$$\begin{array}{ccc} \theta_1 & \theta_1' & \theta_1'' \\ \tilde{\sigma}_1 = [u_1 & u_1' & u_1] \end{array} \qquad \begin{array}{ccc} \theta_2 & \theta_2' & \theta_2'' \\ \tilde{\sigma}_2 = [u_2 & u_2' & u_2] \end{array}$$

there is another equilibrium, namely

$$\begin{array}{ccc} \theta_1 & \theta_1' & \theta_1'' \\ \tilde{\sigma}_1' = [u_1' & u_1' & u_1'] \end{array} \qquad \begin{array}{ccc} \theta_2 & \theta_2' & \theta_2'' \\ \tilde{\sigma}_2' = [u_2' & u_2' & u_2'] \end{array}$$

in which state c obtains when agents' characteristics are σ_1 and σ_2, even though $c \notin f(v_1(\theta_1), v_2(\theta_2))$. Furthermore, it is also true that the untruthful equilibrium $\tilde{\sigma}'$ Pareto-dominates the truthful equilibrium $\tilde{\sigma}$, so that the latter is not likely to be chosen by the agents.

---

8 For example, for agent 1 with characteristic θ_1 we have $v_1(c \mid \theta_1) = 6 > 5 = 1/4 v_1(a \mid \theta_1) + 1/2 v_1(b \mid \theta_1) + 1/4 v_1(a \mid \theta_1)$, and so on.

5 THE STRONG REVELATION PRINCIPLE UNDER INCOMPLETE INFORMATION

In this section we give a condition which guarantees that given a mechanism g that implements a SCR f in Bayesian strategies, there exists a direct mechanism h which not only implements f truthfully, but also implements f.

The condition can be motivated by reference to our previous example. There the untruthful equilibrium for the direct mechanism h does not have a corresponding equilibrium for g because in this mechanism the optical strategy for agent 1 with characteristic θ_1 against strategy s_2' is not s_1' but s_1'', a strategy which is not available to agent 1 in the mechanism h, and similarly for agent 2. This suggests that if any strategy which is lost in moving to a direct mechanism h is dominated by some strategy available in h, then any equilibrium for h would have a corresponding equilibrium for g. Since g implements f, it follows that h would also implement f.

Theorem 5.1 (strong revelation principle for direct mechanisms). *If g is a mechanism that implements the SCR f in Bayesian strategies, and there exists $\sigma \in B(g)$ satisfying*

(D) *for all $i \in I$, $\theta_i \in \Theta_i$, and $s_i \in S_i$ there exists $\theta_i' \in \Theta_i$ such that*

$$v_i\left[g(\sigma_i(\theta_i'),\ \sigma_{-i}(\theta_{-i})) \mid \theta_i\right] \geqslant v_i\left[g(s_i, \sigma_{-i}(\theta_{-i})) \mid \theta_i\right] \text{ for all } \theta_{-i} \in \Theta_{-i},$$

then there exists a direct mechanism h which (truthfully) implements f in Bayesian strategies.

Proof. Let us define $h = g \circ \sigma$. By Theorem 3.1 we have $\hat{\sigma} \in B(h)$, so that $B(h)$ is not empty. Thus to prove that h implements f it suffices to show that for any $\hat{\sigma}' \in B(h)$ we have $\sigma \circ \hat{\sigma}' \in B(g)$.[9] Suppose not. Then there exists some $i \in I$, $\theta_i \in \Theta_i$, and $s_i \in S_i$ such that

$$\int v_i\left[g(s_i, \sigma_{-i}(\hat{\sigma}_{-i}'(\theta_{-i}))) \mid \theta_i\right]\, d\mu_i(\theta_{-i} \mid \theta_i)$$
$$> \int v_i\left[g(\sigma_i(\hat{\sigma}_i'(\theta_i)), \sigma_{-i}(\hat{\sigma}_{-i}'(\theta_{-i}))) \mid \theta_i\right]\, d\mu_i(\theta_{-i} \mid \theta_i).$$

Now by assumption (D) for any $i \in I$, $\theta_i \in \Theta_i$, and $s_i \in S_i$ there exists $\theta_i' \in \Theta_i$ such that

$$v_i\left[g(\sigma_i(\theta_i'), \sigma_{-i}(\hat{\sigma}_{-i}'(\theta_{-i}))) \mid \theta_i\right] \geqslant v_i\left[g(s_i, \sigma_{-i}(\hat{\sigma}_{-i}'(\theta_{-i}))) \mid \theta_i\right]$$

for all $\theta_{-i} \in \Theta_{-i}$, which implies

$$\int v_i\left[g(\sigma_i(\theta_i'), \sigma_{-i}(\hat{\sigma}_{-i}'(\theta_{-i}))) \mid \theta_i\right]\, d\mu_i(\theta_{-i} \mid \theta_i)$$
$$\geqslant \int v_i\left[g(s_i, \sigma_{-i}(\hat{\sigma}_{-i}'(\theta_{-i}))) \mid \theta_i\right]\, d\mu_i(\theta_{-i} \mid \theta_i).$$

---

9 This is because $h(\hat{\sigma}'(\theta)) = g(\sigma \circ \hat{\sigma}'(\theta))$ for all $\theta \in \Theta$, and by assumption g implements f.

Hence we have

$$\int v_i\,[g(\sigma_i(\theta_i'),\,\sigma_{-i}(\hat{\sigma}_{-i}(\theta_{-i})))\mid\theta_i]\,d\mu_i(\theta_{-i}\mid\theta_i)$$
$$>\int v_i\,[g(\sigma_i(\hat{\sigma}_i'(\theta_i)),\,\sigma_{-i}(\hat{\sigma}_{-i}'(\theta_{-i})))\mid\theta_i]\,d\mu_i(\theta_{-i}\mid\theta_i).$$

But by the definition of h we have $g(\sigma_i(\theta_i'),\,\sigma_{-i}(\hat{\sigma}_{-i}'(\theta_{-i})))=h(\theta_i',\,\hat{\sigma}_{-i}'(\theta_{-i})$ and $g(\sigma_i(\hat{\sigma}_i'(\theta_i)),\,\sigma_{-i}(\hat{\sigma}_{-i}'(\theta_{-i})))=h(\hat{\sigma}_i'(\theta_i),\,\hat{\sigma}_{-i}'(\theta_{-i}))$, so we conclude

$$\int v_i\,[h(\theta_i',\,\hat{\sigma}_{-i}'(\theta_{-i}))\mid\theta_i]\,d\mu_i(\theta_{-i}\mid\theta_i)>\int v_i\,[h(\hat{\sigma}_i'(\theta_i),\,\hat{\sigma}_{-i}'(\theta_{-i}))\mid\theta_i]\,d\mu_i(\theta_{-i}\mid\theta_i),$$

which contradicts $\hat{\sigma}'\in B(h)$. ‖

Assumption (D) is clearly satisfied if no strategies are lost in moving to the direct mechanism h, because there we can always choose $\theta_i'\in\Theta_i$ such that $\sigma_i(\theta_i')=s_i$. This gives the following result, which was independently derived by Postlewaite and Schmeidler (1984).

Corollary 5.1. *If g is a mechanism that implements the SCR f in Bayesian strategies, and there exists $\sigma\in B(g)$ satisfying*

(D) *for all $i\in I$ we have $\sigma_i(\Theta_i)=S_i$,*

then there exists a direct mechanism h which (truthfully) implements f in Bayesian strategies.

Assumption (D) may also be shown to be satisfied if in the mechanism g every agent always has a dominant strategy. Thus we have the following result, which was previously noted by Repullo (1985).

Corollary 5.2. *If g is a mechanism that implements the SCR f in Bayesian strategies, and there exists $\sigma\in B(g)$ satisfying assumption (DS), then there exists a direct mechanism h which (truthfully) implements f in Bayesian strategies.*

Proof. For any $i\in I$, $\theta_i\in\Theta_i$, and $s_i\in S_i$ let $\theta_i'=\theta_i$. By assumption (DS) strategy $\sigma_i(\theta_i')=\sigma_i(\theta_i)$ is dominant for agent i with characteristic θ_i, so that $v_i\,[g(\sigma_i(\theta_i'),\,\sigma_{-i}(\theta_{-i}))\mid\theta_i]\geqslant v_i\,[g(s_i,\,\sigma_{-i}(\theta_{-i}))\mid\theta_i]$ for all $\theta_{-i}\in\Theta_{-i}$). Hence the result follows from Theorem 5.1. ‖

Next we consider the conditions which guarantee that given a mechanism g that implements a SCR f in Bayesian strategies, there exists a subdirect mechanism k which also implements f.

Theorem 5.2 (strong revelation principle for subdirect mechanisms). *If g is a mechanism that implements the SCR f in Bayesian strategies, and there exists $\sigma\in B(g)$ satisfying assumptions (U) and (D), then there exists a subdirect mechanism k which (truthfully) implements f in Bayesian strategies.*

Proof. Let us define $k=g\circ\sigma\circ\gamma$, where $\gamma:U\to\Theta$ is defined as in Theorem 3.2. Then we have $\tilde{\sigma}\in B(k)$, so that to prove that k implements f

it suffices to show that for any $\tilde{\sigma}' \in B(k)$ we have $\sigma \circ \gamma \circ \tilde{\sigma}' \in B(g)$.[10] Suppose not. Then there exists some $i \in I$, $\theta_i \in \Theta_i$, and $s_i \in S_i$ such that

$$\int v_i [g(s_i, \sigma_{-i}(\gamma_{-i}(\tilde{\sigma}'_{-i}(\theta_{-i})))) \mid \theta_i] d\mu_i(\theta_{-i} \mid \theta_i)$$
$$> \int v_i [g(\sigma_i(\gamma_i(\tilde{\sigma}'_i(\theta_i))), \sigma_{-i}(\gamma_{-i}(\tilde{\sigma}_{-i}(\theta'_{-i})))) \mid \theta_i] d\mu_i(\theta_{-i} \mid \theta_i).$$

Now by assumption (D) for any $i \in I$, $\theta_i \in \Theta_i$, and $s_i \in S_i$ there exists $\theta'_i \in \Theta_i$ such that

$$v_i [g(\sigma_i(\theta'_i), \sigma_{-i}(\gamma_{-i}(\tilde{\sigma}'_{-i}(\theta_{-i})))) \mid \theta_i] \geq v_i [g(s_i, \sigma_{-i}(\gamma_{-i}(\tilde{\sigma}'_{-i}(\theta_{-i})))) \mid \theta_i]$$

for all $\theta_{-i} \in \Theta_{-i}$, which implies

$$v_i [g(\sigma_i(\theta'_i), \sigma_{-i}(\gamma_{-i}(\tilde{\sigma}'_{-i}(\theta_{-i})))) \mid \theta_i] d\mu_i(\theta_{-i} \mid \theta_i)$$
$$\geq \int v_i [g(s_i, \sigma_{-i}(\gamma_{-i}(\tilde{\sigma}'_{-i}(\theta_{-i})))) \mid \theta_i] d\mu_i(\theta_{-i} \mid \theta_i).$$

Hence we have

$$\int v_i [g(\sigma_i(\theta'_i), \sigma_{-i}(\gamma_{-i}(\tilde{\sigma}'_{-i}(\theta_{-i})))) \mid \theta_i] d\mu_i(\theta_{-i} \mid \theta_i)$$
$$> \int v_i [g(\sigma_i(\gamma_i(\tilde{\sigma}'_i(\theta_i))), \sigma_{-i}(\gamma_{-i}(\tilde{\sigma}'_{-i}(\theta_{-i})))) \mid \theta_i] d\mu_i(\theta_{-i} \mid \theta_i).$$

But by the definition of k we have

$$g(\sigma_i(\theta'_i), \sigma_{-i}(\gamma_{-i}(\tilde{\sigma}'_{-i}(\theta_{-i})))) = g(\sigma_i(\gamma_i(v_i(\theta'_i))), \sigma_{-i}(\gamma_{-i}(\tilde{\sigma}'_{-i}(\theta_{-i}))))$$
$$= k(v_i(\theta'_i), \tilde{\sigma}'_{-i}(\theta_{-i}))$$

and

$$g(\sigma_i(\gamma_i(\tilde{\sigma}'_i(\theta_i))), \sigma_{-i}(\gamma_{-i}(\tilde{\sigma}'_{-i}(\theta_{-i})))) = k(\tilde{\sigma}'_i(\theta_i), \tilde{\sigma}'_{-i}(\theta_{-i})),$$

so we conclude

$$\int v_i [k(v_i(\theta'_i), \tilde{\sigma}'_{-i}(\theta_{-i})) \mid \theta_i] d\mu_i(\theta_{-i} \mid \theta_i)$$
$$> \int v_i [k(\tilde{\sigma}'_i(\theta_i), \tilde{\sigma}'_{-i}(\theta_{-i})) \mid \theta_i] d\mu_i(\theta_{-i} \mid \theta_i),$$

which contradicts $\tilde{\sigma}' \in B(k)$. ‖

As before, assumption (D) is clearly satisfied if no strategies are lost in moving to the subdirect mechanism k. This gives the following result.

Corollary 5.3. *If g is a mechanism that implements the SCR f in Bayesian strategies, and there exists $\sigma \in B(g)$ satisfying assumptions (U) and (D), then there exists a subdirect mechanism k which (truthfully) implements f in Bayesian strategies.*

As noted above, assumptions (U) and (D) may be shown to be satisfied if in the mechanism g every agent always has a dominant strategy. Thus we have the following result.

---

10 This is so because $k(\tilde{\sigma}'(\theta)) = g(\sigma \circ \gamma \circ \tilde{\sigma}'(\theta))$ for all $\theta \in \Theta$, and by assumption g implements f.

Corollary 5.4. *If g is a mechanism that implements the SCR f in Bayesian strategies, and there exists $\sigma \in B(g)$ satisfying assumption* (DS), *then there exists a subdirect mechanism k which* (*truthfully*) *implements f in Bayesian strategies.*

6   THE WEAK REVELATION PRINCIPLE UNDER COMPLETE INFORMATION

In this section we first show that any environment with complete information may be interpreted as a special case of an environment with incomplete information. We then apply Theorems 3.1 and 3.2 to this special case to obtain the weak principle for direct and subdirect mechanisms under complete information.

As explained in Section 2, in environments with incomplete information each agent i has a characteristic θ_i which determines a utility function $v_i(\theta_i)$ on the set A and a probability measure $\mu_i(\theta_i)$ on the set Θ_{-i}. Now suppose that for any $\theta \in \Theta$ we have

$$\mu_i(\theta'_{-i} \mid \theta_i) = \begin{cases} 1, & \text{if } \theta'_{-i} = \theta_{-i} \\ 0, & \text{otherwise.} \end{cases}$$

for all $i \in I$ and $0'_{-i} \in \Theta_{-i}$. In this case each agent i not only knows his own characteristic θ_i but also the characteristics θ_{-i} of the other agents. In particular he knows their utility function $v_{-i}(\theta_{-i})$, and so we have a complete information environment.

It is interesting to notice that in this case we can assume, without loss of generality, that for any $\theta \in \Theta$ there is some $u \in U$ such that $\theta_i = u$ for all $i \in I$, where $v_i(\theta_i) = u_i$ and

$$\mu_i(\theta'_{-i} \mid \theta_i) = \begin{cases} 1, & \text{if } \theta_j = u \text{ for all } j \neq i. \\ 0, & \text{otherwise} \end{cases}$$

Thus for each agent i the space Θ_i of his possible characteristics becomes the set U.

In this situation a Bayesian equilibrium for the game defined by a mechanism g reduces to a vector of strategy rules $\sigma \in \Sigma(g)$ such that for all $i \in I, u \in U$, and $s_i \in S_i$ we have

$$u_i\,[g(\sigma_i(u), \sigma_{-i}(u))] \geqslant u_i\,[g(s_i, \sigma_{-i}(u))],$$

which implies $\sigma(u) \in N(g, u)$ for all $u \in U$. Conversely, if $\sigma(u) \in N(g, u)$ for all $u \in U$ it is clear that $\sigma \in B(g)$. Thus we conclude that $B(g) = N(g) = \Pi_{u \in U} N(g, U)$, and so it follows that implementation in Bayesian strategies becomes implementation in Nash strategies.

Now we are ready to establish the following results.

Theorem 6.1 (weak revelation principle for direct mechanisms). *If g is a mechanism that implements the SCR f in Nash strategies, there exists a direct mechanism h which truthfully implements f in Nash strategies.*

The proof is identical to that of Theorem 3.1.

It should be noticed that in the direct mechanism h the strategy set S_i for each agent i is given by the set U. In other words, each agent is asked to report what he knows, namely, the entire vector of utility functions.

Theorem 6.2 (weak revelation principle for subdirect mechanisms). *If g is a mechanism that implements the SCR f in Nash strategies, and there exists $\sigma \in N(g)$ satisfying*

$$(U') \quad \text{for all } i \in I \text{ and } u, u' \in U \text{ we have } \sigma_i(u) = \sigma_i(u') \text{ whenever } u_i = u_i',$$

then there exists a subdirect mechanism k which truthfully implements f in Nash strategies.

The proof is identical to that of Theorem 3.2.

Assumption (U') may be shown to be satisfied if in the mechanism g every agent always has a dominant strategy. Thus we have the following result.

Corollary 6.3. *If g is a mechanism that implements the SCR f in Nash strategies, and there exists $\sigma \in N(g)$ satisfying*

$$(DS') \text{ for all } i \in I, u \in U, s_i \in S_i \text{ and } s_{-i} \in S_{-i} \text{ we have } u_i[g(\sigma_i(u), s_{-i})] \geqslant u_i[g(s_i, s_{-i})],$$

then there exists a subdirect mechanism k which truthfully implements f in Nash strategies.

As in the case of Theorem 3.1, Theorem 6.1 does not imply that for environments with complete information there is no loss of generality in restricting attention to direct mechanisms, since there is nothing that guarantees that agents will always choose to play the truthful Nash equilibrium when alternative untruthful equilibria exist. Thus in the following section we consider the analogues of Theorems 5.1 and 5.2 for implementation in Nash strategies.

7 THE STRONG REVELATION PRINCIPLE UNDER COMPLETE INFORMATION

In this section we first give a condition which guarantees that given a mechanism g that implements a SCR f in Nash strategies, there exists a direct mechanism h which not only implements f truthfully, but also implements f.

Theorem 7.1 (strong revelation principle for direct mechanisms). *If g is a mechanism that implements the SCR f in Nash strategies, and there exists* $\sigma \in N(g)$ *satisfying*

(D′) *for all* $i \in I$, $u_i \in U_i$, *and* $s_i \in S_i$ *there exists* $u' \in U$ *such that* $u_i [g(\sigma_i(u'), \sigma_{-i}(u''))] \geqslant u_i [g(s_i, \sigma_{-i}(u''))]$ *for all* $u'' \in U$,

then there exists a direct mechanism h which (truthfully) implements f in Nash strategies.

The proof is identical to that of Theorem 5.1.

Assumption (D′) is clearly satisfied if no strategies are lost in moving to the direct mechanism h, because then we can always choose $u' \in U$ such that $\sigma_i(u') = s_i$. This gives the following result which was independently derived by Hurwicz (1982).

Corollary 7.1. *If g is a mechanism that implements the SCR f in Nash strategies, and there exists* $\sigma \in N(g)$ *satisfying*

(D′) *for all* $i \in I$ *we have* $\sigma_i(U) = S_i$,

then there exists a direct mechanism h which (truthfully) implements f in Nash strategies.

Assumption (D′) may also be shown to be satisfied if in the mechanism g every agent always has a dominant strategy. Thus we have the following result, which was previously noted by Repullo (1985).

Corollary 7.2. *If g is a mechanism that implements the SCR f in Nash strategies, and there exists* $\sigma \in N(g)$ *satisfying assumption* (DS′), *then there exists a direct mechanism h which (truthfully) implements f in Nash strategies.*

The proof is identical to that of Corollary 5.2.

Next we consider the conditions which guarantee that given a mechanism g that implements a SCR f in Nash strategies, there exists a subdirect mechanism k which also implements f.

Theorem 7.2 (strong revelation principle for subdirect mechanisms). *If g is a mechanism that implements the SCR f in Nash strategies, and there exists* $\sigma \in N(g)$ *satisfying assumptions* (U′) *and* (D′), *then there exists a subdirect mechanism k which (truthfully) implements f in Nash strategies.*

The proof is identical to that of Theorem 5.2.

As in the case of Theorem 5.2, from Theorem 7.2 we obtain the following results.

Corollary 7.3. *If g is a mechanism that implements the SCR f in Nash strategies, and there exists* $\sigma \in N(g)$ *satisfying assumptions* (U′) *and* (D′), *then there exists a subdirect mechanism k which (truthfully) implements f in Nash strategies.*

Corollary 7.4. *If g is a mechanism that implements the SCR f in Nash strategies, and there exists $\sigma \in N(g)$ satisfying assumption (DS'), then there exists a subdirect mechanism k which (truthfully) implements f in Nash strategies.*

8 CONCLUDING REMARKS

The main results of the paper can be summarized as follows. Firstly, we have shown that if a SCR f can be implemented in Nash strategies (under complete information) or in Bayesian strategies (under incomplete information) by an indirect mechanism:

a   there exists a direct mechanism (i.e. one in which agents report their characteristics) which truthfully implements f in Nash or Bayesian strategies; and

b   if there exists $\sigma \in B(g)$ satisfying assumption (U), there exists a subdirect mechanism (i.e. one in which agents report their preferences) which truthfully implements f in Nash or Bayesian strategies.

Secondly, we have noted that the mechanisms given by (a) and (b) do not necessarily implement f in Nash or Bayesian strategies. Finally, we have shown that if there exists $\sigma \in B(g)$ satisfying assumption (D)

c   the direct mechanism given by (a) also implements f in Nash or Bayesian strategies; and

d   the subdirect mechanism given by (b) also implements f in Nash or Bayesian strategies.

These results are important because they qualify the standard use of the (weak) revelation principle in the literature. Thus, if we want to know whether a particular SCR can be implemented it is not in general sufficient to construct a direct mechanism which truthfully implements it.[11] There are, however, two exceptions to this negative conclusion. Firstly, when there is only one agent, it is clear that multiple equilibria are not really a problem, since the agent is always indifferent between them, and so we can assume that he chooses the truthful equilibrium.[12] Secondly, when we have enough structure so as to ensure that truth-telling is the unique equilibrium, it is clear that truthful implementation coincides with implementation.

11 In particular, in the case of social choice functions (i.e. singleton-valued SCRs) it is not sufficient to check whether a set of incentive-compatibility constraints are satisfied.
12 See, for example, Baron and Myerson (1982).

REFERENCES

Baron, D. P. and Myerson, R. B. 1982: Regulating a monopolist with unknown costs. *Econometrica*, **50**, 911-30.

Dasgupta, P., Hammond, P. and Maskin, E. 1979: The implementation of social choice rules: some general results on incentive compatibility. *Review of Economic Studies*, **46**, 185-216.

Harris, M. and Townsend, R. M. 1981: Resource allocation under asymmetric information. *Econometrica*, **49**, 33-64.

Harsyani, J. C. 1967-68: Games with incomplete information played by 'Bayesian' players (Parts I-III). *Management Science*, **14**, 159-82, 320-34 and 486-502.

Holmstrom, B. and Myerson, R. B. 1983: Efficient and durable decision rules with incomplete information. *Econometrica*, **51**, 1799-1819.

Hurwicz, L. 1982: *Profiles as Canonical Strategy Domains for Nash Implementability*, Mimeo.

Laffont, J.-J. and Maskin, E. 1982: The theory of incentives: an overview. In W. Hildenbrand (ed.) *Advances in Economic Theory*. Cambridge: Cambridge University Press.

Maskin, E. 1983: The theory of implementation in Nash equilibrium: a survey. In L. Hurwicz, D. Schmeidler and H. Sonnenschein (eds) *Social Goals and Social Organization: Essays in Memory of Elisha A. Pazner*. Cambridge: Cambridge University Press.

Myerson, R. B. 1983: Bayesian equilibrium and incentive compatibility: an introduction. In L. Hurwicz, D. Schmeidler and H. Sonnenschein (eds) *Social Goals and Social Organization: Essays in Memory of Elisha A. Pazner*. Cambridge: Cambridge University Press.

Postlewaite, A. and Schmeidler, D. 1984: Implementation in differential information economies. *CARESS Working Paper*, University of Pennsylvania.

Repullo, R. 1985: Implementation in dominant strategies under complete and incomplete information. *Review of Economic Studies*, **52**, 223-9.

9

Optimal Incentive Schemes with Many Agents

D. Mookherjee

The Grossman–Hart principal–agent model of moral hazard is extended to the multiple agent case to explore the use of relative performance in optimal incentive contracting. Under the assumption that the principal chooses incentive schemes to implement agent actions as Nash equilibria, necessary and sufficient conditions are derived for the optimality of independent contracts, of rank-order tournaments, and for attainability of the first-best. In this context the relation of the principal's welfare to the correlation between the underlying randomness in outputs of different agents is also investigated. Finally, some problems with the Nash equilibrium implementation assumption are discussed.

1 INTRODUCTION

In this paper we extend the Grossman–Hart analysis of the principal agent problem to a multiple-agent setting. In this version of the problem, a risk-neutral principal is assumed to observe the output or a performance index for each (risk-averse) agent; the output of any agent depends on a privately observable action chosen by the agent and an exogenous random variable (the realization of which is not observed either by the principal, or by the agent before choosing its action). We especially focus attention on the role of relative performance evaluation in optimal incentive contracts, and the way this depends on properties of the underlying production technology and (the joint distribution of) the random variables affecting the outputs of different agents.

In Section 2 of the paper we consider the principal's problem of finding an optimal incentive scheme and an action tuple for agents, subject to the constraint that the latter be implemented as a Nash equilibrium between agents

For helpful discussions I would like to thank Professors Partha Dasgupta, Ken Binmore and Oliver Hart. I am also grateful to Professor Peter Hammond and two anonymous referees for their comments.

by the chosen incentive scheme (where agents must attain at least their reservation utilities). A characterization of optimal incentive schemes is derived, analogous to the Grossman–Hart characterization for the single-agent problem. This characterization is then utilized to find sufficient and (generically) necessary conditions for (a) optimal contracts for any agent to be independent of the performance of other agents, and (b) optimality of rank-order tournaments (where payments depend solely on ordinal comparisons of output across agents). We then describe a necessary and sufficient condition for the principal to extract maximum advantage from relative performance clauses, i.e. achieve the first-best level of expected utility in the multi-agent situation. An implication of this result is that (under fairly weak conditions) perfect correlation in the underlying production uncertainties for different agents enables the principal to attain the first best if and only if sufficiently heavy penalties can be inflicted on agents. We then enquire what happens in intermediate cases of non-perfect correlation. It turns out that while in general the principal's welfare is a continuous function of the correlation coefficient, it is not always non-decreasing in the latter (because the correlation coefficient is not a general measure of association between two random variables, but rather a measure of linear association between them).

In Section 3 we briefly discuss problems that may arise in assuming that the principal is content to 'implement' action tuples as Nash equilibria, ignoring the possibility that there may exist other Nash equilibria which all agents may prefer to the one the principal wishes implemented. Finally, Section 4 contains some concluding comments.

Similar multi-agent problems have been studied by Nalebuff and Stiglitz (1983), Green and Stokey (1983) and Holmstrom (1982). The Nalebuff–Stiglitz and Green–Stokey models are different in one essential respect from the one we are considering. In their models the output of each agent depends on its effort and on the realization of two random variables. One of these is a common shock whose realization is observed by all agents before choosing their respective effort levels (but not by the principal); while the other is an idiosyncratic shock specific to each agent, distributed independently across different agents and unobserved by agents before choosing effort levels. The common shock observed by different agents before choosing effort introduces an additional informational asymmetry between principal and agents of a kind that is absent in our model. In this respect our model is similar to one of the models in Holmstrom (1982), and the relation between Holmstrom's and our results will be pointed out as we go along.

2   NASH EQUILIBRIUM IMPLEMENTATION

There are two agents denoted $k = 1, 2$; the analysis generalizes straightforwardly to the case of any finite number of agents. There exists for each agent

k a finite set $Q^k = [q_1^k, \cdot, q_{n_k}^k]$ of possible outputs, a finite set A_k of possible actions, a random variable θ_k (with finite range H_k) and a production function $f_k(a_1, a_2, \theta_k): A_1 \times A_2 \times H_k \to Q^k \cdot f_k$ determines for any pair of actions a_1 and a_2 for the two agents, and any realization of θ_k, a unique output for agent k. θ_1 and θ_2 have a joint probability distribution represented by $g(\theta_1, \theta_2)$. The production functions f_1 and f_2 and the joint distribution g of θ_1 and θ_2 induce a probability distribution over output pairs (q^1, q^2) for any given action pair (a_1, a_2). We use $\pi_{ij}(a_1, a_2)$ to denote the probability of output pair (q_i^1, q_j^2) resulting if the actions chosen are (a_1, a_2).

Each agent $k(=1, 2)$ has a von Neumann–Morgenstern utility function U^k which is additively separable in action chosen by k, and payment received:

$$U^k(a_k, I^k) = V^k(I^k) - G^k(a_k)$$

where possible payment I^k by the principal ranges over some closed interval $[\underline{I}, \bar{I}]$ of the real line. Agent k has reservation utility $\underline{U}^k$. The principal's benefit function is defined over the outputs of the two agents $(\bar{B}(q^1, q^2))$ or over the action chosen by agents $(B(a_1, a_2))$; the latter makes sense when a_k is the output of agent k and θ_k is a random measurement error. The principal is assumed to be risk neutral, concerned solely with the maximization of expected benefits minus expected compensation payments. Hence if $\bar{B}(q^1, q^2)$ is the benefit function of the principal, we may define $B(a_1, a_2)$ to be the expected benefit of the principal when actions chosen by agents are (a_1, a_2):

$$B(a_1, a_2) = \Sigma\Sigma_{(i,j)} \pi_{ij}(a_1, a_2) \bar{B}(q_i^1, q_j^2).$$

In order to simplify the notation we shall make the inessential assumption that the two agents are identical (some examples will however involve non-identical agents), and hence have the same utility function $U(a, I) = V(I) - G(a)$, and the same reservation utility $\underline{U}$. One basic assumption that will be employed throughout the analysis is:

Assumption 1. V is continuous, strictly increasing and concave over $[\underline{I}, \bar{I}]$. If $\underline{v} = V(\underline{I})$, and if $\underline{a} \in A$ minimizes $G(a)$ over A (i.e. $\underline{a}$ is the least costly action for the agent), then $\underline{v} - G(\underline{a}) < \underline{U}$. Further, for any $a \in A$ there exists $I \in [\underline{I}, \bar{I}]$ such that $V(I) - G(a) = \underline{U}$.

In the first-best situation the principal can observe actions chosen by agents; the second and third part of Assumption 1 ensures that the principal can then write contracts forcing any agent to choose any feasible action that guarantees the agent its reservation utility. If agent k were to be required to choose a_k, the principal would pay agent k a sum of

$$C_{FB}(a_k) = V^{-1}(\underline{U} + G(a_k)) \equiv h(\underline{U} + G(a_k)), \quad \text{where } h \equiv V^{-1}$$

if it chooses a_k, and $\underline{I}$ otherwise. Hence the first-best cost to the principal of getting action pair (a_1, a_2) implemented is $[C_{FB}(a_1) + C_{FB}(a_2)]$, and the first-best action pair (a_1^*, a_2^*) is that which maximizes the principal's net benefit $[B(a_1, a_2) - C_{FB}(a_1) - C_{FB}(a_2)]$ over $A \times A$.

In the second-best situation where the principal cannot observe the actions chosen by agents, it can base payments to the agents only on their outputs. An incentive scheme for agent k is thus an $(n_1 n_2)$ dimensional vector $I^k = \{I_{ij}^k\} \in [\underline{I}, \bar{I}]^{n_1 n_2}$, where I_{ij}^k is the payment given to agent k if output pair (q_i^1, q_j^2) results. Given a pair (I^1, I^2) of incentive schemes and actions (a_1, a_2) chosen by agents, the principal incurs an expected cost of

$$\tilde{C}(a_1, a_2, I^1, I^2) = \Sigma\Sigma_{(i,j)} \pi_{ij}(a_1, a_2) (I_{ij}^1 + I_{ij}^2).$$

The principal will then choose a pair (I^1, I^2) of incentive schemes and an action pair (a_1, a_2) for the agents in order to maximize net expected benefit $[B(a_1, a_2) - \tilde{C}(a_1, a_2, I^1, I^2)]$ over $A \times A$, subject to the constraint that (a_1, a_2) is a Nash equilibrium for the agents under (I^1, I^2), and that they attain an expected utility of at least $\underline{U}$ at this equilibrium. Analogous to the Grossman–Hart analysis of the one-agent problem, this maximization can be decomposed into two stages: (a) Given any action pair (a_1, a_2), find the incentive scheme (I^1, I^2) that minimizes expected principal's cost $\tilde{C}(a_1, a_2, I^1, I^2)$ subject to the Nash incentive compatibility condition, and the reservation utility constraint. Proposition 1 below demonstrates that there exists a solution to this cost minimization problem whenever the feasible set is non-empty. The minimized expected cost of implementing (a_1, a_2) is denoted by $C(a_1, a_2)$, which may be called the second-best cost function for the principal. (b) At the second stage, the principal chooses the second-best action pair (a_1, a_2) i.e. which maximizes the principal's expected net benefit $[B(a_1, a_2) - C(a_1, a_2)]$ over $A \times A$.

In our model the set of possible actions A is finite; hence given the existence of a second-best cost function there always exists a second-best incentive scheme and action pair $(\tilde{a}_1, \tilde{a}_2)$.[1] The important point to note is that the qualitative properties of the optimal incentive scheme can be deducted from the first-stage cost minimization problem for the implementation of $(\tilde{a}_1, \tilde{a}_2)$. This problem can formally be written as follows:

Choose I^1, I^2 to minimize $\Sigma\Sigma_{(ij)} \pi_{ij}(\tilde{a}_1, \tilde{a}_2)(I_{ij}^1 + I_{ij}^2)$ subject to:

$$\Sigma\Sigma_{(ij)} \pi_{ij}(\tilde{a}_1, \tilde{a}_2) V(I_{ij}^K) - G(\tilde{a}_K) \geqslant \underline{U} \quad \text{for } K = 1, 2$$

---

1 Using arguments analogous to those in Grossman–Hart (1983), the existence of a second-best incentive scheme can be shown even when the set A of feasible actions is not finite. However the finiteness of the set of possible outputs is essential for existence (if agent's utility V for money is unbounded below), as this rules out situations discussed by Mirrlees (1975) where the principal can get arbitrarily close to the first-best by choosing 'heavy' punishments on outcomes with arbitrarily small probability, and paying according to the first-best sharing rule elsewhere.

$$\Sigma\Sigma_{(ij)}\,\pi_{ij}(a,\tilde{a}_2)\,V(I_{ij}^1) - G(a) \leqslant \Sigma\Sigma_{(ij)}\,\pi_{ij}(\tilde{a}_1,\tilde{a}_2)\,V(I_{ij}^1) - G(\tilde{a}_1)$$
$$\text{for all } a \in A \tag{9.1}$$

$$\Sigma\Sigma_{(ij)}\,\pi_{ij}(\tilde{a}_1,a)\,V(I_{ij}^2) - G(a) \leqslant \Sigma\Sigma_{(ij)}\,\pi_{ij}(\tilde{a}_1,\tilde{a}_2)\,V(I_{ij}^2) - G(\tilde{a}_2)$$
$$\text{for all } a \in A$$

$$I_{ij}^k \in [\underline{I},\bar{I}] \text{ all } i,j,k$$

As in the analysis of Grossman and Hart, it is convenient to take the principal's control variables to be output contingent agent utilities for money $(\boldsymbol{v}^1, \boldsymbol{v}^2)$ where $v_{ij}^k = V(I_{ij}^k)$, rather than monetary payments I_{ij}^k. (1) can then be rewritten as (where $h \equiv V^{-1}$ and $\bar{v} = V(\bar{I})$):

Choose $\boldsymbol{v}^1, \boldsymbol{v}^2$ to minimize $\Sigma\Sigma_{(ij)}\,\pi_{ij}(\tilde{a}_1,\tilde{a}_2)\,[h(v_{ij}^1) + h(v_{ij}^2)]$ subject to:

$$\Sigma\Sigma_{(ij)}\,\pi_{ij}(\tilde{a}_1,\tilde{a}_2)\,v_{ij}^k - G(\tilde{a}_k) \geqslant \underline{U} \text{ for } k = 1, 2$$

$$\Sigma\Sigma_{(ij)}\,[\pi_{ij}(a,\tilde{a}_2) - \pi_{ij}(\tilde{a}_1,\tilde{a}_2)]\,v_{ij}^1 + G(\tilde{a}_1) - G(a) \leqslant 0 \text{ for all } a \in A \tag{9.2}$$

$$\Sigma\Sigma_{(ij)}\,[\pi_{ij}(\tilde{a}_1,a) - \pi_{ij}(\tilde{a}_1,\tilde{a}_2)]\,v_{ij}^2 + G(\tilde{a}_2) - G(a) \leqslant 0 \text{ for all } a \in A$$

$$v_{ij}^k \in [\underline{v}, \bar{v}] \text{ all } i,j,k.$$

We can now derive the basic characterization of optimal incentive schemes:

Proposition 1. *If the feasible set in* (9.2) *is non-empty, there exists a solution to* (9.2). *If V is strictly concave, the optimal incentive scheme is unique (almost everywhere under* $(\tilde{a}_1,\tilde{a}_2)$). *Optimal incentive schemes are characterized by the following necessary and sufficient conditions (assuming interior solution):*

There exist scalars $\tilde{\lambda}_1, \tilde{\lambda}_2$ *and real valued functions* $\alpha_1(a), \alpha_2(a)$ *defined on A, such that*

$$\pi_{ij}(\tilde{a}_1,\tilde{a}_2)\,h'(v_{ij}^1) = \tilde{\lambda}_1\,\pi_{ij}(\tilde{a}_1,\tilde{a}_2) - \Sigma_{a \in A}\,\alpha_1(a)\,[\pi_{ij}(a,\tilde{a}_2) - \pi_{ij}(\tilde{a}_1,\tilde{a}_2)]$$

$$\pi_{ij}(\tilde{a}_1,\tilde{a}_2)\,h'(v_{ij}^2) = \tilde{\lambda}_2\,\pi_{ij}(\tilde{a}_1,\tilde{a}_2) - \Sigma_{a \in A}\,\alpha_2(a)\,[\pi_{ij}(\tilde{a}_1,a) - \pi_{ij}(\tilde{a}_1,\tilde{a}_2)]$$
$$\tag{9.3}$$

$$\alpha_1(a)\,\{\Sigma\Sigma_{(ij)}\,[\pi_{ij}(a,\tilde{a}_2) - \pi_{ij}(\tilde{a}_1,\tilde{a}_2)]\,v_{ij}^1 + G(\tilde{a}_1) - G(a)\} = 0,$$
$$\alpha_1(a) \geqslant 0 \text{ for all } a \in A$$

$$\alpha_2(a)\,\{\Sigma\Sigma_{(ij)}\,[\pi_{ij}(\tilde{a}_1,a) - \pi_{ij}(\tilde{a}_1,\tilde{a}_2)]\,v_{ij}^2 + G(\tilde{a}_2) - G(a)\} = 0,$$
$$\alpha_2(a) \geqslant 0 \text{ for all } a \in A. \tag{9.4}$$

At the optimum if action $\tilde{a}_k\,(k = 1, 2)$ *is not the least cost action for agent k in A, there exists at least one action* $a \in A$ *with* $G(a) < G(\tilde{a}_k)$ *such that* $\alpha_k(a) > 0$, *i.e. agent k is indifferent between* $\tilde{a}_k$ *and a.*

Proposition 1 is proved in the Appendix. The Kuhn–Tucker conditions (9.3) and (9.4) characterize optimal incentive schemes. Note that for outcomes with zero probability under $(\tilde{a}_1, \tilde{a}_2)$, each agent can be paid $\underline{I}$ without loss of generality), while for outcomes with positive probability under $(\tilde{a}_1, \tilde{a}_2)$, payments satisfy (where $\lambda_k = \tilde{\lambda}_k - \Sigma_{a \in A} \alpha_k(a)$)

$$h'(v_{ij}^1) = \lambda_1 - \Sigma_{a \in A} \alpha_1(a) \frac{\pi_{ij}(a, \tilde{a}_2)}{\pi_{ij}(\tilde{a}_1, \tilde{a}_2)}$$

$$h'(v_{ij}^2) = \lambda_2 - \Sigma_{a \in A} \alpha_2(a) \frac{\pi_{ij}(\tilde{a}_1, a)}{\pi_{ij}(\tilde{a}_1, \tilde{a}_2)}. \tag{9.5}$$

The significant feature of (9.5) is that the dependence of incentive payments (to agent 1 for instance) on outputs of the two agents occurs through the likelihood ratio terms $[\pi_{ij}(a, a_2)/\pi_{ij}(a_1, a_2)]$. This allows us to derive conditions for the optimality of independent contracts and of rank order tournaments, analogous to Holmstrom's (1982) characterizations in terms of sufficient statistics.

To investigate the optimality of independent contracts, we shall utilize the following assumption:

Assumption 2. Either $[\pi_{ij}(\hat{a}, \tilde{a}_2) \mid \pi_{ij}(a, \tilde{a}_2]$ is independent of j for all pairs $(\hat{a}, a)$ of possible actions for agent 1, or no pair at all.

Assumption 2 rules out situations where the likelihood ratio terms appearing in the characterization of optimal incentive schemes for agent 1 have different qualitative properties (in terms of dependence on agent 2's output) for different alternative (to $\tilde{a}_1$) actions a.

Proposition 2. *A sufficient condition for optimal payments to agent 1 to be independent of agent 2's output is that $\pi_{ij}(a_1, \tilde{a}_2)$ admits the factorization (for all $a_1 \in A$):*

$$\pi_{ij}(a_1, \tilde{a}_2) = H(q_i^1, q_j^2, \tilde{a}_2) F(q_i^1, a_1, \tilde{a}_2). \tag{9.6}$$

If Assumption 2 holds, (9.6) is also (generically) necessary for agent 1's optimal payments to be independent of 2's output.

The proof of the sufficiency part of Proposition 2 is straightforward: (9.6) implies that the likelihood ratio terms appearing in the expression for 1's optimal payments are all independent of j, agent 2's output. For the converse, v_{ij}^1 at the optimum is independent of j if $\Sigma_{a \in A} \alpha_1(a) [\pi_{ij}(a, \tilde{a}_2) \mid \pi_{ij}(\tilde{a}_1, \tilde{a}_2)]$ is independent of j. Given Assumption 2, $[\pi_{ij}(\hat{a}, \tilde{a}_2) \mid \pi_{ij}(\tilde{a}, \tilde{a}_2)]$ is independent of j for all pairs $(\hat{a}, \tilde{a})$ of possible actions for agent 1 (which in turn is equivalent to condition (9.6)), unless the Lagrange multiplier vector $\{\alpha_1(a)\}$ is such that even with every component of the likelihood ratio vector $\{\pi_{ij}(a, \tilde{a}_2) \mid \pi_{ij}(\tilde{a}_1, \tilde{a}_2)\}$ varying with j, their inner product is independent of j. The latter situation can arise only by accident, so the necessity of condition (9.6) for optimality of independent contracts is generic.[2] Assumption 2 is required for the necessity result, since in its absence it is possible that $[\pi_{ij}(a, \bar{a}_2) \mid \pi_{ij}(\bar{a}_1, \bar{a}_2)]$ is independent of agent 2's output j for just those actions a for agent 1 for which the Lagrange multiplier $\alpha_1(a)$ is positive, not for other actions and thus (9.6) does not hold; such cases do not seem very interesting.

The interpretation of condition (9.6) is familiar from the work of Holmstrom (1979, 1982) and Gjesdal (1982). We can imagine the principal is facing a statistical decision problem of estimating agent 1's action a, from observations on outputs (q^1, q^2) of the two agents, given the knowledge that agent 2 is choosing $\bar{a}_2$. Then (9.6) requires agent 2's output q_j^2 to be uninformative for agent 1's action, i.e. agent 1's output q^1 must be a sufficient statistic for a_1. Agent 2's output should influence agent 1's compensation only if it communicates information about the latter's action.[3]

It is clear that if production functions are separable in actions (absence of production externalities) then independence of θ_1 and θ_2 implies the optimality of independent contracts: the joint distribution of (q^1, q^2) given (a_1, a_2) will then decompose into the production of the marginal distributions of q^1 (given a_1) and q^2 (given a_2). An interesting question is whether (in the separable production case) independence of θ_1 and θ_2 is necessary for independent contracts to be optimal. Theorem 7 in Holmstrom (1982) shows using the first-order condition approach that independent contracts are optimal (with separable production) only if θ_1 and θ_2 are independent; his proof implicitly assumes that the production functions are invertible for the random shock, given output and action, (i.e. $f_k^{-1}(q^k, a_k)$ is well defined). One can construct examples where in the absence of this invertibility property, independent contracts are optimal despite the non-independence of θ_1 and θ_2. Hence one may examine whether invertibility of production functions implies the validity of the result when the first-order condition approach is not adopted. The following example demonstrates that this is not always the case.

Example 1. θ_1 takes four possible values x_1, x_2, x_3, x_4; θ_2 takes three possible values y_1, y_2, y_3, where $0 < x_1 < x_2 < x_3 < x_4$. $0 < y_1 < y_2 < y_3$ and

$$(x_1 + x_2 + x_3 + x_4)(y_1^2 + y_2^2 + y_3^2) = 1.$$

2 The necessity result will not hold only if the Lagrange multiplier vector $\{\alpha_1(a)\}$ is orthogonal to the difference between the likelihood ratio vectors between every pair of outputs for agent 2. Such situations can be ruled out by the assumption that there exist at least n pairs of outputs for agent 2 for which the corresponding differences in the likelihood ratio vectors are linearly independent, where n is the total number of possible actions for agent 1.

3 This result does not generalize to the situation where agents' preference over income lotteries is dependent on action; see Gjesdal (1982).

The probability function g is

$$g(x_1, y_j) = (y_j)^2 x_1 - \sigma y_j,$$

$$g(x_2, y_j) = (y_j)^2 x_2 + \sigma y_j,$$

$$g(x_3, y_j) = (y_j)^2 x_3,$$

$$g(x_4, y_j) = (y_j)^2 x_4,$$

where σ is some positive number less than $y_1 x_1$. Hence g is a valid probability function and θ_1 and θ_2 are not independent. The set of possible actions for 1 is $A_1 = \{\underline{a}, \bar{a}\}$ where $G(\underline{a}) < G(\bar{a})$; $Q_1 = \{z_1, z_2, z_3, z_4\}$ and the production function for 1 is

$$f_1(\underline{a}, x_1) = z_1, \quad f_1(\underline{a}, x_2) = z_2, \quad f_1(\underline{a}, x_3) = z_3, \quad f_1(\underline{a}, x_4) = z_4;$$

$$f_1(\bar{a}, x_1) = z_1, \quad f_1(\bar{a}, x_2) = z_2, \quad f_1(\bar{a}, x_3) = z_4, \quad f_1(\bar{a}, x_4) = z_3.$$

Q_2 is $\{w_1, w_2, w_3\}$ and agent 2's production function satisfies $f_2(\bar{a}_2, y_1) = w_1, f_2(\bar{a}_2, y_2) = w_2, f_2(\bar{a}_2, y_3) = w_3$. Though both production functions are invertible for θ_k given a_k, the optimal payment to agent 1 is independent of 2's output. If the principal wishes agent 1 to choose $\underline{a}$ his least cost action, it is optimal for agent 1 to be paid a constant sum. If, on the other hand, agent 1 is to choose $\bar{a}$, optimal incentive payments depend on the likelihood ratio $[\pi_{ij}(\underline{a}, \bar{a}_2) \mid \pi_{ij}(\bar{a}, \bar{a}_2)]$, and this ratio takes the value 1 whenever 1's output q^1 is either z_1 or z_2, value (x_3/x_4) when q^1 is z_3 and (x_4/x_3) when q^1 is z_4, i.e. is independent of 2's output.

To rule out the phenomenon depicted in this example, we need the following condition:

Assumption 3. Given any two realizations $\hat{\theta}_1$, $\tilde{\theta}_1$ of θ_1, there exist possible actions $\hat{a}_1, \tilde{a}_1$ for agent 1 such that $f_1(\hat{a}_1, \hat{\theta}_1) = f_1(\tilde{a}_1, \tilde{\theta}_1)$.

Assumption 3 is violated in Example 1 for the pairs (x_1, x_2) of possible realizations of θ_1.

Proposition 3. *Let Assumptions 2 and 3 hold and assume that production functions are separable in actions, and invertible in the random shock, i.e. $f_k(a_k, \hat{\theta}) \neq f_k(a_k, \tilde{\theta})$ whenever $\hat{\theta} \neq \tilde{\theta}$, for any $a_k \in A$. Then for agent 1's optimal contract to be independent of 2's output, it is (generically) necessary that θ_1 and θ_2 are independent.*

Proof. Using Proposition 2, Assumption 2 implies that for 1's optimal contract to be independent of 2's output it is generically necessary that $[\pi_{ij}(a, \bar{a}_2) \mid \pi_{ij}(\bar{a}_1, \bar{a}_2)]$ is independent of j (over all output pairs (q_i^1, q_j^2) with positive probability under $(\bar{a}_1, \bar{a}_2)$) for every action $a \in A$. The invertibility of f_1 and f_2 implies that whenever $f_1^{-1}(\hat{a}, q_i^1)$ and $f_1^{-1}(a^*, q_i^1)$ are non-empty, $[g(f_1^{-1}(\hat{a}, q_i^1), f_2^{-1}(\bar{a}_2, q_j^2))/g(f_1^{-1}(a^*, q_i^1), f_2^{-1}(\bar{a}_2, q_j^2))]$ is independent of q_j^2 for all pairs $\hat{a}, a^*$ of possible actions for agent 1. If θ_1 and θ_2 are not independent there exist $\hat{\theta}_1, \theta_1^*$ such that $[g(\hat{\theta}_1, \theta_2)/g(\theta_1^*, \theta_2)]$ depends on θ_2. By Assumption 3 there exist actions $\hat{a}$ and a^* for agent 1 such that $f_1^{-1}(\hat{a}, q_i^1) = \hat{\theta}_1$, $f_1^{-1}(a^*, q_i^1) = \theta_1^*$, so we obtain a contradiction. ‖

Assumption 3 (in addition to invertibility of production functions) thus ensures that independent contracts are suboptimal whenever θ_1 and θ_2 are dependent and there are no production externalities. Whenever Assumption 3 is violated, one can construct examples along the lines of Example 1 where this result does not hold. Assumption 3 is not a particularly natural assumption from the economic point of view; it is satisfied for instance when the production function is symmetric in action and random shock, and the set A of possible actions is identical to the set H of possible realizations of θ_1. Hence it appears that the independence of random shocks is not in general necessary for the optimality of independent contracts with separable production, though the pattern of dependence between θ_1 and θ_2 that permits the necessity result to be violated must be quite special.[4]

Next we obtain conditions for the optimality of rank-order tournaments, where incentive payments are based solely on ordinal comparison of output across agents. Let $\delta(q_i^1, q_j^2)$ denote the rank of agent 1's output (so $\delta = 1$ if $q_i^1 > q_j^2$, 2 if $q_i^1 < q_j^2$ and equal to 0 if $q_i^1 = q_j^2$); a rank-order tournament bases compensations to agents solely on the realization of δ. We use the following assumption analogous to Assumption 2 to rule out relatively uninteresting cases:

Assumption 4. Conditional on the value of $\delta(q_i^1, q_j^2)$, the likelihood ratio $[\pi_{ij}(\hat{a}, \tilde{a}_2) | \pi_{ij}(a, \tilde{a}_2)]$ is independent of the outcome pair (i, j) either for all action pairs $(\hat{a}, a)$ for agent 1 or none at all.

Proposition 4. *A sufficient condition for optimal payments to agent* 1 *to solely depend on the rank* $\delta(q_i^1, q_j^2)$ *of his output relative to agent* 2*'s is that* $\pi_{ij}(a_1, \tilde{a}_2)$ *admit the factorization (for all* $a_1 \in A$*):*

$$\pi_{ij}(a_1, \tilde{a}_2) = K(q_i^1, q_j^2, \tilde{a}_2) L(\delta(q_i^1, q_j^2), a_1, \tilde{a}_2). \qquad (9.7)$$

4 If production is non-separable (i.e. the action of any agent affects not only its own output, but also that of the other agent), it is natural to expect independent contracts not to be optimal even if θ_1 and θ_2 are independent, for one agent's output will then be informative about the other agent's action. However, in the special case where θ_2 is uniformly distributed (i.e. in this discrete framework, the marginal probability of any two values in the support of the distribution of θ_2 are the same) and agent 2's production function f_2 is one-to-one between θ_2 and q_2 (given any pair of actions of the two agents), an independent contract for agent 1 is still optimal when θ_1 and θ_2 are independent. However in this extreme situation the output of agent 2 fails to be informative for agent 2's action as well, and agent 2's optimal payment depends on agent 1's output, but is independent of its own output.

If Assumption 4 *holds,* (9.7) *is also* (*generically*) *necessary for agent* 1's *optimal payments to depend only on* δ.

The proof of this proposition is analogous to the proof of Proposition 2, and is omitted. It shows that the condition for optimality of rank-order tournaments is that the outputs of different agents communicate information about agent actions only through their ordinal rankings. It must be the case that any agent by changing its action unilaterally cannot alter the relative probability of 'winning' (or 'losing') by different margins; it can only thereby alter the probability of its winning (by whatever margin). It is difficult to imagine a wide variety of realistic circumstances where cardinal output comparisons convey no statistical information at all about actions chosen by various agents, whereas ordinal comparisons do. However, one situation where (9.7) is satisfied is depicted in Example 3 in Section 3.

We now proceed to obtain a characterization of situations where the principal can attain the first best in a multi-agent situation, assuming that agents are strictly risk-averse. To introduce the result we need the following notation and definitions. $J(\tilde{a}_1, \tilde{a}_2)$ denotes the set $\{(i,j) \mid \pi_{ij}(\tilde{a}_1, \tilde{a}_2) > 0\}$, i.e. the support of (q^1, q^2) given $(\tilde{a}_1, \tilde{a}_2)$. $P_1(a; \tilde{a}_1, \tilde{a}_2)$ denotes $[\Sigma \Sigma_{(i,j) \in J(\tilde{a}_1, \tilde{a}_2)} \pi_{ij}(a, \tilde{a}_2)]$, the probability of the occurrence of outcomes in the support of (q^1, q^2) under $(\tilde{a}_1, \tilde{a}_2)$, when agent 1 decides to choose action a rather than $\tilde{a}_1$, and agent 2 continues with $\tilde{a}_2$. Hence $[1 - P_1(a; \tilde{a}_1, \tilde{a}_2)]$ is the probability that a unilateral switch in action by agent 1 from $\tilde{a}_1$ to a will be detected by the principal. $P_2(a; \tilde{a}_1, \tilde{a}_2)$ can be defined analogously for agent 2.

The maximum punishment $\underline{v}(= V(\underline{I}))$ that can be inflicted on agent k is said to be 'sufficiently heavy' if

$$\underline{v} \leqslant \min_{a \in M_k(\tilde{a}_1, \tilde{a}_2)} \left[\underline{U} + G(a) - \frac{P_k(a; \tilde{a}_1, \tilde{a}_2)}{[1 - P_k(a; \tilde{a}_1, \tilde{a}_2)]} [G(a) - G(\tilde{a}_k)] \right]$$

$$(9.8)$$

where

$$M_k(\tilde{a}_1, \tilde{a}_2) = \{a \in A \mid P(a; \tilde{a}_1, \tilde{a}_2) < 1, G(a) < G(\tilde{a}_k)\},$$

the set of all actions less costly to agent k than $\tilde{a}_k$ which if chosen instead of $\tilde{a}_k$ will be detected by the principal with positive probability. (9.8) has no particular natural economic interpretation; it serves merely to impose an upper bound on $\underline{v}$. We can now derive

Proposition 5. *A sufficient condition for the principal to attain the first-best, i.e.* $C(\tilde{a}_1, \tilde{a}_2) = C_{FB}(\tilde{a}_1) + C_{FB}(\tilde{a}_2)$, *is that both of the following conditions be satisfied:*

(a) (*for* $k = 1, 2$) $P_k(a; \tilde{a}_1, \tilde{a}_2) < 1$ *for every* $a \in A$ *with* $G(a) < G(\tilde{a}_k)$, *i.e. if agent* k *switches to any action less costly than* $\tilde{a}_k$, *it will be detected by the principal with positive probability.*

(b) *the maximum punishment that can be inflicted on either agent is sufficiently heavy.*

If V is strictly concave, and $\bar{a}_k$ is not least cost for k ($= 1, 2$), then (a) *and* (b) *are also necessary for attainability of the first-best.*

Proof. We shall only prove the necessity part because the sufficiency result is fairly obvious. Given strict concavity of V the principal can attain the first-best only if each agent is paid a constant sum with probability one under $(\bar{a}_1, \bar{a}_2)$; hence without loss of generality, agent k will be paid $h(U + G(\bar{a}_k)) \equiv C_{FB}(\bar{a}_k)$ whenever the output pair is in $J(\bar{a}_1, \bar{a}_2)$, and $\underline{I}$ whenever (q_i^1, q_j^2) is impossible under $(\bar{a}_1, \bar{a}_2)$. Such an incentive scheme must implement $(\bar{a}_1, \bar{a}_2)$ as a Nash equilibrium. So agent 1 for example should not benefit by unilaterally switching to any action other than $\bar{a}_1$; i.e. for all $a \in A$:

$$\sum\sum_{(i,j)} \pi_{ij}(a, \bar{a}_2)\, v_{ij}^k - G(a) = P_k(a; \bar{a}_1, \bar{a}_2)[U + G(\bar{a}_1)]$$
$$+ [1 - P_k(a; \bar{a}_1, \bar{a}_2]\, v - G(a) \leqslant \underline{U} \quad (9.9)$$

for which both (a) and (b) are necessary. ∥

Proposition 5 says that with strictly risk averse agents, the first-best can be attained by the principal if and only if any shirking by either agent on its own can be detected and punished suitably. An interesting corollary to this result is that under the invertibility of production functions and sufficiently heavy punishments, perfect correlation between θ_1 and θ_2 implies that the principal can attain the first-best.

Corollary. *Suppose that $f_k(a_1, a_2, \hat{\theta}_k) \neq f_k(a_1, a_2, \bar{\theta}_k)$ whenever $\hat{\theta}_k \neq \bar{\theta}_k$ and $f_1(\hat{a}, a_2, \theta) \neq f_1(\bar{a}, a_2, \theta)$, $f_2(a_1, \hat{a}, \theta) \neq f_2(a_1, \bar{a}, \theta)$ whenever $\hat{a} \neq \bar{a}$. Then, if θ_1 and θ_2 are perfectly correlated and maximum punishments are heavy enough, the principal can attain the first-best.*

This is because the invertibility of f_k in θ_k and perfect correlation between θ_1 and θ_2 implies the existence of a function $q^2 = q^2(q^1, a_1, a_2)$ that output pairs (q^1, q^2) satisfy with probability one, and the invertibility of f_k in a_k then implies that the shifting support (condition (a) in Proposition 5) property is satisfied. Note however that if sufficiently heavy punishments cannot be inflicted on (strictly risk averse) agents then Proposition 5 implies that it will not be possible for the principal to attain the first-best, even with perfect correlation.

Hence in the perfect correlation case the principal can extract maximum advantage from using the performance of other agents as a benchmark to evaluate the performance of any agent. In such situations the advantage may be strong enough for a principal with one agent to hire an additional agent and have the same task duplicated.[5] The case of perfect correlation may how-

5 For an example see the earlier version of this paper, Mookherjee (1982).

ever seem a rather extreme one and unlikely to be satisfied exactly in most situations of interest. In the proof of the attainability of the first-best with perfect correlation, we utilized the shifting support property that is an implication of perfect correlation and invertibility of production functions. It is possible that the correlation between θ_1 and θ_2 be 'near' -1 or $+1$, and yet the shifting support property not be satisfied. An interesting question is whether in such situations the principals will be able to attain a welfare level 'near' the first-best level. Mathematically this is the question whether the principal's welfare is continuous in the correlation between θ_1 and θ_2. In the following Proposition we establish that if the probability function $\pi_{ij}(a_1, a_2)$ depends continuously on some real parameter ρ, then (under weak conditions) the principal's welfare is also continuous in ρ.

Proposition 6. *Assume that the probability of any output pair (q_i^1, q_j^2) given actions (a_1, a_2) depends continuously on some real parameter ρ, and represented by the function $\pi_{ij}(a_1, a_2, \rho)$. If $\Pi(a_1, a_2, \rho)$ denotes the probability distribution of (q^1, q^2), i.e. the vector $\{\pi_{ij}(a_1, a_2, \rho)\}$, assume that*

$$\Pi(a_1, a_2, \rho) \neq \Pi(\hat{a}_1, \hat{a}_2, \rho) \text{ whenever } (a_1, a_2) \neq (\hat{a}_1, \hat{a}_2). \qquad (9.10)$$

Then if the set of feasible incentive schemes implementing $(\tilde{a}_1, \tilde{a}_2)$ is non-empty for every value of ρ, the principal's second-best level of welfare is continuous in ρ, and the set of optimal incentive schemes is upper semi-continuous in ρ.

Proposition 6 is proved in the Appendix. It shows that continuous changes in the probability distribution over output pairs generally lead to continuous changes in the principal's welfare, and also in the optimal incentive scheme (almost everywhere) if it is unique almost everywhere. Hence with near perfect correlation, the principal can approximately attain the first-best with an incentive scheme that is 'close' to the optimal scheme under perfect correlation.

Another interesting question in this context is whether the principal's welfare is non-decreasing in the absolute value of the correlation between θ_1 and θ_2. This question has implications for the prior problem of defining the domain of tasks or monitoring technologies for different agents. However as it stands the question does not make clear which properties of the probability distribution of (θ_1, θ_2) (such as moments up to second order, or all moments of the marginal distributions of θ_1 and θ_2) should be held fixed as the correlation between them is changed. The weakest proposition one may investigate is with respect to the effects of an increase in the absolute correlation between θ_1 and θ_2 keeping their respective marginal distributions unchanged. It turns out that it is possible for the principal's welfare to decrease with such an increase in the absolute correlation; this is illustrated in the following example.

Example 2. Agent 1 has a set A_1 of feasible actions, and $\underline{a}_1$ is the least cost action for 1. Agent 2 can choose only one of two possible actions $\underline{a}_2, \bar{a}_2$ where $G(\underline{a}_2) < G(\bar{a}_2)$. θ_1 can take four possible values $\pm 1, \pm 2$ each with probability $\frac{1}{4}$, while θ_2 can take two possible values 1, 4 each with probability $\frac{1}{2}$. Agent 1 has production function $f_1(a_1, \theta_1) = a_1 \theta_1$, while agent 2's output can take either of two distinct values y_1, y_2 and $f_2(\underline{a}_2, 1) = f_2(\bar{a}_2, 4) = y_1$, $f_2(\underline{a}_2, 4) = f_2(\bar{a}_2, 1) = y_2$. The principal's benefit function is linear in the outputs of the two agents $\tilde{B}(q^1, q^2) = \alpha_1 q^1 + \alpha_2 q^2$, where α_1 and α_2 are such that the first-best solution involves agent 1 choosing the least cost action $\underline{a}_1$, and agent 2 its high cost action $\bar{a}_2$.

Consider first the situation where $\theta_2 = (\theta_1)^2$, i.e. θ_1 and θ_2 are perfectly related, but their correlation is 0. In this situation the principal can attain the first-best because agent 1 can be paid a constant sum $C_{FB}(\underline{a}_1)$, the realization of θ_1 and hence of θ_2 inferred from agent 1's output (since its action is known to be $\underline{a}_1$) and this information can be used to force agent 2 to choose $\bar{a}_2$ at first-best cost. Now suppose the joint distribution of θ_1 and θ_2 changes to: $g(1, 4) = g(1, 1) = g(2, 4) = g(-2, 1) = \frac{1}{6}, g(1, 1) = g(-1, 4) = g(2, 1) = g(-2, 4) = \frac{1}{12}$, so the marginal distributions of θ_1 and θ_2 are unchanged but θ_1 and θ_2 are now positively correlated. The principal cannot now infer the realization of θ_2 from that of θ_1, and the shifting support property (a) in Proposition 5 is not satisfied; hence the first-best cannot now be attained.

Example 2 illustrates the point that the correlation coefficient is a measure of linear association between two random variables, and it is possible that two variables become more closely related to one another (non-linearly) and the absolute value of their correlation declines. Hence the correlation between θ_1 and θ_2 has no necessary connection (in general) to the informativeness of q^2 as a signal for a_1. It would be interesting to obtain conditions under which this connection can be made or to relate the principal's welfare to some general (yet simple) measure of association.

3 MULTIPLE EQUILIBRIUM PROBLEMS

The analysis in the preceding section assumed that the principal is content with choosing incentive schemes for which the action-pair to be implemented is a Nash equilibrium for the agents. There are two possible problems with this approach: (a) for the chosen incentive scheme there may be other Nash equilibrium action pairs, some of which may be strictly preferred by both agents to the one the principal wishes implemented, and (b) if the agents can collude in their choice of action pairs, i.e. play a cooperative rather than a non-cooperative game, they may end up choosing a different action pair.

The first of these problems is illustrated in the following example.

Example 3. The two agents are identical, and θ_1 and θ_2 are perfectly correlated. The production functions are such that the principal can infer from observing outputs which agent chose the action involving greater effort.

$$\pi_{ij}(a_1, a_2) = 0$$

if and only if either

$$\text{(i)} \quad q_i^1 < q_j^2 \quad \text{and} \quad G(a_1) \geqslant G(a_2),$$

or

$$\text{(ii)} \quad q_i^1 > q_j^2 \quad \text{and} \quad G(a_1) \leqslant G(a_2) \tag{9.12}$$

or

$$\text{(iii)} \quad q_i^1 = q_j^2 \quad \text{and} \quad G(a_1) \neq G(a_2).$$

Then the principal can sustain any action pair (a_1, a_2) with $a_1 = a_2 = \hat{a}$, say, as a Nash equilibrium at first-best cost with the following tournament: a price of $C_{FB}(\hat{a})$ to the winner, or to both in case of a tie, and a payment of $\underline{I}$ to the loser. However with this incentive scheme any other action pair (a^*, a^*) with $G(a^*) < G(\hat{a})$, is also a Nash equilibrium where both agents attain an expected utility of $[\underline{U} + G(\hat{a}) - G(a^*)]$, greater than what they achieve at $(\hat{a}, \hat{a})$. In fact if $\underline{a}$ is the least costly action for the agents, $(\underline{a}, \underline{a})$ is a Nash equilibrium which Pareto-dominates all other Nash equilibria, and in this sense is the most natural action pair to be implemented under the above incentive scheme. However the principal will be unable to detect from observing outputs that agents are choosing their least costly actions rather than $\hat{a}$.

In some special cases, however, a carefully designed tournament can implement any symmetric action pair as a Nash equilibrium that Pareto-dominates all other Nash equilibria. For instance consider the case where there is 'increasing marginal disutility of effort', i.e. where the set of possible actions can be listed $\{a_1, a_2, a_3, \ldots\}$ and

$$G(a_{l+2}) - G(a_{l+1}) > G(a_{l+1}) - G(a_l) > 0 \quad \text{for all } l = 1, 2, \ldots \tag{9.13}$$

In this case a principal wishing to implement action pair (a_l, a_l) can choose the tournament where the winner's prize is $h(\underline{U} + G(a_l) + g)$, the loser gets $\underline{I}$, and in the event of a tie both receive $h(\underline{U} + G(a_l))$; g is any number lying between $[G(a_l) - G(a_{l-1})]$ and $[G(a_{l+1}) - G(a_l)]$.

But there are also cases where for *any* tournament that implements (a_l, a_l) as a Nash equilibrium (where both agents receive at least $\underline{U}$), the least effort pair (a_1, a_1) is a Nash equilibrium that Pareto-dominates (for the agents) all other Nash equilibria. For instance, consider the case of 'constant marginal disutility of effort' where

$$G(a_{l+2}) - G(a_{l+1}) = G(a_{l+1}) - G(a_l) = k > 0 \quad \text{for all } l = 1, 2, \ldots \tag{9.14}$$

To see this, consider any tournament which pays $h_W = h(U_W)$ to the winner, $h_T = h(U_T)$ to both agents in case of a tie, and $h_L = h(U_L)$ to the loser. Let g_R denote $(U_W - U_T)$ and q_l denote $(U_T - U_L)$, so the tournament is uniquely described by U_T, g_R and g_L. A necessary and sufficient condition for such a tournament to sustain (a_l, a_l) as a Nash equilibrium (where both agents attain at least $\underline{U}$) is then

$$U_T \geqslant \underline{U} + G(a_l), \quad g_R \leqslant k, \quad g_L \geqslant (l-1)k. \qquad (9.15)$$

But for any tournament satisfying (9.15), any symmetric action pair (a_m, a_m) with $m < l$ is also a Nash equilibrium where both agents are strictly better off than at (a_l, a_l). Hence when (9.14) holds, the principal should no longer choose a tournament form for the incentive contract if complete shirking by the agents is to be avoided.

The above example also demonstrates the vulnerability of tournaments to collusion among agents, contrary to Holmstrom's (1982) claim that rank-order tournaments induce a zero-sum game between agents and are hence collusion proof. It is possible for both agents to reduce their effort levels in step with each other and leave the probability distribution of compensations to each unchanged.

The question then arises whether it is possible to obtain some general insights into the properties of optimal incentive schemes that implement action pairs as equilibria that possess stronger stability properties than Nash equilibria. If agents play a non-cooperative game while choosing their respective actions, it is not clear which equilibrium concept is suitable. Should the principal seek to implement a given action pair as a Nash equilibrium not Pareto-dominated by any other Nash equilibrium, or as a Nash equilibrium that Pareto-dominates all other Nash equilibria? While the latter approach would 'implement' the action pair in question more naturally, it would also prove more expensive for the principal. Certain analytical problems arise with the general formulation of either approach. It turns out that the corresponding constraint sets for the principal's cost minimization problem are not closed; hence the existence of an optimal incentive scheme cannot be guaranteed, and neither is any simple characterization available for optimal contracts when they do exist.[6]

In the case where the agents can monitor each other's actions and collude in their choice of actions by making binding agreements, there also does not appear to be any natural equilibrium concept that the principal can employ (especially since agent utilities are non-transferable). For a formulation of the problem where the principal seeks to implement action pairs as a strong equilibrium (a concept due to Aumann (1959)) in the two-agent case, the reader may consult Mookherjee (1982).

6 For further details see Mookherjee (1982).

4 CONCLUSION

We have explored a number of issues in connection with the use of relative performance in optimal incentive contracting. Under the assumption that the principal is content to implement agent actions as Nash equilibria, necessary and sufficient conditions were derived for the optimality of independent contracts, of rank-order tournaments, and for attainability of the first-best. In this context we also investigated the relation of the principal's welfare to the correlation between the underlying randomness in (measured) outputs of different agents. However the incentive schemes optimal for Nash equilibrium implementation that base rewards on relative performance may suffer from vulnerability to collusion among agents, or even from implementation by (non-cooperative) agents of alternative action tuples that are detrimental to the principal's interests. In particular rank-order tournaments may suffer from both these problems, and may actually be rendered unusable in some situations. However, no satisfactory theory seems available to analyse these implementation problems in general, and future research in this area will be valuable. It will also be interesting to explore the implications of the analysis of this and related papers to more specific areas such as the design of reward structures to innovative activity in a market setting (Stiglitz 1982) or to the optimal division of tasks within an organization.

APPENDIX

Proof of Proposition 1. If V is linear, there exists a solution to (9.12) since $\Sigma\Sigma_{(i,j)} \pi_{ij}(\bar{a}_1, \bar{a}_2) v_{ij}^k$ equals $(\bar{U} + G(\bar{a}_k))$ over the constraint set (for $k = 1, 2$). So suppose V is not linear. Define $J(\bar{a}_1, \bar{a}_2) = \{(i,j) \mid \pi_{ij}(\bar{a}_1, \bar{a}_2) > 0\}$. Since the constraint set is closed, it suffices to show that feasible incentive schemes are bounded over $J(\bar{a}_1, \bar{a}_2)$. This is because incentive schemes that are equal almost everywhere under action pair $(\bar{a}_1, \bar{a}_2)$ lead to the same expected cost for the principal. Now $[\Sigma\Sigma_{(i,j) \in J(\bar{a}_1, \bar{a}_2)} \pi_{ij}(\bar{a}_1, \bar{a}_2)(v_{ij}^1 + v_{ij}^2)]$ is bounded below by $[\underline{U} + G(\bar{a}_1) + \underline{U} + G(\bar{a}_2)]$ in the constraint set. Since h is convex and non-linear, it follows from a result of Bertsekas (1974) that unbounded sequences of incentive schemes defined on $J(\bar{a}_1, \bar{a}_2)$ cause $[\Sigma\Sigma_{(i,j) \in J(\bar{a}_1, \bar{a}_2)} \pi_{ij}(\bar{a}_1, \bar{a}_2)(h(v_{ij}^1) + h(v_{ij}^2))]$ to tend to $+\infty$. Hence the constraint set can be bounded on $J(\bar{a}_1, \bar{a}_2)$ without loss of generality, and there exists a solution to (9.2).

The convexity of the objective function, and linearity of all constraints in (9.2) implies that the Kuhn–Tucker conditions (9.3) and (9.4) are necessary and sufficient for the optimality of an incentive scheme. The last part of the Proposition follows from arguments similar to those in Proposition 6 in Grossman and Hart. ‖

Proof of Proposition 6. First introduce the notation ($k = 1, 2$):

$$Y^k(a_1, a_2, \boldsymbol{v}^k, \rho) = \Sigma\Sigma_{(i,j)} \, \pi_{ij}(a_1, a_2, \rho) \, v_{ij}^k - G(a_k) - \underline{U}.$$

Then the constraint set (denoted $0(\bar{a}_1, \bar{a}_2, \rho)$) in (9.2) for any value of ρ can be written as the cartesian product of $0^1(\bar{a}_1, \bar{a}_2, \rho)$ and $0^2(\bar{a}_1, \bar{a}_2, \rho)$ where

$$0^1(\bar{a}_1, \bar{a}_2, \rho) = \{\boldsymbol{v}^1 \in [\underline{v}, \bar{v}]^{n_1 n_2} \mid Y^1(\bar{a}_1, \bar{a}_2, \boldsymbol{v}^1, \rho) = 0, \, Y^1(a, \bar{a}_2, \boldsymbol{v}^1, \rho) \leqslant 0$$

$$\text{for all } a \in A\}$$

and $0^2(\bar{a}_1, \bar{a}_2, \rho)$ is defined analogously. Now $Y^1(a_1, a_2, \boldsymbol{v}^1, \rho) = 0$ for any action pair (a_1, a_2) is the equation of a hyperplane in $R^{n_1 n_2}$. So $0^1(\bar{a}_1, \bar{a}_2, \rho)$ is the intersection of a collection of half spaces, and the hyperplane $Y^1(\bar{a}_1, \bar{a}_2, \boldsymbol{v}^1, \rho) = 0$.

We establish first that $0^1(\bar{a}_1, \bar{a}_2, \rho)$ is lower semi-continuous in ρ. So let $\boldsymbol{v}^1 \in 0^1(\bar{a}_1, \bar{a}_2, \rho)$ and $\{\rho_n\}$ be a sequence converging to ρ. If $\boldsymbol{v}^1$ is an interior point of $0^1(\bar{a}_1, \bar{a}_1, \rho_n)$ then it is clear that for sufficiently large n, we can find $\boldsymbol{v}_n^1$ in the interior of $0^1(\bar{a}_1, \bar{a}_2, \rho_n)$ such that $\{\boldsymbol{v}_n^1\}$ converges to $\boldsymbol{v}^1$. If $\boldsymbol{v}^1$ is a boundary point of $0^1(\bar{a}_1, \bar{a}_2, \rho)$ then $\boldsymbol{v}^1$ must be a solution to a set of linear equations:

$$Y^1(\bar{a}_1, \bar{a}_2, \boldsymbol{v}^1, \rho) = 0$$

$$Y^1(a, \bar{a}_2, \boldsymbol{v}^1, \rho) = 0 \text{ for all } a \in \hat{A}, \text{ some subset of } A. \tag{9.11}$$

(9.10) implies that $\boldsymbol{v}^1$ must also be the unique solution to (9.11). However, there may exist more than one possible subset $\hat{A}$ of A with property (9.11).

If there exists only one such subset $\hat{A}$, we can take the sequence $\{\boldsymbol{v}_n^1\}$ defined by the (unique) solution to

$$Y^1(\bar{a}_1, \bar{a}_2, \boldsymbol{v}_n^1, \rho_n) = 0, \, Y^1(a, \bar{a}_2, \boldsymbol{v}_n^1, \rho_n) = 0 \quad \text{for all } a \in \hat{A}. \tag{9.16}$$

This sequence converges to $\boldsymbol{v}^1$ because $\Pi(a_1, a_2, \rho)$ is continuous. Since $Y^1(a, \bar{a}_2, \boldsymbol{v}^1, \rho) < 0$ for all $a \in (A \backslash \hat{A})$ it follows that for all large n, $Y^1(a, \bar{a}_2, \boldsymbol{v}_n^1, \rho_n) < 0$ for all such a. Hence $\boldsymbol{v}_n^1 \in 0^1(\bar{a}_1, \bar{a}_2, \rho_n)$ for all large n.

Now suppose that there exists more than one subset $\hat{A}$ of A for which (9.11) is true. Let I be a subset of the set of natural numbers such that $\{\hat{A}_i \mid i \in I\}$ is the collection of such subsets. For any $i \in I$, the unique solution $\boldsymbol{v}_{n,i}^1$ to (9.16) with $\hat{A}$ replaced by $\hat{A}_i$, will converge to $\boldsymbol{v}^1$. However, $\boldsymbol{v}_{n,i}^1$ may not belong to $0^1(\bar{a}_1, \bar{a}_2, \rho_n)$. Since $0^1(\bar{a}_1, \bar{a}_2, \rho_n)$ is non-empty, the boundary of the set $\{\boldsymbol{v} \in [\underline{v}, \bar{v}]^{n_1} \mid Y^1(a, \bar{a}_2, \boldsymbol{v}, \rho_n) \leqslant 0 \text{ for all } a \in A\}$ must intersect the hyperplane $Y^1(\bar{a}_1, \bar{a}_2, \boldsymbol{v}, \rho_n) = 0$. Hence for any large n, there exists $i(n) \in I$ such that $\boldsymbol{v}_{n, i(n)}^1 \in 0^1(\bar{a}_1, \bar{a}_2, \rho_n)$. We can then choose a sequence $\{\boldsymbol{v}_n^1\}$ such that $\boldsymbol{v}_n^1 \in 0^1(\bar{a}_1, \bar{a}_2, \rho_n)$ for all n, and $\boldsymbol{v}_n^1 = \boldsymbol{v}_{n, i(n)}^1$ for all large n, which converges to $\boldsymbol{v}^1$. This establishes the lower semi-continuity of $0^1(\bar{a}_1, \bar{a}_2, \rho)$ in ρ.

A similar argument establishes the lower semi-continuity of $0^2(\bar{a}_1, \bar{a}_2, \rho)$ and hence of $0(\bar{a}_1, \bar{a}_2, \rho)$ in ρ. Since $0(\bar{a}_1, \bar{a}_2, \rho)$ is upper semi-continuous in ρ, and the principal's objective function $\Sigma\Sigma_{(ij)} \pi_{ij}(\bar{a}_1, \bar{a}_2, \rho) [\bar{B}(q_i^1, q_j^2) - I_{ij}^1 - I_{ij}^2]$ is continuous in ρ, the result follows from the Theorem of the Maximum.　‖

REFERENCES

Aumann, R. J. 1959: Acceptable points in general cooperative n-person games. In R. D. Luce and A. W. Tucker (eds). *Contributions to the Theory of Games IV*. Princeton: Princeton University Press, 287–324.

Bertsekas, D. 1974: Necessary and sufficient conditions for existence of an optimal portfolio. *Journal of Economic Theory*, 8, 235–47.

Gjesdal, F. 1982: Information and incentives: the agency information problem. *Review of Economic Studies*, 49, 373–90.

Green, J. and Stokey, N. 1983: A comparison of tournaments and contracts. *Journal of Political Economy*, 349–64.

Grossman, S. J. and Hart, O. D. 1983: An analysis of the principal agent problem. *Econometrica*, 7–46.

Holmstrom, B. 1979: Moral hazard and observability. *Bell Journal of Economics*, 79–91.

Holmstrom, B. 1982: Moral hazard in teams. *Bell Journal of Economics*, 324–40.

Mirrlees, J. 1975: *The Theory of Moral Hazard and Unobservable Behaviour, Part I*. Mimeo. Oxford: Nuffield College.

Mookherjee, D. 1982: Optimal incentive schemes in multiagent situations. *Discussion Paper No. 82/57, ICERD*, London School of Economics.

Nalebuff, B. and Stiglitz, J. 1983: Prizes and incentives: towards a general theory of compensation and competition. *Bell Journal of Economics*, 21–43.

Stiglitz, J. 1982: Theory of competition, incentives and risk. Paper prepared for International Economic Association Conference, Ottawa.

Index